Confederate Crackers and Cavaliers

Cataloging-in-Publication Data

McWhiney, Grady.
    Confederate crackers and cavaliers / Grady McWhiney.
    p. cm.
    ISBN 1-893114-25-2—ISBN 1-893114-27-9 (pbk.)

    1. Southern States--Civilization—1775-1865. 2. Southern
States—Social life and customs—1775-1865. 3. Confederate States of
America—Social conditions. 4. Confederate States of America—
Politics and government. 5. United States—History--Civil War,
1861-1865—Campaigns. 6. United States—History--Civil War,
1861-1865--Biography. 7. Generals—Confederate States of America
—Biography. 8. Statesmen—Confederate States of America—
Biography. 9. Leadership—Confederate States of America—History.
I. Title.

    F213 .M378 2002
    975'.03—dc21

                             2002005193
                                     CIP

McMurry Station, Box 637
Abilene, TX 79697-0637

Printed in the United States of America

ISBN 1-893114-27-9
10 9 8 7 6 5 4 3 2 1

Book Designed by Rosenbohm Graphic Design

All inquiries regarding volume purchases of this book should be
addressed to McWhiney Foundation Press, McMurry Station, Box 637,
Abilene, TX 79697-0637.
Telephone inquiries may be made by calling (915) 793-4682

Confederate Crackers and Cavaliers

Grady McWhiney

McWhiney Foundation Press
McMurry University
Abilene, Texas

Contents

Map Key

Geography

Trees

Marsh

Fields

Strategic Elevations

Rivers

Tactical Elevations

Fords

Orchards

Political Boundaries

Human Construction

Bridges

Railroads

Tactical Towns

Strategic Towns

Buildings

Church

Roads

Military

Union Infantry

Confederate Infantry

Cavalry

Artillery

Headquarters

Encampments

Fortifications

Permanant Works

Hasty Works

Obstructions

Engagements

Warships

Gunboats

Casemate Ironclad

Monitor

Tactical Movements

Strategic Movements

Maps by
Donald S. Frazier, Ph.D.
Abilene, Texas

Maps

Figures

Foreword

In his half-century career as an eminent and highly respected Civil War historian and teacher, Grady McWhiney has never shied away from thinking original themes and articulating them in bold prose. From the pen of this master historian has come some of the most provocative writing of the main currents and meanings of the Civil War in the South.

His two most influential and innovative works, *Cracker Culture: Celtic Ways in the Old South* and *Attack and Die: Civil War Military Tactics and the Southern Heritage* (coauthored with Perry D. Jamieson), are landmarks in Civil War historiographical thinking and writing. In the first he powerfully propounds the thesis that both the North and the South were shaped by the nature of their immigration into not only two separate geographical regions but also two distinct cultures. The South was settled mainly by Celts—people from Scotland, Ireland, Wales, and Cornwall—the North mainly by English and Germanic immigrants. They were distinct and different cultures in the Old World, and they were distinct and different cultures in the New World too, carrying the same antagonisms. And this shaped the way they lived and the society each developed—in the North, a Roundhead culture wed to a sturdy work ethic; in the South, a Cavalier culture distinguished by a more leisurely, courtly, and aristocratic way of life based on having somebody else do the work. This central difference in their distinct social and cultural histories was an important part of *why* the sections fought a war against one another.

In *Attack and Die*, McWhiney with equal power explains that these social and cultural differences also dictated *how* they fought that conflict. Ignoring new advances in the technology of warfare, Southerners fought as Cavaliers, attacking nearly impregnable Federal defenses in bold, disastrous charges. Attacking in this heartbreakingly outmoded, outdated manner against vastly improved weaponry—the rifle having replaced the smoothbore musket—they died in appalling numbers, nearly bleeding the Confederacy to death during the first three years of the war. As McWhiney and Jamieson clearly explain, it was a very Celtic/Cavalier way of fighting.

McWhiney has also written—in books and many essays— fine studies of some of these bold, latter-day cavaliers: Robert E. Lee, P.G.T. Beauregard, Joseph E. Johnston, Leonidas Polk, Braxton Bragg, and the president of the Confederacy, Jefferson Davis, himself the embodiment of this Celtic spirit. In the essays in this collection, McWhiney devotes much thought to Davis, amounting to an insightful assessment of the man and his contribution to the Lost Cause.

Many of the major McWhiney themes surface again in this book of stimulating essays, an engaging mix of previously published studies and pieces newly written for this volume. In a sense, these essays constitute a sampler of McWhiney's lifework as a Southern scholar and historian. To read them is to revisit his most important themes in Civil War and Southern history. But this collection is not so limited. With the verve and bluntness that typifies all of his writing, he also explores several other themes—as he has done throughout his career—with such divergent subjects as sex, women, and marriage in the South to the first shot in the Civil War and the generalship of U.S. Grant.

What also distinguishes these essays is the writing. Too often historians, who so prize research, neglect writing—not giving it equal importance and priority to the investigation of sources. This can never be said of Grady McWhiney. As a teacher, he has always taught his graduate students to be engaging writers as well as sound researchers. And he has always practiced what he preached. These essays are not only meaty and stimulating but also rewarding and fun to read, rich in quotes that are pointed, relevant, and graphic.

In one of these essays, McWhiney writes delightfully of the legendary and eccentric Southern historian, Francis Butler Simkins, who was his own mentor. The similarities between

McWhiney and that late great historian—excluding the eccentricity—are striking. One scholar called Simkins "one of the most interesting intellectual forces of his generation," an academic who questioned conventional thinking and refused to truckle to historic fads. The same can be said of Grady McWhiney. As a scholar, Simkins stood ahead of most of his contemporaries for his perceptive views and insights, which were often unsettling to Northerners and Southerners alike. The same can be said of McWhiney. Simkins was a teacher who enjoyed nothing more than questioning and offering a fresh look at the past, a historian of an "iconoclastic nature." The same can be said of McWhiney. Simkins was not only a distinguished historian but also a great teacher whose students called him "Doc," the term of affection McWhiney's students now give their own great mentor.

It is a measure of their admiration for him that McWhiney's past students have formed the Grady McWhiney Research Foundation, housed at McMurry University in Abilene, Texas, to perpetuate original study in and stimulating writing about Southern and military history.

That kind of writing, as insightful as it is a pleasure to read, is on abundant display in this masterful collection of essays by the Doc himself.

John C. Waugh

Acknowledgments

Friends—old and new—have helped me write, and I am grateful to them all—masters, associates, doctoral students, all the people one encounters in a half-century of writing and professing. I had two great mentors—Francis Butler Simkins and David H. Donald. They made it possible for me—a country boy, the son of Crackers—to have a wonderful life as a scholar, a life I shared with my wife, Sue, for more than fifty years until her death.

During that time, I could not have had better friends—Ari and Olive Hoogenboom; Forrest and Ellen McDonald; Gary Mills; John and Joan Tricamo; Judith Lee Hallock, my much admired coauthor of Braxton Bragg's biography; John C. Waugh, a great writer and friend, who contributed this book's flattering forward; Drake Bush, my favorite editor, and his wife, Mary, who hosts the best wine parties; and Judy L. Walters, who reads critically whatever I produce, keeps my business records, and listens to my complaints.

Among my former graduate students, I especially appreciate those whose interests I share and whose talent and industry I treasure—Anne Bailey, Perry Jamieson, Dan Sutherland, Steve Hardin, Don Frazier, Robert T. Maberry, Robert Pace, Jeff Kinard, Elizabeth Shorn Mills, Thomas D. Mays, Stanley McGowen, David Coffey, and many others.

I also thank Kevin Brock, the best copyeditor I have ever had; Charlene Cummings for typing this manuscript; and Rosemary Adams for making an important suggestion.

My thanks also go to the original publishers for permission to reprint the following revised essays: "Crackers and Cavaliers," in *Plain Folk of the South Revisited*, ed. Samuel C. Hyde Jr. (Baton Rouge: Louisiana State University Press, 1997), 187–202; "Sex and Chivalry," in *Southerners and Other Americans*, by Grady McWhiney (New York: Basic Books, 1973), 39–60; "Grant's Military Model," in ibid., 61–71; "Jefferson Davis and the Art of War," *Civil War History* 21 (1975): 101-12; "A Tactical Revolution," originally published as "Who Whipped Whom?" ibid. 11 (1965): 5–26; "The First Shot," originally published as "The Confederacy's First Shot," ibid. 14 (1968): 5–14; "Davis and His Generals," in *Southerners and Other Americans*, 83–104; "Beauregard's 'Complete Victory' at Shiloh," *Journal of Southern History* 49 (1983): 421–34; "An 'Unsuccessful' Davis Biographer," *Southern Partisan* 15 (2d Qtr, 1995): 20–26; and "The Unforgiven President," *Journal of Mississippi History* 42 (1980): 111–27.

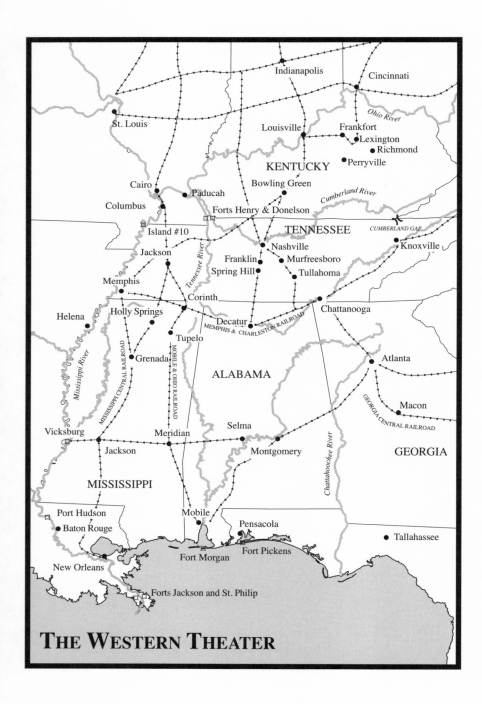

THE WESTERN THEATER

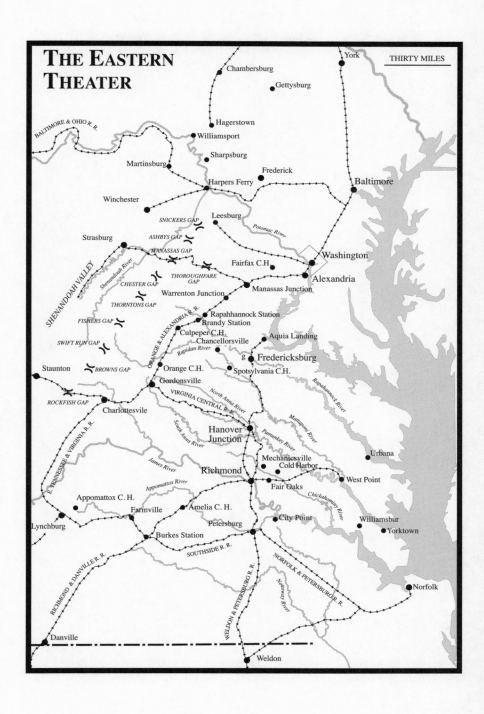

THE EASTERN THEATER

THIRTY MILES

York

Chambersburg

Gettysburg

BALTIMORE & OHIO R. R.

Hagerstown

Williamsport

Sharpsburg

Martinsburg

Frederick

Harpers Ferry

Baltimore

Winchester

Leesburg

SNICKERS GAP

Potomac River

Strasburg

ASHBYS GAP

MANASSAS GAP

Fairfax C.H.

Washington

SHENANDOAH VALLEY

Shenandoah River

CHESTER GAP

THOROUGHFARE GAP

Warrenton Junction

Manassas Junction

Alexandria

THORNTONS GAP

ORANGE & ALEXANDRIA R. R.

FISHERS GAP

Rapahhannock Station

Brandy Station

SWIFT RUN GAP

Culpeper C.H.

Chancellorsville

Aquia Landing

Rapidan River

Staunton

BROWNS GAP

Orange C.H.

g Fredericksburg

Spotsylvania C.H.

Gordonsville

North Anna River

Rappahannock River

ROCKFISH GAP

VIRGINIA CENTRAL R. R.

Charlottesville

E. TENNESSEE & VIRGINIA R. R.

South Anna River

Hanover Junction

Pamunkey River

Mattaponi River

Urbana

James River

Mechanicsville

Cold Harbor

Richmond

West Point

Appomattox River

Fair Oaks

Chickahominy River

Appomattox C. H.

Farmville

Amelia C. H.

City Point

Williamsbur

Lynchburg

Petersburg

Yorktown

Burkes Station

SOUTHSIDE R. R.

RICHMOND & DANVILLER R. R.

WELDON & PETERSBURG R. R.

NORFOLK & PETERSBURG R. R.

Nottoway River

Norfolk

Danville

Weldon

CHAPTER ONE

A Celtic Heritage

Southerners are not like other Americans, and they never have been. Sociologist John Sheldon Reed insists that even today significant cultural differences separate Southerners from Northerners and that many of these differences are just as prevalent now as they have ever been. For example, he claims that the differences between Southern black and white people are fewer than those between white Southerners and white Northerners. In other words, the population of the United States is more culturally divided along regional rather than racial lines. Other studies suggest that cultural variations between Southerners and Northerners are greater than those between males and females, urban and rural residents, Protestants and Catholics, and manual and nonmanual workers.

For more than twenty years, Forrest McDonald and I have contended in articles and books that Americans have been divided by cultural differences for more than three hundred years—that indeed Southerners and Northerners have always been significantly distinct from each other. Their ways and values have been different because their cultural heritages are different. More specifically, we maintain that the North was settled mainly by English and Germanic peoples, who culturally dominated the area, and that the South was settled mainly by Celtic peoples and culturally dominated by them.

For too long historians have accepted the myth that Anglo-Saxons settled and dominated the antebellum South, that the region was and is what one scholar calls "the biggest single WASP nest this side of the Atlantic." Actually, the overwhelming majority of the people who settled the South were not Anglo-Saxons but Celts. They came from Scotland, Ireland, Wales, Cornwall, and the English North Country, and whatever they were—Scots, Scotch-Irish, Irish, Welsh, or Cornish—they shared a culture that was significantly different from English culture.

Just the opposite was true in the Old North, where people of English as well as of other Anglo-Saxon heritages dominated throughout the antebellum period.

The importance of all this is that the cultural antagonisms that had divided Celts from Englishmen in the British Isles for centuries continued in America. I do not mean, of course, that either the Old North or the Old South was totally homogeneous, but the tendency, by and large, was for Celts who settled in the North to become Anglicized and for Englishmen in the South to become Celticized.

The persistence of Celtic and English cultural traits over time and distance is evident in the observations of travelers and other contemporary writers. They found that the characteristic ways and values of antebellum Southerners were remarkably similar to those of the most Celtic people of the British Isles; conversely, the ways and manners of antebellum Northerners were precisely those that seventeenth- and eighteenth-century writers found typical of the most English people of the British Isles. In other words, Celts in the South and Englishmen in the North retained most of their habitual folkways, imposed in large measure their traditions and habits upon their New World environment, and acculturalized within a generation or so most of the outsiders who settled among them.

"Cracker Culture"—the term I use for the Celtic ways that Southerners adopted from their British ancestors—spread from the Southeast to Texas and shaped habits and manners, especially in the backcountry South, throughout the antebellum period. It was the predominant, though not the only, culture of the Old South. For a more detailed examination, see my *Cracker Culture: Celtic Ways in the Old South*, with a prologue by Forrest McDonald, distinguished research professor, University of Alabama (Tuscaloosa: University of Alabama Press, 1988). That volume concentrates on traditions shared by Celts and Southerners and the dissimilarity between them—their ways and values—and those of Englishmen and Northerners.

In this current essay my goals are: one, to examine some of the various ways Southerners adopted from their Celtic ancestors and to contrast them with traditions Northerners acquired from their Anglo-Saxon heritage; and two, to demonstrate by using name analysis where Celts and Englishmen settled in antebellum America.

During the seventeenth and eighteenth centuries, the English became ever more orderly, disciplined, and hard working; indeed, they molded a national society in which they integrated their capitalistic values with the "interests of the individual nuclear family." Regulated by laws, codes of basic values, proverbs, and wise sayings—for example, "keep a stiff upper lip" and "stay steadily at your work"—Englishmen centered their lives on the work ethic.

New Englanders, of course, brought the English work ethic to America. "God sent you not into this world as into a Playhouse, but a Work-house," New England Puritans reminded each other. "Abhor one hour of idleness as you would be ashamed of one hour of drunkenness," a Yankee admonished his son.

In no other part of the world, from the 1600s through the 1800s, was the work ethic more revered than in England and in the northern United States. "English people are naturally industrious—they prefer a life of honest labour to one of idleness," boasted an English journalist. An Austrian, after living ten years in Boston, said of New Englanders that there were "no people on earth with whom business constitutes pleasure, and industry amusement, in an equal degree. Active occupation is not only the principal source of their happiness, but they are absolutely wretched without it, and know but the *horrors* of idleness."

Celts and Southerners were quite different. Male Southerners and their Celtic ancestors believed that people who worked when they did not have to were crazy; they much preferred to enjoy life while their animals, their women, or their slaves made a living for them.

Various observers from the twelfth through the eighteenth centuries emphasized that Celts were a lazy, herding people who preferred their pastoral ways to tillage agriculture, towns, and business. Later travelers described the Irish as "slothful," "the most improvident people in the whole world," "lazy to an excess"; a people "strangely given to idleness, thinking it the greater wealth to want business and the greatest happiness to have liberty"; "indolent" and willing to "dissipate the hard earnings of to-day regardless of to-morrow" yet without "the haggard money look [so] characteristic of the English." Observers employed almost the exact terms and phrases in depicting the Scots, especially the Highlanders, that were used in describing the Irish. The profit motive and the work ethic simply were not part of Highland culture. As one Highland minister reported at the end of the eighteenth century, "The people being, from their infancy, principally employed in attending cattle, are generally disposed to be idle, and, though able-bodied, continue at hard work with reluctance."

Cracker Southerners were just as leisure oriented as their Celtic ancestors. An observer in the 1850s referred to the typical white Southerners as "the hardy descendants of the early Scotch and Irish settlers. Their learning is seldom such as is seen inside of school-houses; it may not even include an ability to read and write." They were, of course, "good horsemen, marksmen, and hunters," he noted, "but the men, at least, are not remarkable for agricultural industry, for the patient thrift and intelligent skill that make the successful farmer. They are squatters rather than farmers." Moreover, he concluded, "they will not work."

An English traveler reported that everywhere in the North he saw "bustle, and all sorts of industry—men riding about, chopping down forests, building up houses, ploughing, planting, and reaping, [but in the South] all mankind appeared comparatively idle. The whites consider it discreditable to work, and the blacks, as a matter of course, work as little as they can. The free population prefers hunting, and occupy themselves also very much with the machinery of electioneering." A Yankee noted that in the North one servant did the work that it took five to accomplish in the South.

Commenting on how lazy Southerners were, another observer noted that "no Northern farmer" would neglect to build a bridge over a stream that crossed his property; indeed, two "live Yankees" would complete the work in a single day, but "the Southern planter will ford the creek lying between his house & stable a whole life time." The same complaint was made about Highland Scots, whose roads incidentally were equally as bad as those of Ireland and the Old South.

By the capitalistic standards of the antebellum period, nearly all Cracker Southerners were hopelessly backward. They favored rural life and values over urban, frequently opposed such "modern improvements" as railroads and banks, and ranked even middling planters higher on the social scale than the richest merchants and manufacturers. Invariably, antebellum Southerners were described as hospitable and fond of pleasures; they enjoyed what money could buy, but they disdained people who devoted their lives to making money. An eighteenth-century traveler claimed that Southerners "are content if they can but live from day to day; and if they have but enough to pay their merchants and to provide for their pleasures; they are satisfied, and desire nothing more." One Englishman claimed that there was "no part of the world where great wealth confers so little rank, or is attended with so few advantages," as in the South.

"We are a peculiar people, sir!" secessionist Louis T. Wigfall of Texas told an English reporter in 1861. "We are an agricultural people; we are a primitive people. We have no cities—we don't want them. We have no literature—we don't need any yet. We have no press—we are glad of it. We do not require a press, because we go out and discuss all public questions from the stump with our people. We have no commercial marine—no navy—we don't want them. We are better without them. Your ships carry our produce, and you can protect your own vessels. We want no manufactures: we desire no trading, no mechanical or manufacturing classes."

The values of Southerners and Northerners, like those of Celts and Englishmen, were not only different but actually antagonistic. "'Take no thought of the morrow' [is] the motto of the southern population," chided a disciplined Northerner, who charged that the "energies of the South either lie dormant in idleness or [they] are expended in visionary [and reckless] projects for useless luxuries & foolish dissipation." Another Northerner denounced Southern wastefulness. "In New-England," he boasted, "a man may put a hundred dollars in a bridge, a turnpike, a rail-road, a bank, an insurance company, or a mill-dam, and thus blend his private advantage with the public good." But in the South even the small planters squandered more money every year than most New England farmers saved in a "life [time] of toil and close economy."

Northerners often found Southerners, just as Englishmen found Celts, to be careless businessmen. One Yankee claimed that the only "excellent business men in the South" were Northerners and foreigners. Another suggested that Southerners often failed in business because they spent too much time in amusements. "No business," he claimed, "is so important at any time as to prevent them from attending the horse-race, the cock-fight, or any other kind of sport." To illustrate, he described how a clergyman, who was waiting for a train, made the mistake of taking a small item to a blacksmith for repair; the blacksmith, while repairing the item, stopped twice to go watch a cock fight. Not surprisingly, the clergyman missed his train.

"In traveling in the South," observed another Northerner, "you become astonished at the little attention men pay to their business. The idea appears to be very prevalent, that if a business is once started, it must take care of itself." This man had to visit the only two stables in Pine Bluff, Arkansas, several times before he could find either of the proprietors. "One of them had gone into the 'bottom,' on the opposite side of the river, hunting wild turkeys; while the other was enjoying a social glass at a [local] saloon."

When an exasperated Yankee complained that some job had not been finished at the time agreed upon, a complacent Southerner would explain that a "fox [hunting] party came along, and he had to join that,—or the military paraded, which every body must see." A New Englander wrote: "I was employed to superintend the building of a mill [in the South], and fourteen hands were engaged six days in raising it, after it was framed. The dimensions of the building were only 40 by 70 feet, and the same number of hands at the North would have raised it in half a day; but the master workman took two of the hands and went off fishing a part of two days. The crew rested while they were absent. A squirrel ran by one day, and all the men left the mill, and chased him half a mile before they treed him. In this way was much of the time spent."

Neither antebellum Southerners nor their Celtic ancestors were in a hurry. "When God made time, He made plenty of it," remarked an old Irish woman. The offhanded disorderliness of the Southerner was obvious by the odd assortment of things that he kept in his desk. "There," noted a perceptive observer, "you will find his bonds, accounts, receipts, and even his will, jabbed into pigeon-holes lying about loose in the midst of a museum of powder-horns, shot-gourds, turkey-yelpers, flints, screws, popcorn, old horseshoes and watermelon seed."

The carelessness about moneymaking and financial affairs as well as a strong commitment to the leisurely enjoyment of life characterized both Celts and Southerners and set them apart from most Englishmen and Northerners. Consider this description of a week's entertainment: "Coverlets being prepared, morn and even. Wines, newly-opened, being drunk, [hogs and beefs] on spits, tables [full of food]. Companies [of guests] coming to the mansion, [people] discoursing uproariously. A fragrant odor issuing in strength. Airs being played harmoniously. The doors wide open. Waxlights blazing from every wall and chamber. Every moment fresh casks being opened for the multitude, with no ebb in the feast. Strong steeds racing. The loud cry of the chase on the sides of the misty hills." This might have been a report on a party hosted by some antebellum Southern planter, but it is in fact Irish poet Egan O'Rahilly's account of how Daniel O'Callaghen of County Cork, one of Ireland's "big house" gentry, entertained in the eighteenth century.

Celts and Southerners of all social ranks delighted in sensuality; they were hospitable and openhanded. "Their vices," noted a Highland minister, "may be said to be grafted on their virtues." As a visitor remarked of the western Scots, "they covet no Wealth." Nor would they, or any other Celts, let business interfere with their pleasures. A native of the South claimed that the typical Southerner, "whatever may be his engagements, seems never to have any thing to do but to amuse himself and his family and the stranger within his gates." Many a planter "lives an idle, worthless life, too lazy even to fox-hunt," concluded this writer, who admitted that all the poorer white Southerners "seem to care for is to live from hand to mouth; to get drunk, provided they can do so without having to trudge too far after their liquor; to shoot for beef; to hunt; to attend gander pullings; to vote at elections; to eat and to sleep; to lounge in the sunshine of a bright summer's day, and to bask in the warmth of a roaring wood fire, when summer days are over."

Not only were Yankee values different from those of Celts and Southerners; the average Yankee neither looked nor acted like a Celt, but rather like an Englishman. "The persons of the New-Englanders, their complexion, manners, and language, so much resemble those of Englishmen, that the similarity has been the subject of not a little discussion on both sides of the Atlantic," said the president of Yale College in 1812.

Nor did Yankees and Southerners eat the same foods; pork, the mainstay of the Southern diet, was unpopular with Northerners. Yankees, like their English forebears, favored mutton and beef over pork. Antebellum diners at Boston's Revere House, for example, consumed each week seven times as much beef and five times as much mutton as pork. Between 1854 and 1860 the New York livestock market handled a million more sheep than swine, and few of the hogs slaughtered and packed there were for northeastern consumption.

Contemporary observers used different adjectives to describe the Yankee, depending on whether they approved or disapproved, but the essence of the descriptions was the same. Sympathetic observers pictured the Yankee as thrifty, industrious, and ascetic; those more critical saw him as mercenary, hypocritical, and rapacious.

Susan G. Becton, a Southerner who taught school in Paradise, Pennsylvania, reported that

> these complacent Pennsylvanians, who so far from seeing anything singular in the name of their village, have bestowed the same upon a township, and linked to it the equally happy titles of Eden Hall (the village Seminary) and All Saints Church. Congratulate me, my dearest Jane, on having exchanged the rattle snakes and pine trees of

old Carolina (her only productions, one of our teachers coolly informed me) for such bliss, at least *in name*. I have left the pleasures of the [South] behind and am now seeing a new phase of life. And true, democratic life it is; one in which every body labours; the men earning their bread by hard toil, and their wives, alternately mistress & maid, performing with their own hands, the drudgery, which, with us, devolves upon slaves. At first I was rather pleased with this; in the evening I met men, who had worked all day in the field, and they appeared intelligent, educated gentlemen—I saw a lady step from the parlour to the kitchen, and perform her duties with equal ease and facility in each—but six months familiarity banished the illusion. The nobility and elevating influences of labour are lost in the daily, hourly strife with petty cares and means; men become narrow-minded and pernicious; women sink beneath the double burden of natural and assumed duties. Care for the body usurps care for the mind and the tone of society is inevitably lowered. You will think I do not like Penn. No, my dear, I do not.

Other observers stressed the devotion of Yankees to hard work. "A stranger at Boston," noted an antebellum South Carolinian, "soon remarks on the industry of its inhabitants; and their attention to business." Yankees always showed great concern for "those material cares which are disdained by the white population of the South," observed Alexis de Tocqueville. A Boston divine reportedly said of his fellow Yankees, "Prosperity is the goal for which they toil perseveringly from morning until night." Yankees believe "that the getting of money is the chief end of man," confessed a New Englander in an 1858 article on Northern farm life; consequently, "exclusive devotion to labor has been deemed indispensable to success. The maxims of [Benjamin] Franklin have been literally received and adopted as divine truth. We have believed that to labor is to be thrifty, that to be thrifty is to be respectable, that to be respectable is to afford facilities for being still more thrifty; and our experience is, that with increased thrift comes increased labor. This is the circle of our ambition and rewards."

Southerners, like their Celtic ancestors, favored informal and rural ways. Visitors reported that most people in the Old South lived in an unpretentious style, usually in carelessly built cabins, which they scarcely ever improved. A traveler reported as typical a Southern home that "was ventilated on an entirely new principle; that is to say, by wide cracks in the floor, broad spaces between the logs that composed the walls, huge openings in the roof, and a window with a shutter that could not be closed." Southern roads and bridges—where they existed—were as poorly constructed and maintained as those in premodern Scotland and Ireland. This was typical, one man claimed, because Southerners were "extraordinarily indifferent to practical internal improvements."

Cracker home

Despite the informal style of Celts and Southerners, few people anywhere could match their hospitality. Even some of the most critical travelers mentioned the warmth with which Celts and Southerners received them. It was customary in both the Celtic areas of the British Isles and in the antebellum South to overwhelm visitors with food and to encourage them to eat all they could; it was traditional in both places, as an eighteenth-century Scottish lady explained, "to please your company." Travelers could hardly say enough in praise of the kindness of Southerners, who were "ever ready to welcome the wayfarer to their hospitable firesides." "If you are disposed to be convivial," noted a traveler, "you may dine with some one every day." "They welcomed us to everything," confessed another man.

Neither Celts nor Southerners were "bookish"; formal education meant less to them than leaning to master their natural environment. The Southern woman described by a traveler as "sitting with a pipe in her mouth, doing no work and reading no books" doubtless would have agreed with the Southern man who, when asked by a Yankee if he liked to read, replied, "No, it's damn tiresome." It has often been said, only partly in jest, that more Southerners wrote books than read them.

Celts and Southerners were less materialistic—less oriented toward the making of money—than most other Western cultures. Premodern Celts boasted that they coveted no wealth; as pastoralists and warriors, they "despised" trade and what they called "mercenary employments." To show her contempt for money, an eighteenth-century Scottish woman, in the words of her debtor, "lighted her pipe with the note I gave her for the money I owed her." A Yankee observed that Southerners were less impressed by wealth than most other people.

Both Celts and Southerners spent much of their lives out-doors. Expert marksmen and anglers, they hunted and fished regularly and with delight. Fast horses and packs of dogs were as much a part of their lives as hogs and cattle. In the antebellum South, even small boys were experts at hunting and fishing, observed one traveler, who dined on delicious venison and trout brought in by "two little fellows that looked almost too small to shoulder a gun." In a log cabin another visitor counted thirteen "guns hung up along the rafters or stacked up in the only two rooms of the house."

Neither Celts nor their Southern descendants regarded their ways as unusual or reprehensible. Laziness and a lack of ambition—which good Englishmen and Yankees considered deplorable—were viewed differently by traditional Celts and antebellum Southerners. They delighted in their livestock culture and their comfortable customs. Being lazy did not mean to them being indolent, shiftless, slothful, and worthless; it meant being free from work, having spare time to do as they pleased, being at liberty, and enjoying their leisure. They saw no point in working when their livestock would make their living; they thought anyone who worked when he did not have to was insane.

Southerner and his dogs

Nor did they see reason to have more than what they could eat, drink, wear, or ride. Unlike conscientious Englishmen or Northerners, when Celts or Southerners said they were being lazy, they were not reproaching themselves but merely describing their state of comfort. They suffered no guilt when spending their time pleasantly—hunting, fishing, dancing, drinking, gambling, eating, fighting, or just loafing and talking.

These were the characteristic ways of most of the people who fought as Confederates in the 1860s. They fought not just to protect their homes and families but also to prove their courage, protect their right to live as they pleased, and to disassociate themselves from people they distrusted.

Some hard evidence on where the ancestors of most antebellum Southerners migrated from may be more persuasive than the impressions of contemporary observers that Southern ways and traditions were Celtic.

Using the term "Celtic" does not mean to suggest a common genetic pool, for the people under discussion were clearly of different genetic mixtures. The Welsh are obviously of different genetic stock than the Irish, and the Highland Scots have bloodlines different from Lowlanders. Rather, these people shared a common cultural heritage—customary lifestyles, attitudes, and ways of doing things. Even in this sense, of course, the various peoples identified here as Celts were far from identical. But after a great deal of study, I have concluded that it is legitimate to consider them as a single cultural group, different from the English—much in the same way that Western culture is seen as distinct from Islamic culture while recognizing that Italians and Swedes differ from one another even as do Libyans and Turks. A more accurate phraseology than "Celtic," in the sense that I use the term, would be "people from the British Isles who were historically and culturally non-English"—but somehow that phrase seems less catchy.

Establishing who settled when and where in America is more difficult than one might imagine; determining the national or ethnic composition of a sizable number of Americans is arduous. Ideally, the information would be recorded in the census, but this was not done until later in the nineteenth century. Alternatively, the ethnic composition of the population might be reconstructed from lists of arriving immigrants, but only fragmentary records exist for the colonial and early national periods. No systematic recording of the arrival of immigrants was required by law until 1819.

The resulting records are useless in analyzing the ethnic makeup of the Southern population because so few migrants came to the South after 1800. Only about 4.2 percent of the white people in the South in 1850 were foreign born, and most of them were concentrated in such urban places as New Orleans, Mobile, and Charleston.

Since records of early settlers are either unavailable or sketchy, I have relied on name analysis. Tracing ancestry is both complex and inexact, but fairly reliable approximations can be reached if the list of European names is full and accurate, if the body of American names being analyzed is large enough to absorb invariable flukes and exceptions, and if a rigorous methodology is formulated.

Wherever possible, the work of other scholars has been relied upon, but in addition to this, three methods of name analysis have been used. The focus here is on what these methods of name analysis reveal rather than on the techniques involved.

One method, a projection technique, reveals that sectionalism based upon settlement patterns existed throughout the United States at the time the first federal census was taken in 1790. Well over three-quarters of the people living in New England were of English origins. New York, having originally been a Dutch colony, retained a large Dutch component in its population; but the single largest group, composing something over two-fifths of the people, was English. Pennsylvania was heterogeneous: two-fifths of the people were of Celtic origins, one-third were German, fewer than one-fifth were English. Elsewhere, the farther south and west from Philadelphia, the more Celtic the population: in the Upper South, Celts and Englishmen each constituted about two-fifths of the population; in the Carolinas, more than half the people were Celtic, and Celts outnumbered Englishmen five to three.

Even more significantly, Celts completely dominated the frontier from Pennsylvania southward, an area where they constituted from 60 to nearly 100 percent of the total population. In such interior North Carolina districts as Hillsborough, Celts composed nearly 100 percent of the population, and in some western Virginia counties, Scots and Irish alone numbered nearly 80 percent of residents.

Using the projection technique to analyze the censuses of 1810, 1830, and 1850 reveals that the Celtic portion of the entire Southern white population stabilized at about 60 percent; the English portion stabilized at about 20 percent; and the remainder were largely of German, French, or Spanish origins. In New England and the upper Middle West, the English continued to constitute about three-quarters of the population until the 1840s, when the arrival of numerous refugees from the Irish potato famine changed the ratio to about 60–40 percent English.

My conclusions on settlement patterns are supported by other studies. Charles Banks, for instance, in his work on English immigrants to New England between 1620 and 1650, indicates that none came from Ireland, Scotland, or Wales, and only 185 of 2,885 originated in the Celtic fringe; 71 percent came from the east and southeast of England. Conversely, in an analysis of 7,359 references to seventeenth-century Virginians, John E. Manahan finds that 90 percent came from Cornwall, Wales, Ireland, or elsewhere along the Celtic fringe.

Additional studies also confirm that many more Celts settled in the antebellum South than traditional sources acknowledge. In 1850 some 25,000 or more Irish lived in New Orleans, a quarter of that city's residents; and even in Apalachicola, Florida, the Irish were the largest foreign-born element in the population.

Not all of the Irish in the South arrived in the late antebellum period, nor were they confined to urban areas. One investigator found records of "a great infusion of Irish" into the South throughout the colonial period. Another writer concludes that thousands of Irish were transported to America between 1703 and 1775 and that many settled in Virginia, the Carolinas, and Georgia. And yet another scholar estimates that in 1790 Irish settlers constituted 26 percent of the population of South Carolina and 27 percent of that in Georgia.

Many of these Irish have been overlooked by historians who have assumed incorrectly that, during the colonial period of American settlement, all natives of Ireland outside Ulster were devout Catholics. "The passionate and exemplary attachment of the Irish nation to the Catholic faith dates from a later time," writes a distinguished Irish historian about the seventeenth and eighteenth centuries; "the real contest was between Englishmen and Irishmen rather than Protestants and Catholics. . . . In Ireland in the seventeenth century . . . the Irish laity were still for the most part only passively and traditionally Catholic."

Nor did the situation change during the first part of the nineteenth century. "The figures on church attendance in pre-famine Ireland indicate that only thirty-three percent of the Catholic population went to mass," notes an eminent authority. "Most of the two million Irish who emigrated between 1847 and 1860 were part of the pre-famine generation of nonpracticing Catholics, if indeed they were Catholics at all." Not until the later part of the nineteenth century, long after most of the Irish who came to the South had migrated, did the "devotional revolution" turn Ireland into a country of churchgoers who equated Irish nationalism with Roman Catholicism.

Irish settlers in the South, especially those who arrived during the seventeenth and eighteenth centuries, suffered little cultural shock. Nominal Catholics at best, they mixed with the Scotch-Irish and Scots, people with whom they had shared traditions and ways for centuries; feuded and stole each other's

livestock, just as they had always done; and helped spread
Celtic culture across the Southern backcountry. The evidence
indicates that large numbers of Irish simply adopted the religion
of their Southern neighbors. For example, Andrew Leary
O'Brien was born in County Cork, Ireland, in 1815; migrated to
South Carolina; married a local girl; and converted to her
Methodist faith. A Catholic bishop, after traveling in the antebellum South, maintained "that, calculating from the names of the
people, no less than forty thousand had lost the Faith in the Carolinas and Georgia." Later, a British Catholic observed that the
South was full of Irish names. "No doubt," he wrote, "the
[Protestant] missionaries on circuit baptized the children and
grandchildren of Irish who had not brought their women or
their priests. [Baptist ministers], Wesleyan ministers, Methodist
bishops, bear Irish names—Healy, Murphy, Connor. Their blood
could only have come from Ireland. One of these Irish patriarchs
. . . did meet a priest after fifty years, and could only present two
grownup generations of Methodists."

A second method of name analysis, an apportionment system, also suggests that a Celtic cultural hegemony existed in the
South. Some sample results: An examination of the names
recorded in the early censuses of three Georgia counties reveal
that fewer than one-third of the families listed were English;
more than half were Celtic. Of the families identified as being of
British extraction, 62 percent were Celtic and 38 percent were
English. A similar pattern was found in Lowndes County, Mississippi, where an examination of the 1,616 families listed in the
1850 census reveals that more than half were Celtic and only
one-third were English. Of the families identified as British, 61
percent were Celtic and 39 percent were English.

The significance of these figures from Georgia and Mississippi becomes clear when one looks at the ethnic pattern in a comparable Northern area. For example, Eaton County in central
Michigan was settled between 1834 and 1860 primarily by people from New England, New York, and Ohio. Nearly half of the

first 2,175 families to acquire land in the county were of English ancestry; fewer than one-third were of Celtic ancestry. Of the families identified as British, fully 61 percent were of English extraction and only 39 percent were Celtic. This is the exact reverse of the Southern pattern.

In an effort to overcome some of the biases inherent in the apportionment technique, another method of name analysis was used. I compiled a list of 2,468 names that are common to and peculiar to the shires of the south and east of England. To see just how many of these names, supposedly the most English of English names, were represented in the antebellum South, I compared them with the 20,000 or so names listed in the U.S. census of Alabama in 1850. I also compiled a list of 1,087 different names, almost all of them Celtic, found on gravestones in the counties of Antrim and Down in northern Ireland, which I also compared with the Alabama census of 1850. The results: 84 percent of the Celtic names but only 43 percent of the English names were also found in Alabama.

Such ratios of Celts to Englishmen as the various name-analysis methods reveal suggest that the North and the South were settled and dominated numerically during the antebellum period by different people with significantly different cultural backgrounds. This is not to suggest that either North or South was totally homogeneous: there were hustlers, go-getters, eccentrics, hard workers, and even literate people sprinkled through the South. Similarly, there were individuals and groups in the North that resisted amalgamation. Some Scotch-Irish in New England, for example, refused from the outset to fit into Puritan society. But the tendency, by and large, was for Celts in the North to become Anglicized and for Englishmen in the South to become Celticized.

The persistence of Celtic and English cultural traits over time and distance is evident in the observations of travelers and other contemporary writers. The ways and values that they found characteristic of antebellum Southerners were the same ones that seventeenth- and eighteenth-century observers reported peculiar to the most Celtic people of the British Isles; conversely, the observed ways and manners of antebellum Northerners were precisely those that seventeenth- and eighteenth-century writers found typical of the most English people of the British Isles. In other words, Celts in the South and Englishmen in the North retained most of their folkways, imposed in large measure their traditions and habits upon their New World environment, and acculturated within a generation or so most of the outsiders who settled among them.

The Celtic ways that Southerners adopted from their British ancestors spread from the Southeast to Texas and shaped habits and manners, especially in the backcountry South, throughout the antebellum period. It was the predominant, though not the only, culture of the Old South. Besides Crackers, the Old South contained a number of cultures, including some Cavaliers.

CHAPTER TWO
Crackers and Cavaliers

Confederate military leaders, like most historic figures, varied as much in manners and characteristics as they did in appearance and brains. Some were polished, worldly, and sophisticated; others seemed scarcely more than violent rustics. A number could be described simply as bold countrymen who displayed remarkable courage in battle. So gallant were a few that contemporaries called them "Cavaliers" even if their family background, social standing, and conduct sometimes fell below Cavalier standards.

Not many genuine Cavaliers inhabited the Old South or the Confederate States of America, but by 1861 the Cavalier ideal enjoyed a revered place in Southern popular culture. After writers romanticized plantation life, abolitionists helped distort the Cavalier image by picturing the Old South as a three-tiered society comprised of arrogant, aristocratic planters; "mean poor whites"; and cruelly treated black slaves.

Many Southerners believed that after the English Civil War one of the contesting factions, the Roundheads, who supported the Parliament, had colonized the American North and another, the Cavaliers, Royalists who supported the crown, had settled in the South. According to this view, Yankees descended from Puritan Roundheads and Southerners from more aristocratic Cavaliers.

That such beliefs rested more on myth than reality dissuaded few believers; the Cavalier cult depicted Southerners not as they were but as the depicter portrayed them. Just before the Civil War, Southerner Daniel R. Hundley wrote in considerable exaggeration: "The Southern Gentleman is usually possessed of an equally faultless physical development. His average height is about six feet, yet he is rarely gawky in his movements, or in the least clumsily put together; and his entire physique conveys . . . an impression of firmness united to flexibility."

According to yet another contemporary: "The Southern aristocrat trained his sons in a code of behavior which was self-consciously chivalric. The items in this code were noblesse oblige, a sense of personal and family honor, and above all, a due and proper regard for the beauty and virtue of white women."

But disagreement existed on what constituted Cavalier characteristics. In Virginia fiction Cavaliers were "expected at all times to be graceful and dignified, as well as courteous and thoughtful. They sought to attain qualities of fortitude, temperance, prudence, justice, . . . and courtesy."

Scholars acknowledge that plantation conditions fostered outdoor living, which in turn encouraged familiarity with horses and guns and thus stimulated interest in the profession of arms. Slavery required patrols and militia units to cope with threats of servile insurrection, and the lack of commercial and industrial opportunities in the Old South's agrarian economy helped turn many young Southerners toward military careers. All these activities promoted the Cavalier image, as did such trappings of chivalry as attention to manners, stately ladies, lavish hospitality, heraldry and ancestry, romantic oratory and place naming, dueling, military affairs, and the use of horses in hunting, tournaments, and racing. The horse and horsemanship were inextricably linked to the chivalric ideal, and the cult of manners became so intertwined with concepts of personal honor and integrity that all appeared part of a single theme. Because the planter class regarded a business career with disdain, their sons rarely considered occupations other than law, politics, plantation management, or the military.

A nineteenth-century biographer defined George Washington as a Cavalier, not just because he was brave and inspired confidence but also because he displayed self-control and regularity of character as well as tenderness and compassion rather than ambition. Washington possessed two additional Cavalier traits of significance: "he lived on his horse and idolized his mother and his wife."

Early in the Civil War, Southern journalist Thomas C. DeLeon encountered Frank, "an old chum" whom he considered an authentic Cavalier, on a train wearing the dress of a Georgia battery's first sergeant. Frank was "rushing a carload of company property to Richmond." As the train got underway, "Cicero, Frank's ancient black Man Friday, 'dispensed hot coffee and huge hunks of bread and ham; and a violin and two good voices among the Crescents [Louisiana troops on the way to Richmond from Pensacola] . . . made the time skim along far faster."

"How is it you haven't your commission?" one of the Creoles asked Frank, who had been promised a commission. His "careless reply" was: "Pledges are not commissions . . . I got tired of waiting the Secretary [of War's] caprices, . . . so one day I went to the War Department and demanded either my sheepskin, or a positive refusal. I got only more promises; so I told the Sec. I needed no charity from the government, but would present it with a company! Then, to be as good as my word, I sold some

cotton and some stock, equipped this company and—*voila tout!*"
"But you are not commanding your company?" asked the Creole. "Couldn't do it, you see," replied Frank. "Wouldn't let the
boys elect me an officer and have the Sec. think I had *bought* my
commission! But, old fellow, I'll win it before the month is out;
and, if God spares me, mother shall call her boy Colonel Frank,
before Christmas!"

DeLeon lamented: "Poor Frank! Before the hoped for day his
bones were bleaching. . . . One morning [on] the retreat from
Yorktown [he received] . . . a bullet in his brain. He was one of
many, but no truer heart or readier hand were stilled in all the
war."

Following the conflict, John A. Wise mentioned the influence
of Sir Walter Scott's fiction in shaping not only his own views
but also those of many other Southerners. He listed the following traits as desirable not just for Virginia Military Institute
cadets but something all Southern Cavaliers and gentlemen
should also practice: "courtesy, self-respect, deference to superiors, contempt for effeminacy or cowardice, a dauntless courage,
a joyous simple outlook, a healthy love of life, tempered by the
romantic code of [Sir Walter Scott's] Fitz-James. Such, my comrades," insisted Wise, "is the ideal Cadet, as you and I love to
picture him."

Not every Cavalier, of course, met these standards. In 1860
one of the Old South's most popular magazines admitted that
"Cavaliers had many human failings; they were indeed earthy,
they fought, they drank, they swore, they loved." A Yankee writing after the war asserted: "the central trait of the 'chivalrous
Southron' is an intense respect for virility. If you will fight, if
you are strong and skillful enough to kill your antagonist, if you
can govern or influence the common herd, if you can ride a dangerous horse over a rough country, if you are a good shot or an
expert swordsman, if you stand by your own opinions unflinch-
ingly, if you do your level best on whisky, if you are a devil of a
fellow with women, if, in short, you show vigorous masculine

attributes, he will grant you his respect."

The real Cavalier, not the character of fiction or idealization but the flesh and blood man, may not have been so different from another stereotyped Southerner, the Cracker, with whom Cavaliers shared a cause and a culture. At the time of the Civil War, the overwhelming majority of white residents of the Confederacy—most planters, farmers, and plain folk; indeed, everyone except a few aristocrats, some townsfolk and professionals, and a sprinkling of foreigners and unacculturated Yankees—were part of Cracker culture, whether they acknowledged it or not. Some Crackers were rich, others poor, and still others neither; but they all more or less acted alike and shared the same values. And that is the point: the word "Cracker" did not signify an economic condition; rather, it defined a culture. Scotch-Irish settlers, "in whose dialect a *cracker* was a person who talked boastingly," brought the term to the South, where during the colonial period it became associated mainly with Scottish, Scotch-Irish, Irish, or Welsh herdsmen of Celtic origins. "The Cracker was typically a Scotch-Irishman," noted one scholar. In 1766 a colonial official informed the Earl of Dartmouth: "I should explain to your Lordship what is meant by Crackers, a name they have got from being great boasters; they are a lawless set of rascals on the frontiers of Virginia, Maryland, the Carolinas, and Georgia, who often change their place of abode." A German visiting the Carolina backcountry found longhorn cattle, swine, and slovenly people whom he identified as Crackers. A Spanish official reported in 1790 the "influx [into Florida] of rootless people called *Crackers*." He described them as rude and nomadic, excellent hunters but indifferent farmers who planted only a few patches of corn, and people who kept "themselves beyond the reach of all civilized law."

"Cracker" became part of the American vocabulary, but almost always it has been used disparagingly to describe the mudsills of the South. Contemporaries and scholars alike usually equated Crackers with poor whites. Few writers chose, as did historian Lewis C. Gray, to distinguish between the two: "The distinctive characteristics of the poor whites were recognized in the various special appellations by which they were contemptuously known in different parts of the South, such as, 'piney-woods people,' 'dirt-eaters,' 'clay-eaters,' 'tallow-faced gentry,' 'sand-hillers,' and 'crackers.' The term *crackers*, however, was sometimes applied also to mountaineers and other small farmers." Gray acknowledged that many of the Old South's herdsmen were called Crackers. To most travelers in the antebellum South and the Confederacy, especially those from England and the North, a Cracker was any Southerner whose ways differed significantly from their own, and many visitors to the South delighted in laughing and sneering at the rustic ways of such people.

It is understandable why visitors usually failed to distinguish between Crackers and poor whites, for both shared the same culture: all poor whites were Crackers even though not all Crackers were poor whites. Frederick Law Olmsted, an observant Yankee who visited the South in the 1850s, noted that some Crackers "owned a good many negroes, and were by no means so poor as their appearance indicated." Crackers all shared the common heritage of being Southerners. "We do not remember ever to have seen [poor whites] in the New-England States," remarked Southerner Daniel Hundley in 1860. "They are . . . found in Ohio, Pennsylvania, Indiana, and all States of the [Old] North-west, though in . . . these last they came originally from the South." The characteristics of poor whites drawn up by Hundley, which match a list compiled much later by Lewis Gray, credit them with being courageous, lazy, lustful, quarrelsome, violent, ignorant, superstitious, drunkards, gamblers, and livestock thieves. Both observers agreed that poor whites were unconcerned with money. "Dollars and dimes," Hundley claimed, "they never bother their brains any great deal about." The list compiled by Hundley and Gray, allowing for exaggeration, is a fair but incomplete outline of Cracker traits.

The easiest way to understand Cracker characteristics, and indeed to understand Cracker culture, may be to contrast again (as in chapter 1) some of the major differences between antebellum Southerners and Northerners. A wide range of observers generally described Southerners as more hospitable, generous, frank, courteous, spontaneous, lazy, lawless, militaristic, wasteful, impractical, and reckless than Northerners, who were in turn more reserved, shrewd, disciplined, enterprising, acquisitive, careful, frugal, ambitious, pacific, and practical than Southerners. The Old South was a leisure-oriented society that fostered idleness and gaiety, where people favored the spoken word over the written and enjoyed their sensual pleasures. Family ties reportedly were stronger in the South than in the North; Southerners, whose values were more agrarian than those of Northerners, wasted more time and consumed more tobacco and liquor and were less concerned with the useful and the material. Yankees, conversely, were cleaner, neater, more puritanical, less mercurial, better educated, more orderly and progressive, worked harder, and kept the Sabbath better than Southerners.

These characterizations, which attempt to distinguish Rebs from Yanks, also suggest similarities between Cavaliers and Crackers. No individual Southerner—Cracker, Cavalier, or whatever—possessed all of the peculiarities described, but Cavaliers and Crackers shared with most other white Southerners such ideals as hospitality, frankness, generosity, and courtesy; they sanctioned a leisure-oriented, agrarian society with strong family ties in which people favored the spoken word over the written and enjoyed their sensual pleasures, delighting in music, dancing, gambling, hunting, fishing, horse racing, talking, telling stories, eating, drinking, smoking, chewing tobacco or dipping snuff; they shared a strong sense of personal and family honor, and tended to be rash, violent, and brave.

Some Confederate military leaders possessed traits that failed to enhance their careers. A striking example: Maj. Gen.

George B. Crittenden, eldest son of Sen. John J. Crittenden of Kentucky. The younger Crittenden had demonstrated courage in 1842 by joining Col. William Fisher's disastrous Texan filibuster expedition into Mexico. Captured and compelled by the Mexicans to draw beans from a jar to decide which of the adventurers would be executed, Crittenden picked a white bean, which meant he would be spared; he gave it to a friend and then was lucky enough to select another white bean. Brevetted for heroic conduct during the Mexican War, against his father's advice he joined the Confederacy. After the Confederate disaster at Mill Springs in early 1862, where he was accused of being "in a beastly state of intoxication" during the battle, Crittenden received command of a corps in Gen. Albert Sidney Johnston's army, but on April 1, 1862, Maj. Gen. William J. Hardee found him drunk and his command in a "wretched state of discipline." Arrested on the spot, censured by a court-martial, and pronounced unfit for command by Gen. Braxton Bragg, Crittenden resigned his commission in October 1862.

There were plenty of drunks in the Confederacy, and far too many of them held high military command. Generals Roswell Ripley and Nathan G. Evans were two of the army's "most notorious drunkards." Brig. Gen. Henry Hopkins Sibley was another; after his failure to take New Mexico for the Confederacy, his uncontrolled drinking cost him his command. Maj. Gen. Benjamin Franklin Cheatham, commanding a division in the Army of Tennessee, attacked lackadaisically at Murfreesboro, sending "his brigades . . . into action individually rather than simultaneously—and he was drunk," as General Bragg and others charged him with being on other occasions. Officers found ardent secessionist John Dunovant too inebriated to attack and "lying drunk by the roadside" instead of leading his regiment forward during the Secessionville campaign. Arrested and imprisoned, he was later released and promoted to brigadier general. Dunovant died in 1864, leading his brigade in a headlong charge; his biographer noted that "Dunovant commanded troops in heavy fighting only four days of the entire war, three of them defeats. It is difficult reconciling [praise for him] . . . with the reality of Dunovant lying drunk on the . . . Road and lying dead after a foolhardy frontal foray. Brave the brigadier unquestionably was, but his bravery was the rashness of irresponsibility."

Hardly anything appears more extreme than contrasting the reckless Dunovant and the dutiful Robert E. Lee, the epitome of Cavalier virtues. Son of Revolutionary War hero "Light Horse Harry" Lee and "one of the finest women the State of Virginia ever produced," Robert Edward Lee established his military reputation during the Mexican War. For twenty months he served on Maj. Gen. Winfield Scott's staff and worked in close proximity with the army's commander. Scott reported that Lee "greatly distinguished himself" during the siege of Veracruz. At Cerro Gordo, Scott based his victorious strategy on the reconnaissance made by Lee, who again received Scott's praise along with promotion to the brevet rank of major for his gallant and meritorious conduct. Lee further distinguished himself on the march to Mexico City by twice crossing the difficult terrain of the Pedregal on a dangerous reconnaissance that Scott called "the greatest feat of physical and moral courage [ever] performed by any individual." Lee received two additional brevet promotions for heroic conduct in Mexico. Jefferson Davis recalled that Lee "came from Mexico crowned with honors, covered by brevets, and recognized . . . as one of the ablest of his country's soldiers." A fellow officer observed that General Scott had an "almost idolatrous fancy for Lee, whose military genius he estimated far above that of any other officer of the army." In an official letter Scott referred to Lee as "the very best soldier that I ever saw in the field."

Almost everyone who knew Lee held him in high regard. A family friend once spoke of young Robert's "amiable disposition, & his correct and gentlemanly habits." One of his early teachers said that Lee "was a most exemplary student in every respect. He was never behind time at his studies; never failed in a single recitation; was perfectly observant of the rules and regulations of the Institution; was gentlemanly, unobtrusive, and respectful in all his deportment to teachers and fellow-students. His specialty was *finishing up*. He imparted a finish and a neatness, as he proceeded, to everything he undertook."

Lee passed through West Point in four years without receiving a single demerit, a remarkable accomplishment. Gen. Joseph E. Johnston, who was a classmate of Lee's at the academy, claimed that "no other youth or man so united the qualities that win warm friendship and command high respect. For he was full of sympathy and kindness, genial and fond of gay conversation, and even of fun, that made him the most agreeable of companions, while his correctness of demeanor and language and attention to all duties, personal and official, and a dignity as much a part of himself as the elegance of his person, gave him a superiority that every one acknowledged. He was the only one of all the men I have known who could laugh at the faults and follies of his friends in such a manner as to make them ashamed without touching their affection for him, and to confirm their respect and sense of his superiority."

Audacity, the military characteristic that most influenced Lee's generalship, was not exclusively a Cavalier trait. Crackers often were as bold as Cavaliers. Whether Lee's audacity, which sometimes bordered on recklessness, was simply part of his heritage or something he learned from Scott is less important than understanding that long before the conflict of the 1860s, Robert E. Lee was committed to aggressive warfare. From the outset of the Confederacy's struggle for independence, Lee suggested offensives to President Davis and urged other generals to be bold and aggressive. "What genius! What audacity in Lee!" exclaimed war clerk John B. Jones during the Seven Days campaign.

A member of Lee's staff told Brig. Gen. E.P. Alexander that "if there is one man in either army, Confederate or Federal, head and shoulders above every other in audacity, it is Gen. Lee! His name might be Audacity. He will take more desperate chances and take them quicker than any other general in this country, North or South." And "General Lee, . . . not excepting [Stonewall] Jackson, was the most aggressive man in his army," concluded Maj. Gen. Henry Heth. "No one ever went to General Lee and suggested an aggressive movement who was not listened to attentively."

President Davis observed that after the war some critics charged Lee "with 'want of dash.' I wish to say," Davis announced, "that I never knew Lee [to] decline to attempt anything that man may dare." The president's wife agreed. "General Lee was not given to indecision," she remembered, "and they have mistaken his character who supposed caution was his vice. He was prone to attack."

Other generals may have been as aggressive as Lee, but his boldness, revered by both Cavaliers and Crackers, established a model that Southerners appreciated and honored. Audacity not only characterized Confederate heroes; it united even such diverse Southerners as James Johnston Pettigrew and Nathan Bedford Forrest.

Pettigrew, who was killed in action during the retreat from Gettysburg, personified the Cavalier ideal and practiced the highest standards of Southern chivalry. "One of the finest scholars ever to attend the University of North Carolina," he graduated first in the class of 1847. After dabbling in such intellectually satisfying pursuits as writing, college teaching, law, politics, and travel, he turned to the study of warfare. What he lacked in formal training, he learned from reading and observation. Pettigrew served as both a private and a colonel; for a time, modesty forced this slender Cavalier to refuse President Davis' attempt to promote him from colonel to general. At the battle of Seven Pines, Pettigrew fell with a neck wound that appeared to be fatal, yet before the action ended he suffered another wound, a bayonet slash in the leg, and capture. Following his exchange, he led both a brigade and a division through the carnage at Gettysburg. On the march to Pennsylvania, he remarked, "life was only to be desired for what could be accomplished in it and death only to be dreaded for what had been done amiss." For himself, Pettigrew said, he was ready to die at any time, at that very moment, if he could do so with honor and usefulness. He meant it. Bold and aggressive, he courted combat. "We whipped the Yankees," he stated, "every time we could get at them." At Gettysburg, as his men cheered and his division prepared to charge, he rode up and down the battle line, a perfect target for sharpshooters. Later, while he was rallying troops, his horse was shot from under him and canister shattered his right hand, but Pettigrew was among the last to leave the field. "None had more deeply at heart . . . the cause for which he shed his blood," wrote a friend. "He gave himself up to it wholly, with all his fine energies, extraordinary talents, and the courage of a heart literally

**Nathan Bedford Forrest *(Cracker)* and
James Johnston Pettigrew *(Cavalier)***

ignorant of fear. I have never met with one who fitted more entirely my 'beau ideal' of the patriot, the soldier, the man of genius, and the accomplished gentleman."

General Forrest never spoke the language of a Cavalier, nor did he dress or act like one. He was a Cracker, and he proudly wore the habits and manners of one.

His Cracker heritage hid his military skills. Forrest once replied to Gen. John Hunt Morgan's question of how he achieved his victories. "Oh," said Forrest, "I just took the short cut and got there first with the most men." Gen. James R. Chalmers of Mississippi once reported that, as Forrest prepared to lead his men against some Federal forces, "a badly demoralized and evidently panic-stricken soldier" tried to speak to the cavalry commander. Forrest "seized the soldier by the collar, threw him down, dragged him to the side of the road, . . . picked up a piece brush that was convenient, proceeded to give him one of the worst thrashings I have ever seen a human . . . get." Finally, the general let the soldier loose. "Now, damn you, go back to the front and fight; you might as well be killed there as here, for if you ever run away again you will not get off so easy."

A young woman in northern Alabama discovered that Forrest was direct but warm and friendly. He and his men were after some Yankees who had just crossed a river bridge and had set it on fire. At the home of Emma Sansom, near the bridge, Forrest and his men stopped. "I and my men will protect you; can you show me another way to cross the river," Forrest asked. Emma did not hesitate. Despite frightening her mother, the girl jumped up behind the general and directed him to a ford. There they saw some Yankees on the other side of the river. He told her, stepping to the front, "I am glad to have you for a pilot, but I am not going to make breastworks of you." On the way back to her house, Forrest asked her name and for a lock of her hair. Back at Sansom's house, the general left a note thanking her and asking a favor: "one of my bravest men has been killed," he wrote and requested that she see that "he is buried in a nearby graveyard."

Forrest, perhaps the ideal Cracker and surely a violent and an aggressive one, seemed to have little in common with General Pettigrew except courage. Son of a backcountry Scotch-Irish blacksmith, Forrest had raised livestock, sold slaves, and killed his uncle's murderer before turning his talents to slaughtering Yankees. When called upon to defend the Confederacy, both Johnston Pettigrew and Bedford Forrest, despite their differences, reacted with equal bravery.

So did many other Southerners. Courage may not have been universal throughout the Old South, but a remarkable number of Confederate military leaders displayed a willingness to die in battle. More than half of all Confederate generals—235 of 425—managed to get themselves killed or wounded in combat. "I have to stay in the forefront to make these men fight," confessed Brig. Gen. James Dearing. "I'll get myself killed." In the last days of the war, this "reckless, handsome boy" did just that—he died in combat.

He was not alone. Brig. Gen. Samuel Garland, Jr., a graduate of the Virginia Military Institute and a descendant of Pres. James Madison, suffered several wounds before receiving a fatal one at South Mountain. Garland was "the most fearless man I ever knew," insisted Maj. Gen. D.H. Hill, and General Lee called Garland a "brave and accomplished officer." Brig. Gen. States Rights Gist, a wealthy South Carolinian whom General P.G.T. Beauregard regarded as "able and brave," died at Franklin while leading a charge on foot after his horse had been killed. Brig. Gen. Tom Green, a native Virginian, spent most of his life in Texas, where he participated in the battle of San Jacinto and in nine Indian and Mexican campaigns. He served in the war with Mexico and fought during the Civil War in the invasion of New Mexico, the liberation of Galveston, and in Louisiana. Described as "upright, modest, and with the simplicity of a child," Green "rejoiced in combat," noted his commanding officer, Maj. Gen. Richard Taylor. "His men adored him, and would follow wherever he led; but they did not fear him, for, though he scolded at them in action, he was too kind-hearted to punish breaches of discipline. In truth, he had no conception of the value of discipline in war, believing that all must be actuated by . . . devotion to duty." General Green died, leading his men "in his accustomed fearless way," while attacking a Union gunboat.

Not every brave man died the first time he was shot. Twenty-one of the seventy-seven Confederate generals who were killed or mortally wounded in battle had been shot at least once before they received their fatal injuries; some had been hit two or more times. William D. Pender survived three wounds before an artillery shell shattered his leg and killed him at Gettysburg. Stephen D. Ramseur recovered from wounds received at Malvern Hill, Chancellorsville, and Spotsylvania, only to die at Cedar Creek. A remarkable number of Confederate generals received multiple wounds yet survived the war: thirty-one were wounded twice, eighteen three times, and a dozen were hit four or more times. Generals Clement A. Evans, William ("Extra Billy") Smith, and William H. Young were wounded five times. Young was hit in the shoulder and had two horses shot from under him at Murfreesboro; he was hit in the leg at Jackson and in the chest at Allatoona, where another horse was shot from under him and he was captured. Generals John R. Cooke, William R. Terry, and Thomas F. Toon were wounded seven times, but the record seems to have been set by William Ruffin Cox, who joined the 2d North Carolina Infantry as a major in 1861 and fought throughout the war with the Army of Northern Virginia. He was wounded eleven times.

A mere listing of courageous Confederates would take days. Even brief sketches of selected bravery omit more heroes than they include. Brig. Gen. Junius Daniel, West Point graduate and Louisiana planter, returned to his native North Carolina at the war's outset to command a regiment. Promoted to brigade command, he died leading his men at Spotsylvania. Brig. Gen. Richard Brooke Garnett, a Virginia gentleman, injured when his horse had kicked him a few days earlier and made it impossible for him to walk, rode into battle at Gettysburg, where his brigade constituted the center of Pickett's massive assault. Garnett may have been the only Confederate in the charge to stay mounted throughout. As the assaulting column neared the crest of Cemetery Hill, he and his horse disappeared in the smoke and confusion. No one ever saw him again, "only his bloodied horse running to the rear."

Heroes became commonplace. Consider three Confederate generals named Gordon. First captured near Cumberland Gap in 1862, George Washington Gordon of Tennessee, after being exchanged, suffered a serious wound "while gallantly leading his regiment" at Murfreesboro. Promoted to brigadier general, he led troops in the deepest penetration of the Union center during the battle of Franklin, where he was again wounded and captured. Brig. Gen. James B. Gordon of North Carolina received J.E.B. (Jeb) Stuart's praise for disregarding wounds and continuing "by his brave example and marked ability to control the field" until he fell mortally wounded. And Maj. Gen. John B. Gordon of Georgia, who rose to prominence in the Army of Northern Virginia, first demonstrated his courage and leadership at Sharpsburg, where five bullets struck him. "Not to promote him," an officer wrote, "would have been a scandal."

During action in East Tennessee, Brig. Gen. Archibald Gracie Jr., after taking a rifle bullet in his arm, had the wound dressed and then went back into combat, where he received a more serious wound; he lived until 1864, when an exploding shell killed him in the Petersburg trenches.

A deadly assault at Atlanta—only one of many—cost Brig. Gen. Daniel C. Govan's Arkansas brigade half of its thousand men, but they captured eight artillery pieces, numerous wagons loaded with ammunition, and seven hundred Yankees, many of them members of the 16th Iowa. After the war Govan attended a reunion of the 16th Iowa and returned the regiment's captured colors.

Brig. Gen. Hiram B. Granbury, a Mississippian who migrated to Texas in the early 1850s, led his Texans at New Hope Church in "a dashing charge on the enemy, driving them from the field." At Franklin, leading yet another charge, he died within a few yards of the Federal breastworks.

At Shiloh a bullet hit Brig. Gen. Henry W. Allen, then a colonel and commander of the 4th Louisiana Infantry, in the mouth and tore away part of his cheek. Despite his wound, he continued to lead his regiment, recalled an officer, "like a whirlwind into the thick of the battle." Later, while directing an attack on an enemy battery at Baton Rouge, Allen rode to within fifty feet of the guns before being hit by canister. The blast killed his horse and permanently crippled Allen, who walked on crutches for the rest of his life. Elected governor of Louisiana in 1863, he resigned from the army and devoted himself to performing the miracle of securing supplies and industries for his state. An Allen biographer proclaimed him "spectacular," and Douglas Southall Freeman called Allen "the single great administrator produced by the Confederacy."

Many senior officers could say that they were lucky to survive the war. South Carolina Cavalier Wade Hampton, whom Jeb Stuart called "a brave and distinguished officer," had hunted bears with a butcher knife before the Civil War. A soldier described Hampton leading a charge as "a veritable god of war." Maj. Gen. Bryan Grimes of North Carolina had seven horses killed under him during the war, yet he received only one wound.

Two generals named Gregg were not so lucky. Alabamian John Gregg, described as "personally without fear" and who had migrated to Texas before the war, sustained a severe wound at Chickamauga, led the furious charge of the Texas Brigade in the Wilderness, and survived until he directed an assault on the Charles City Road south of Richmond. Maxcy Gregg was equally courageous. He led his brigade of South Carolinians with such dash at Gaines's Mill that a contemporary called him "the sublimest spectacle I ever saw." At Second Manassas, Gregg strode among his men, waving an ancestral sword and shouting,

"Let us die here, my men, let us die here." Many did, contributing significantly to winning the victory. Gregg received a painful wound at Sharpsburg and a mortal one at Fredericksburg, where he managed to drag himself to his feet, wave his hat, and cheer on the Confederate counterattack. As his men charged the Federals, Gregg died holding on to a sapling.

Brig. Gen. William R. "Dirty Shirt" Scurry, who was born in Tennessee but grew to manhood in Texas, became a hero at Glorieta Pass during the New Mexico campaign and demonstrated his courage on several other occasions until he was mortally wounded at Jenkins' Ferry. Refusing to be taken to the rear, where surgeons might have saved his life, he bled to death on the battlefield.

Just as valiant were two generals named Adams. Daniel W. Adams of Louisiana, who had killed a newspaper editor in a duel before the Civil War, received three wounds while fighting for the Confederacy. "It is difficult for me to decide which the most to admire, his courage in the field or his unparalleled cheerfulness under suffering," wrote Gen. D.H. Hill. At Shiloh, while directing a charge, Adams received a wound in the head that cost him his right eye. He received his second wound leading an assault at Murfreesboro and his third at Chickamauga, where he was captured. Brig. Gen. John Adams of Tennessee, son of an Irish-immigrant father, had received a brevet promotion for gallantry during the Mexican War. Wounded in the arm early in the battle of Franklin, Adams refused to leave the field, where his shattered brigade lost 450 men. Instead, he rode up to the Federal breastworks and tried to leap his horse over them. A hail of bullets met the general and his horse, which fell on the mortally wounded Adams, who remained conscious for a time and bravely told a Yank, "It is the fate of a soldier to die for his country."

Many Southerners bled and died for their country during the 1860s. The typical Confederate military leader either died in battle or suffered one or more wounds during the war; whether predominately Cracker or Cavalier, he needed courage because his men demanded it and because he demanded it of himself. Individual honor, of course, required bravery, but so did family, clan, and community. Unwilling to face their peers in disgrace, most Confederates despised cowards and dreaded dishonor more than death. A foreign visitor recorded Col. George Grenfell's explanation "that the only way in which an officer could acquire influence over the Confederate soldier was by his personal conduct under fire. They hold a man in great esteem who in action sets them an example of contempt for danger; but they think nothing of an officer who is not in the habit of *leading* them. In fact such a man could not possibly retain his position. Colonel Grenfell's expression was, 'every atom of authority has to be purchased by a drop of your blood.'" In other words, Confederate military leaders—whether Cavaliers or Crackers—preferred death in battle to the white feather of cowardice.

CHAPTER THREE
Sex and Chivalry

Friends and enemies of the U.S. Military Academy agreed that West Point—where the overwhelming majority of the officers of the "old army" began their military careers between the ages of fifteen and twenty—left its mark upon these young men. Their experience at the academy, it might be argued, was somewhat analogous to the "frontier experience" described by Frederick Jackson Turner. At West Point, cadets were stripped of their previous habits and ways and reshaped by an environment that stressed discipline and conformity.

Instructors insisted that they could (and did) homogenize the "most heterogeneous [material] imaginable—youth of good education, poor education, no education at all; from the plow, the office, the machine shop, luxury, destitution, competence; with brilliant, mediocre, or little ability; with high moral development, or with tendencies colored by demoralizing environment; with strict and with lax views of the obligations of truth. From these are . . . weeded out the impossible, and the rest are . . . molded

[into] men." Academy authorities boasted that "no other institution in the world has so strongly impressed its stamp upon the whole body of its alumni."

Above all, they and others asserted, the West Point experience created officers and gentlemen of high moral character. "The Military Academy stands primarily for *character*," stated the institution's centennial history; "the paramount feature of West Point's work is its character developing and forming power." Antebellum observers, one historian noted, "seldom failed to be impressed with the character of the officers who were their hosts." A visitor praised the officer corps for "its moral character, its spirit of discipline, and its sentiment of honor and patriotism." Another traveler described the young West Point graduate he met on the upper Mississippi River as "a gentleman, . . . high minded, honorable, strictly honest and correct in all his deportment."

To test this generalization, I have examined the attitudes and actions of West Point graduates regarding sex, women, and marriage. These topics were selected for investigation because sexual behavior was considered one of the strongest indicators of character in the nineteenth century. If the West Point experience actually produced a uniform value structure, this homogeneity should be apparent in the sex life of "old army" officers.

The relatively isolated location of West Point as well as the academy's restrictive routine limited contact between antebellum cadets and females and doubtless encouraged what an instructor called the "clean habits of life." "The moral discipline of the institution is perfect," announced the Board of Visitors in 1828, "the avenues to vice are closed, and the temptations to dissipation . . . have been vigilantly guarded against." "Our recreations are very few," complained a cadet in 1830. "They consist chiefly in walking over a plain about 800 yards in diameter & in the enjoyment of each other's society (which, to me at least, is rather more of a bore than anything else) when it is not study hours or drill. . . . By far the most profitable & pleasant of our time is . . . spent in the mess hall. There are a very few ladies in the Point & those, who are here, are pretty old & ugly which is not at all congenial with my taste." Girls attended such occasions as the annual fall dance, but usually females were so scarce at West Point that cadets practiced dancing with each other. "It is rather dry business dancing without ladies," admitted one young man.

The scarcity of girls at the academy probably caused cadets to act with more than usual adolescent awkwardness when in the company of females. "I forgot to describe my meeting with Miss Margaret Robinson," wrote Cadet Edmund Kirby Smith in 1844. "A party of us had taken a stroll through the woods Saturday afternoon to breathe the fresh air, gather chestnuts & on our return in passing a party of ladies & officers I heard someone exclaim—why really there's Edmund Smith. In consternation at being caught in such a plight for I was rather dishabille & with a mouth full of chestnuts I shook her warmly by the hand, but in my first attempt to express my pleasure at the meeting out flew the chestnuts bountifully distributed on all sides; had it not been for her open countenance beaming with delight I should have felt rather awkward—as it was I had a hearty laugh over it on my return to quarters."

Another cadet complained: "There is so little variety in the dismal routine of a cadet's life. We live isolated as it were in this insulated spot. There is little or no intercourse existing between the Cadets & the citizens living on the point. The small number of citizens & the ill breeding of some of the cadets (many of whom are perfect boors) render it probable that the nonintercourse will continue. We are never allowed to leave the point during the academic term."

The wives of army officers who lived at or visited West Point unquestionably taught the cadets much of what they knew about females. "Mrs. [Winfield] Scott and her daughters have been creating quite an excitement here," noted a cadet in 1844. "If I was the Old General I should be dreadfully jealous—Mrs.

Scott holds her levee to forty or fifty Cadets. . . . Gives them parties, sends them daily fruit, cakes &c.—and never seems at ease
till she gets a crowd of Cadets (her heart's corps as she calls
them) around her. She is very much liked and would make quite
a popular superintendent." Other army wives also entertained
cadets, though usually less elaborately than Mrs. Scott. "I spent
a pleasant afternoon with . . . [the wife of Gen. Edmund Pendle-
ton Gaines] and another lady, whose name I have forgotten,"
reported Cadet Alexander McRae, who was not attracted to all
females. "Mrs. G asked me to take her daughter (a child of about
14 or 15) to the ball, and dance with her; which I, as politely as
possible, declined."

In 1833 a foreign visitor charged that the contact between
cadets and women at West Point was not always innocent. "As
no watch is kept over the cadets at night," claimed an Englishman, "some leave their rooms and repair to haunts of dissipation among the hills, known only to themselves, where they
meet women of loose character, eat pork and molasses, drink,
and chew tobacco."

Some cadets undoubtedly engaged in heterosexual intercourse while at West Point, but opportunities for coitus were
probably infrequent. "We are kept tremendously strict, I assure
you," announced one cadet. Another lad reported that life at the
military academy consisted of "temperance, cleanliness, and
regular diet." Yet in 1846 a cadet reportedly sneaked two prosti-
tutes into his room, where he kept them overnight. They were
discovered the next morning, and he was forced to resign from
the academy.

Surely talk and teasing about sexual experiences, real and
imagined, abounded among cadets. At least one such incident
led to violence. When a cadet from South Carolina suggested
that Emory Upton had been intimate with Negro girls at Oberlin
College, which he had attended before coming to West Point,
Upton challenged his accuser to a duel. They fought with
swords in the dark; Upton was slightly wounded.

A few homosexual relationships probably developed. Though I have discovered no overt acts mentioned in letters, it seems unlikely that none occurred among young men living in such close contact over a prolonged period of time. Latent homosexuality, if nothing more, seems indicated in the letters of Cadet Stephen Dodson Ramseur to his friend David Schenck. Some of the phrases Ramseur used were: "remember, my dear Dave, that in my breast beats a heart that will ever cling to you"; "I know you, Dave, and I love you"; "whenever I write to you my blood rapidly approaches the boiling point"; and "I love you as ever."

Ramseur confessed: "I wish that I could change my pen & paper for a seat by your side. I could say many things that I can not write; and then to look upon your dear face, to feel the warm grasp of your hand and to hear kind words of Hope & encouragement that you always bestow upon me. Would not all this make my heart overflow and would I not then be able to express how dearly I love you." On March 27, 1858, he wrote, "Would that I could tell you the depth and intensity of the affection I feel for you. . . . But it is impossible for me to portray the depth of the affection I bear you. *You know it is tender* and deep." And on January 5, 1859, Ramseur admitted: "my Dear Old Dave! God Bless you! I wish I could *sleep with you tonight.* We would sleep a heap wouldn't we? How I long to hear of your adventures you! Patience! There's a good time coming!"

Ramseur's youthful difficulty in establishing his male sexual identity, perhaps exacerbated by the scarcity of females at Davidson College and at West Point, apparently eased as time passed. Before his death at Cedar Creek in 1864, Ramseur married and fathered a child.

Masturbation and nocturnal (perhaps even spontaneous) emissions probably were the most common sexual outlets for cadets. One young man recalled "the most beautiful creature" he ever beheld. "I have dreamed of her several times," he confessed. Another cadet revealed in a letter to a relative just how strong his fantasies of females were. "I do think there are some of the prettiest girls in Virginia that have flourished since the days of Helen," he wrote, "Angelic creatures! At this moment me thinks I see you standing in all the array of loveliness . . . , your alabaster skin—the auburn locks describing curves of unimagined beauty as they pang in graceful negligence over foreheads too pure for earthly mould. Oh! Oh! Oh how I do wish you all had but one mouth and that I could kiss it. Happy—thrice happy—would I be. I must hold in though. I am like gun powder whenever the subject is broached—off like lightning."

Yet if one cadet considered his stay at West Point sexually frustrating, another cadet apparently thought otherwise. "I frequently refer to the four years spent at the Military Academy as the happiest period of my life," stated John S. Hatheway in 1852.

After their graduation from West Point, officers usually enjoyed more frequent and freer contact with women. "I have [already] been to one party in the city," announced Lt. Lafayette McLaws just after his arrival in Baton Rouge. "The ladies are not handsome, of their other qualifications I cannot say anything for my acquaintance does not as yet extend beyond a mere party introduction." In 1859, from California, Lt. Edward Dillon wrote: "Benecia contains I presume as large a number of respectable women as any place in Cal, and it was with some regret that I left it. Besides a number of resident ladies, it boasts two female academies, where you may find the sex, of all colors, nations, and degrees, from the pure Castillian to the christianized China-woman."

Officers were socially acceptable in nearly any society; consequently, wherever they were stationed, they got to know the local females. "I am perfectly delighted with Louisville & the only drawback to my pleasure is the anticipation of having to return to the frontier to fried bacon and Indians," admitted Lt. Richard S. Ewell in 1845. "There are a number of *beautiful* women in this place and as unsophisticated a personage as myself would most certainly fall a victim were it not that one heals the wounds left by another." Gen. Philip H. Sheridan recalled that in 1854, when he was a young officer stationed on the southern border, the Mexican commander nearby often held dances to which the Americans were invited. "We generally danced in a long hall on a hard dirt floor," remembered Sheridan.

> The girls sat on one side of the hall, chaperoned by their mothers or some old duennas, and the men on the other. When the music struck up each man asked the lady whom his eyes had already selected to dance with him, and it was not etiquette for her to refuse—no engagements being allowed before the music began. When the dance, which was generally a long waltz, was over, he seated his partner, and then went to a little counter at the end of the room and brought his dulcinea a plate of candies and sweetmeats provided. Sometimes she accepted them, but most generally pointed to her duenna or chaperon behind, who held up her apron and caught the refreshments as they were slid into it from the plate. the greatest decorum was maintained at these dances, primitively as they were conducted; land in a region so completely cut off from the world, their influence was undoubtedly beneficial to a considerable degree in softening the rough edges.

Such limited, though sexually stimulating, contact with women doubtless hurried some young officers toward marriage. In 1859 Lt. Edward Dillon informed his sister that a fellow officer "will marry when he next goes home, since he seems to be scrupulous of late in courting every woman he meets; somebody will surely take him up." And Dillon added, "I want you and mother to prepare some young women, for a favorable reception of myself, and if I don't add the finishing stroke to the work when I get leave, it will be because of utter inability." Another officer explained to his nephew, a West Point cadet, just how to win a girl: "my little horse is beyond compare. I am going to take him away with me, break him & offer him to my sweetheart. I flatter myself she'll never resist the united attractions of myself & Tigertail." To most young officers, marriage apparently seemed desirable. In 1840, West Point cadets debated "whether it would be beneficial to the service to prohibit officers of the army under the rank of captain from being married." The negative side won the debate.

Officers married various types of women for various reasons. Certain men took a calculating, self-interested approach. "How often do unforseen accidents occur to change our most maturely considered plans," observed Lt. Robert Anderson, who had just been assigned to instruct cadets in artillery at West Point. "This winter I had hoped to have seen you—for 1837 I had planned to visit Europe—in 1838 I was to return and forthwith look around for a wife. But here comes a new change over my affairs, should I receive a permanent situation here, I may feel it a duty to my country to consider at once the propriety of taking a wife. I shall make no exertions to change my situation until I consider it a duty," Anderson promised his mother. "Much do I owe to you, my dear Mother, and to my dear Father, for your care and prudent management of me. I expect that you did not whip me as often as I deserved. . . . Never mind I'll have my boys whipped enough to make up for it. If I can find a wife who will educate her children so as to make them as contented as I am (barring a few touches of the rheumatism) I'll marry her directly, even if she has not more than twenty thousand Dollars for her fortune."

Marriage into a wealthy family provided some officers the means they needed to leave the army. Capt. Braxton Bragg admitted in 1848, "I cannot live out of the army, until I get a rich wife." He got one the next year, but he still could not leave the army because, as an officer noted, "her estate is so arranged as to be unavailable to either of them at present." In 1856, soon after his wife received her inheritance, Bragg resigned from the army and, with his wife's money, purchased a large sugar-cane plantation and 105 slaves. Not all officers who married rich women resigned, of course, but those who did apparently were not denounced by their former comrades. One informed his sister in 1859: "Two officers of my Regiment have married and resigned within the last year, and it is likely that one or two more will go and do likewise. I believe you know both [Archibald I.] Harrison & [William H.F.] Lee, both nice gentlemen, whose resignations we all regret, while we must admit, that in marrying rich women, and settling down in a decent country, they have acted most sensibly."

The supply of rich girls was never sufficient to meet the demand; most officers married females of modest or no fortune whom they had known back home or had met at army posts. "I called this afternoon on Capt. [Nathaniel C.] McRae who is now in command at the barracks at Newport opposite this place," a lieutenant wrote from Cincinnati. "His daughter, Miss Virginia, is the belle among the young officers stationed here." From Jefferson Barracks, Missouri, in 1844, Lieutenant Ewell stated: "This is the best country for single ladies I ever saw in my life. They are hardly allowed to come of age before they are engaged to be married however ugly they may be. Except the Misses Garlands I have not seen a pretty girl or [an] interesting one since I have been here." Ewell's standards may have been higher than those of other officers, who often married officers' daughters— one suspects—simply because they were there.

Some ambitious men, no doubt, hoped to win favor by marrying a high-ranking officer's daughter, but many young officers unquestionably were attracted to girls who understood army life. "Every afternoon we have . . . drill," wrote the West Point superintendent's daughter; "it is my favorite military pastime to sit on our piazza and watch it. You would laugh to see the interest I take in it, many of the maneuvers [*sic*], in fact I may say all, are familiar to me, for I have read the 'Tactics,' and sometimes my enthusiastic delight, at some well executed command, causes me to clap my hands, regardless of transgressing the limits of etiquette. But my fondness for the drill is a secret between ourselves, for I would not have civilians know what a thorough army girl I am." Some argued that the daughters of officers were more likely to accompany their husbands to remote outposts, perhaps because they knew what temptations single officers encountered on the frontier.

A traveler lamented that officers were too frequently "exiled" on the frontier, "far removed from cultivated female society, and in daily contact with the refuse of the human race." Lydia Lane, daughter of a major, emphasized the hardship she and other wives of officers experienced living in outposts. She recalled too how one wife, Mrs. Abner Doubleday, "was more afraid of a mouse than anything in the world. I remember she had a frame fixed around her bed and covered with netting to keep them out. She did not seem to dread snakes at all, nothing but an awful mouse!"

Some officers, for various reasons, were in no hurry to marry. Many were simply too poor. A large number of the West Point cadets, though from middle-class families, could expect little or no financial aid from home. Many, probably a majority, of the cadets were at the military academy because it was free; their families could not afford to educate them elsewhere. In 1831 Cadet Benjamin S. Ewell refused to ask for summer leave because the expenses of the trip home "would require a much larger sum than the present condition of Mother's finances would admit of her sending." He also refused to borrow money from his sister. "I am very much obliged to you for your generous offer," he informed her, "but I could not think of depriving you of the pittance you have earned." It was quite common for junior officers to be in debt for some time following their graduation from the military academy. In 1839 Cadet William T. Sherman asked his mother for "$5 to satisfy some little debts." He promised to repay her as soon as he received his commission as a lieutenant. Then his income—"upwards of $700 yearly inde-

pendent of quarters and fuel"—would "be amply sufficient" for
a single man stationed at one of "the Western posts. To be sure,"
admitted Sherman, "the outfit upon graduation will be quite
heavy but it is generally so arranged as to be paid for gradually
at different periods of the year." In 1835 Lt. Robert Anderson
asked his mother: "Will you promise, if I can marry well, that
you will come and spend some of the summer months with
your new daughter? Remember that [my brothers] John,
Charles, and William only got married by accident before I did. I
have always been well disposed in that way, and have been prevented by untoward circumstances, such as having no house to
live in, not having pay enough to support a wife &c."

A few simply considered marriage unsuitable to army life.
"A beautiful life this military life of ours isn't it?" asked Maj.
John S. Hatheway. "Such variety, such unexpected incidents,
here today, gone yesterday. Still to a good for nothing old bachelor (like myself) who has no one but himself and soldiers to care
for it is not without its attractions, far from it, but it is no place
for a family, the army. I have come to that conclusion from long
experience and mature deliberation, and I *think* I may safely say,
so long as your brother John is an officer of the U.S. Army so
long you may write him down 'Old Bachelor.'"

Others remained single because they were too occupied at
the moment with other activities. Upon being assigned to duty
as an instructor at West Point, Lt. Edmund Kirby Smith confided
to his diary: "in truth I have avoided society and pass the
greater portion of my time in my own room. . . . I feel a distaste
for the gaities and enjoyments of society and much prefer the
quiet and seclusion of my own room. Moreover I came to West
Point solely for the purpose of study and improvement, and care
not for flitting away my time in idle and ceremonious calls of
society." To a nephew who accused him of being more interested
in women than in war, Lt. Joseph E. Johnston replied: "no, no,
Pres: women are pleasant & attractive creatures, beyond denial.
When one has nothing else to think of, or to excite him—but

those who believe such a story know me little. There are not—
never were—women enough in the world to allure me from the
chance of one hostile shot."

The reactions of officers to Indian women were as varied as to
white women. "Many of the Officers have Cherokee Mistresses, a
scrape I intend to keep out of both on account of my purse and
taste," announced one lieutenant. "Occasionally a good looking
half breed may be seen but generally they are a dirty set and all
have a smoky odor about them which is particularly disagreeable to me at the distance of ten yards for I was never closer."

A number of men, of course, got much closer to the "dusky
damsels" than the fastidious lieutenant. In 1847 an Oregon set-
tler wrote: "I am decidedly opposed to military posts among
Indians. *A dragoon camp is the gate of hell*—the wickedest place I
ever saw." And a soldier admitted: "As a general rule, the Indians resent any special attention to the young females of their
race by the white man. Only long residence among them, and a
line of conduct on the part of the white man that wins their confidence, is this race prejudice overcome. It is well understood
among them that a large majority of soldiers—at least ninety-
nine out of a hundred—who seek the society of their girls do so
merely to spend agreeably the passing hour, and that their special attention cannot be relied on as indicating any desire for
marital relations." One officer who married an Indian was so
ostracized by his fellow officers that he secured a transfer and
abandoned his wife and child. She followed, however, and her
devotion impressed him so much that he resigned his commission and settled with her and the child in Galena, Illinois.

Wherever they were stationed, officers who wanted tempo-
rary relationships with women could usually find them. "I have
not yet procured you a bedfellow for the coming winter," the
chief justice of Utah Territory apologized to an officer in 1858. "I
have spoken to one woman and she says if her husband is
agreed to it she would like to go but not until she is freed from
her present *interesting* condition. She says she has a sister who is

the 2nd wife of an old *Cap* and she has one child and wants to leave him and she will send and inquire if she will cook and wash for you. I think she will do—I told her sister to let me know. I think also that if she does not succeed in that *quarter* I will in some other—hold *on a little*." From Louisville in 1845, Lt. Richard Ewell wrote: "somebody rapped at my door just then & lo and behold a waiter came in with a bouquet of the finest flowers with a card on which was written in a *female hand* 'From a friend, a Cincinnati bouquet.' These ladies do certainly plague one out of his life. . . . The Bouquet . . . came I presume from a widow whom I have, or rather who has been sparking me & who at present is on a visit to Cin'ti. She is rich and is engaged to be married but like most widows is fond of a flirtation. Do you remember [Franklin] Saunders who graduated at West Point in 37 & belonged to your section? He was regularly victimized by this same widow." Later Ewell wrote: "I am obliged to you for your offer to select a finer specimen of the genus woman that can be found in New Mex., but as you have not seen these latter I doubt your capability of judging. Yet awhile these are good enough for me."

Officers usually were more demanding when they sought wives. One man revealed his views in discussing his sister and her boyfriend. "Elizabeth does wrong in asking him to ride about with her," he wrote. "It is not at all delicate and Mother ought to put a stop to it. Reports very injurious to Elizabeth's reputation might be the consequence. . . . In this 'world that we live in' too much care cannot be taken to prevent malicious reports being spread—and a female ought to be particularly cautious," he concluded. Most officers probably agreed that a virtuous reputation for a woman was a valuable commodity in the marriage market. "A Christian woman is the most Heavenly of earthly creatures," announced Lt. William D. Pender. "Darling," he wrote his wife, "I love you more than I ever knew, and how much superior you are to any of the ladies around you. You have goodness, Oh! how good; intelligence, youth & beauty;

what more could I ask? If I were not satisfied I would indeed, be difficult to please. Please, be assured my own precious wife that I ask for nothing more in my wife." Another officer insisted: "There is something enobling and elevating in the society of refined women which is seen and felt by all who come in contact with them. No garrison is complete without ladies, and there should be a number at every military post."

Yet another officer charged that most army wives were selfish schemers who spent more than their husbands made, drank excessively, and flirted outrageously. "There is a freedom of manners among ladies of the Army that does not obtain in the best civilian society," stated Lt. Duane M. Greene. "Married ladies may accept costly presents and receive little attentions and visits from agreeable bachelors without provoking the jealousy of their husbands or offending the general sense of propriety." The "gay and lighthearted" wives of officers took "advantage of every opportunity for enjoyment"; they regarded "all occasions and circumstances as favorable for 'sport.'" The wife of one post commander boldly walked hand in hand across the parade ground at noon with a bachelor, remembered Greene. Nor was it unusual for wives to "bestow their smiles and approving glances upon the debauches who show the least regard for the proprieties of refined society" or for a woman to get her husband promoted "by the adroit manipulation of her admirers."

The validity of Greene's charges is difficult to determine. Army life—characterized by long and frequent separations of husbands and wives and by the forced familiarity of garrison life, especially on the frontier—unquestionably promoted a certain "freedom of manners." But it is impossible to establish whether the wives of "old army" officers were more adulterous than the wives of antebellum American civilians. The sexual attitudes and actions of army wives, like those of army officers, apparently varied widely.

Even the soundest marriages probably suffered when assignments kept officers apart from their wives and children for a long time. From Mexico City in 1847, Capt. Benjamin Huger wrote a friend: "Personally I should not mind spending a year or two here more or less, but there is the family at home. Boys will grow up—& my presence with them is of great importance. So I am in earnest in asking to be relieved in the spring."

After nearly two years on the West Coast away from his family, Capt. Ulysses S. Grant wrote his wife, "You do not know how forsaken I feel here." To dull his loneliness, he drank; "misery loves company," he noted, "and there are a number in just the same fix with myself, and . . . some who have separated much longer from their families than I have." A few months later, in 1854, the separation became too much for Grant to endure; he resigned his commission.

In 1836 an officer's wife wrote her husband: "You bid me be happy. Dearest, I *cannot* be happy when I am separated from you; for although I may be cheerful, I always feel that there is something wanting—some part of myself missing, dearer than my right arm." The following year she admitted: "You have been gone two weeks, my beloved, and what long, long weeks they have been to me. You bade me forget you dearest, while we are separated, but I can not. I dream of you—think of you always. I frequently take my *siesta* after dinner but I have been thinking of giving it up. I don't like it so much as I did when I had *company*. I dream of you and feel lonely when I wake and find that you are not there."

"Oh! darling you know not what a pleasure looking at your likeness give me," one lieutenant, away on patrol, informed his wife: "It is almost like looking at your self. If I could see that self, but we must make the best of it. We will love each other, enjoy the company of each other so much the more when we meet. How I will pet you, hold you in my lap, in fact do every thing that will please you."

Col. Robert E. Lee told newly wed Mrs. Winfield Scott Hancock: "I understand that you contemplate deserting your post, which is by your husband's side, and that you are not going to California with him. If you will pardon me, I should like to give you a little advice. You must not think of doing this. As one considerably older than Hancock, and having had greater experience, I consider it fatal to the future happiness of young married people . . . to live apart, either for a short or long time."

One officer complained after his arrival at Jefferson Barracks, Missouri, in 1844: "There is no garrison here but a few grass widows belonging to the 2d Regt. & very poor company . . . they make—always grumbling about their Husbands. I never saw a place so well calculated . . . to cure an officer of a matrimonial disposition." Two months later the situation was just as unpleasant. "Several families of the 4th were left here, when the Regiment went to La., expecting the Regt. to return soon," complained a sociable officer, "but their absent Husbands & lovers occupy the thought & conversation so much when one visits them that it is quite a bore to call."

An absence often caused husbands and wives to worry about what their spouses might be doing. To his wife, who had admitted attending a dance while he was away, one officer wrote: "Honey I am glad you do not dance the fancy dances with anyone but me, for I should feel jealous of having anyone but myself putting his arm around your waist. I do not think the less of other ladies for doing those things, but prefer your not doing so. One thing certain Capt. Smith must never do it again. That I am determined upon."

Even Gen. John E. Wool complained to his wife: "I have not received a line from you. . . . If I had not heard from you indirectly I would have concluded you were sick. . . . Miss Foote said she had received a letter from some friend . . . who informed her that she had seen you a short time before at a party . . . , when you looked uncommonly well as *young* and as *beautiful* as anyone in the room, all which has induced me to believe that you have not been sick but probably very busy." At another time the general informed his wife: "Don't be jealous because the old folks are . . . kind to me during my stay in this country, I mean the old Ladies, who think *I look remarkably young considering how old I am.* As for the Young Girls you know I don't look at them however much they may look at me. I always turn my back upon their pretty faces. That is just as you would wish and you know I always do as you wish."

Some officers clearly had reason to be jealous. From New Mexico an officer wrote:

> I believe . . . a man would do better to marry in this country, provided he never was so imprudent as to return home at unreasonable hrs. or when not expected. A Maj. [Oliver L.] Shepherd, Infy. passed the other day with his wife, a Mexican about 15 yrs old when he married 6 or 8 months since. They stopped here during the heat of the day & prospects ahead for him made me feel melancholy. He is a fool & coarse brute & neglects this girl very much. There were scoldings & disputations when they got into the carriage & temper in the greatest abundance. She, raised among those whose virtue was very easy, young & neglected by her husband, who is crass & not agreeable . . . has, as I can see, hardly one chance in fifty of keeping within bounds. The first sproutings looked almost ready to burst forth—I have no doubt when he finds the horns full grown he will make a devil of a fuss just as if they were not entirely owing to his stupid & brutal course.

In 1860 a friend wrote handsome Lt. James B. McPherson, who was stationed in San Francisco: "It is not necessary for me of course, to give you any advice as to your intercourse with women, your experience has doubtless perfected your education. I will merely say to you, never take a *respectable married* woman to an assignation house, & run the risk of detection; rather wait your opportunity at home, & make haste with the operation, after the fashion of the Ram, quick, but *often*."

The brazen conduct of some men shocked their fellow officers. During the Mexican War, Lt. John Pope and another officer were "accused of kidnapping two Mexican women, one 14 yrs old . . . , for carnal purposes. One thing is certain," noted an officer, "the women live with them now, and ride thru the city with them in defiance of decency in an open carriage furnished by the Q[uarter] M[aster] Dept."

Other officers were equally outraged by the adulterous acts of certain army wives. "Men can not fully understand the goodness of a good woman," an officer admitted to his wife. "They are so much our superiors. . . . And oh! darling a bad woman; did you see that Mrs. [John M.] Brannan, wife of Capt. B. who was supposed to have been residing in New York nearly one year ago was seen in Florence[?] with Lt. [Powell T.] Wyman. She ought to be burnt, & he quartered, for after every thing else to have abused the confidence of a brother officer. We of all others ought to protect each others wives, having to place confidence in each other. It seems to me, if I were in poor Brannan's place, I should go crazy, after first committing murder."

Officers tended to caricature women as either devils or angels. Public contact with a loose woman, one whose flirtations and indiscretions might jeopardize the reputation of her husband or companion, was socially and professionally dangerous, though intercourse with such a woman often did not produce guilt or tarnish self-respect. A wife, however, might be placed on a pedestal and idealized. Neither stereotype allowed women the humanity in vice or virtue that men allowed themselves.

A stereotyped view of the opposite sex was not confined to officers, or even to men. The cultural patterns that often encouraged men to treat women as sex objects also encouraged women to see men as lustful and sometimes foolish animals.

The attitude toward men expressed by Eliza Johnston, wife of Col. Albert Sidney Johnston, probably represented the popular biases of her time and sex. From the Texas frontier, she wrote in her diary on March 30, 1856: "I made a discovery through my cook the other day hearing her say a poor woman was very sick in camp with a young baby 5 weeks old and both neglected. I told her to go and see if I could have anything done for her & asked where her husband was. She said she was Lieutenant [Charles W.] Fields mistress & the baby was his. He had taken a woman from her good decent husband in Missouri and brought her here to Texas. Oh! you immoral men what should be your fate for all the sorrow you cause in this world. I never can talk to the man with pleasure or patience again & yet he is considered a gentleman and a fine officer. I do not know why but I had a dislike to that man ever since I first knew him in Austin."

A day later Mrs. Johnston noted:

> Mr. Fields keeps his mistress now openly in the camp. I get all this news from Mrs. Capt. [James] Oak[e]s who I verily believe would cause trouble in Heaven, "memo" I must beware of her. . . . I listen to all, but say nothing. Mrs. Capt. [Innis N.] Palmer had her first babe about 2 weeks since a bride of just a year, and being still in bed she is receiving all the young gentlemen at the post and the strangers of the court martial. What strange things people do. The night of the birth of her babe she was walking the room in great pain when Lieut. [Cornelius] Van Camp knocked at the door. Capt. Palmer foolish man opened the door and asked him to walk in & take a seat, which he did, and the poor woman sat down in an arm chair and dared not even groan. There he sat and talked until at last he remarked her countenance when he said Mrs. Palmer you look sick, shortly after, he left. What a goose the husband is.

Some of these men were shocked by certain sexual habits, especially those of foreigners. "People rarely marry in this region, particularly among the lower class," reported an officer from Baja California. "They 'take on' as a soldier would say.

They don't know what *chastity* is. I have seen mothers selling their daughters for two, three, four and six dollars. I am told that in the Ranchos in the interior it is no uncommon thing for a father to have connection with his daughter. The country is cursed with Mexican blood. Yet I am told that it is virtuous, when compared with some parts of Mexico."

One of the most intolerant officers to observe and comment on the sexual morals of foreigners was Capt. Edmund Kirby Smith, who visited Europe in 1858. In France and Germany, where he saw women working "in the most public places" and "engaged in the legitimate occupations of men," he was disgusted. "Women are thus taken from their household duties and out of their legitimate sphere & forced into positions & occupations, whence they soon lose their modesty & where their morality soon forsakes them," he charged.

On July 9 he noted in his diary: "I have seen in one hour more beautiful women in . . . Vienna than in all the rest of Europe combined, and with it find morality at a lower par than elsewhere; twenty-five out of thirty of the children born here are said to be illegitimate, and intrigue seems to be the order of the day. As a check upon the immorality of the Viennese, the Emperor of Austria was advised to licence houses where women of doubtful character could live together under the surveillance of the Police—he refused, saying 'that in that case he would have to build one grand roof over Vienna & licence the whole city.'" The captain reported special hospitals where unmarried pregnant women went "in the most secret manner" to have their children.

Smith believed "that whilst the public taste was improved the morals must be deteriorated" by the Liechtenstein Art Gallery, which was filled with what he called "lewd & lascivious subjects . . . in all the rich coloring and nudity of nature . . . with the scenes & acts so vividly represented that nothing is left to the imagination. . . . Why the most broken down old blaze could not walk through some of these European galleries, without feeling the blood course through his veins in rapturous excitement," he declared, "and yet the halls swarm with women of every age & clime and sphere of society—the middle age matron and the young girl just budding into womanhood may be seen side by side commenting on and criticizing the rape of . . . Europa, or the more scriptural subject of Susannah and the Elders."

Of all the places in Europe Smith visited, he was most critical of Italy. "The Italian characteristics now first show themselves, rags, garlic & misery—bare legged Lazzeroni and jolly Pappas," he sneered on July 30. After visiting the excavations of Pompeii, he wrote: "I noticed that the houses were generally marked with some sign indicating the occupation of their inmates; the houses of ill-fame were decorated with a huge *indescribable arrangement,* sculptured in stone over the street door, and frequent recurrence of these buildings with sign rampant was quite significant of the tastes of the Pompeians. . . . The pictures (mural or fresco) in many of the houses were good," admitted Smith, "but the large number of licentious and obscene subjects indicated a depraved state of morals and habits. The luxurious and licentious mode of life of the Romans was the cause of their downfall, and its consequence are exhibited in the miserable race which now represent that once great and powerful people. In no other part of the enlightened world has human nature so retrograded; the mass of men are under five feet, and the large proportion of dwarfs and hideous specimens of deformity . . . is as distressing as it is remarkable."

It is impossible to know, of course, just how many officers of the "old army" accepted Captain Smith's code of sexual morality. Some—maybe most—did, but certainly there were exceptions.

Smith saw nothing humorous in sex; to him it was a sober and often an immoral subject. But this was not the case with a number of officers, who considered sex a suitable topic for jokes. "Major [Granville O.] Haller started to York [Pennsylvania] this morning to be married to-morrow to a Miss Cox," an officer informed another. "He has taken a warm time for it and though the nights are now at the shortest I think he will find them long enough." Candidly and with apparent amusement, Ulysses S. Grant wrote his fiancée in 1845: "I was . . . returning [to barracks from New Orleans] between 1 and 2 o'clock at night when I discovered a man and a woman that I thought I knew, footing it to the city carrying a large bundle of clothes. I galloped down to the Barracks to asc[er]tain if the persons that I suspected were absent or not and found that they were. I was ordered immediately back to apprehend them, which by the assistance of some of the City Watchmen I was able to do. I had the man put in the watch house and brought the *lady* back behind me on my horse to her husband, who she had left asleep and ignorant of her absence. Quite an adventure wasn't it?" To a friend, another officer wrote: "[Lt. Truman] Seymour's wife still resembles the barren fig-tree, producing no fruit. It does not proceed from want of moisture about the roots, for Seymour's *root* is kept constantly in motion so his friends say."

When Congressman Daniel E. Sickles killed Philip Barton Key, son of "The Star-Spangled Banner's" author, for seducing Mrs. Sickles, officers differed in their reactions. "I have sent you several copies of the N. Y. Herald, containing the account of the trial of Sickles," wrote one young man. "No doubt the trial is full of interest to you as it is to all. He was acquitted as every one supposed he would be." Another man informed a lieutenant stationed in San Francisco, "I presume the bachelors of your city were very much affected as the young men, or rather single men, of New York which was, that no *unmarried* man was known to have an *erection* for at least *ten days after* the death of poor Barton Key!"

The diverse sexual attitudes and actions revealed in the writings of "old army" officers refute the claim that they were homogenized by the West Point experience. They disagreed on when and on whom to marry, even on whether or not to marry.

Some officers pampered and sheltered their wives; others neglected them. Women were treated as sex objects by certain officers at certain times, but these or other officers often regarded females as companions, as aids in professional or social advancement, or as sources of income. At least some officers copulated with the wives of fellow officers, and others kept mistresses. Frequently, officers denounced each other's actions. Those with robust or indiscriminate tastes were censured by those with more subdued sexual drives, who in turn were laughed at by the bawdy and uninhibited. The range was wide: from an Edmund Kirby Smith, who was disgusted by the "lewd & lascivious" paintings in the Liechtenstein Gallery, to a John Pope, who allegedly kidnapped a fourteen-year-old Mexican girl "for carnal purposes," to a William D. Pender, who uninhibitedly informed his wife: "Speaking of health, I have a cure for the *piles* and if you suffer in the least please try it. Let Marshall get you a tarred rope, such as used about ships—light it, then blowout the flames and smoke your piles. If the first smoking does not cure you try again in a day of so, and if you find it does any good repeat till it ceases to trouble you. Try this, for I know it to be good."

Some officers, of course, avoided any discussion of sex in their letters or diaries; others made only vague or disguised references to the subject. Rarely did those who refused to write openly about sex reveal as clearly through the use of symbolism their conscious or unconscious sexual wishes as did former "old army" officer P.G.T. Beauregard. In 1862, after he had become a Confederate general, Beauregard wrote to the novelist Augusta J. Evans: "Permit me to send you by one of my aids . . . the pen with which I have written all my orders & reports of battles from the fall of Sumter to 'Shiloh' inclusive. It is now like myself, a little the worse for the wear & tear of over 15 months' active service in the cause of our country—but will still do its duty faithfully, if handled with care. I beg you to believe that I do not send it to you, on acct. of the importance I attach to it, but the ladies here seem to prize so highly my *pencil*, that I have been presumptuous enough to think, that one who writes so ably & beautifully as yourself, would probably appreciate still more my *pen*, however unattractive in appearance it may be."

CHAPTER FOUR

Grant's Military Model

The claim is often made that Ulysses S. Grant became a successful general for an astonishing reason—he failed to learn the formal military lessons taught to all pre–Civil War professional soldiers. "In his studies he was lazy and careless," noted a contemporary. "Instead of studying a lesson, he would merely read it over once or twice." Grant's poor scholarship, so the argument runs, left him ignorant of the military theories and practices that more bookish officers memorized. "It is true," writes T. Harry Williams, "that Grant was not versed in doctrine, but his comparative ignorance was an advantage. Other generals were enslaved by their devotion to traditional methods." Grant, however, never allowed military orthodoxy to supersede common sense. In this way, argues Bruce Catton, "Grant was . . . definitely unprofessional. His attitude . . . was much more the attitude of the civilian than the trained soldier." Unburdened by the sterile dogma that handicapped so many of his fellow officers, Grant was thus free to act pragmatically and successfully.

Was Grant as uncommitted to orthodox military doctrines as this thesis suggests? What were his pre–Civil War military experiences? What lessons did he learn and from whom? What did he read on the art of war? Who were his heroes?

The future general in chief spent fifteen years in the army before the Civil War. His military career began as a cadet at West Point in 1839. After four years of study, he graduated from the military academy and was commissioned a brevet second lieutenant in the 4th Infantry in 1843. For the next three years, he was stationed at various posts in Missouri, Louisiana, and Texas. During the Mexican War, Grant served with both Generals

Ulysses S. Grant as a young officer

Zachary Taylor and Winfield Scott and received brevet promotions for gallant conduct in the battles of Molino del Rey and Chapultepec. Even so, it took him ten years to reach the rank of captain. In 1854, after a lonely assignment on the Pacific Coast, he resigned his commission to be with his family.

Grant claimed to have had mixed feelings about a military career. In his *Memoirs,* written some forty years after he was a cadet at West Point, Grant recalled, "A military life had no charms for me, and I had not the faintest idea of staying in the army even if I should be graduated, which I did not expect." But in a letter to a cousin, written soon after Grant arrived at West Point, he announced: "On the whole I like the place very much, so much that I would not go away on any account. The fact is if a man graduates here he [is] safe for life, let him go where he will. There is much to dislike but more to like. I mean to study hard and stay if it be possible."

Despite his promise to study hard, Grant compiled a mediocre record at the military academy. He ranked twenty-first among the thirty-nine cadets in his graduating class. His marks in military subjects during his final year were even less impressive; he ranked twenty-fifth in artillery tactics and twenty-eighth in infantry tactics. "I did not take hold of my studies," Grant later confessed, "in fact I rarely ever read over a lesson the second time during my entire cadetship." Furthermore, he admitted that he had considered the encampments, at which many practical military lessons were taught, "very wearisome and uninteresting."

Historians often assert that the two men who influenced the military thinking of Civil War commanders the most were Henri Jomini and Dennis Hart Mahan. Every graduate of the U.S. Military Academy before 1861, this argument goes, was exposed to the ideas of Jomini, an interpreter of Napoleonic warfare, who was considered the foremost authority on tactics and strategy. One officer remarked that "many Civil War general went into battle with a sword in one hand and Jomini's *Summary of the Art of War* in the other." And in the words of historian T. Harry Williams: "the American who did more than any other to popularize Jomini was Dennis Hart Mahan, who [taught] at West Point . . . [for more than thirty years] and who influenced a whole generation of soldiers. He interpreted Jomini both in the classroom and in his writings. . . . Probably no one man had a more direct and formative impact [than Mahan] on the thinking of the war's commanders."

Yet neither Jomini nor Mahan seems to have had much influence upon Grant's military thinking. The evidence here admittedly is mostly negative. Grant claimed that he had never read any of Jomini's works. There is no reason to doubt this. Jomini's works were all written in French, a language of which Grant had little knowledge. He admitted that, as a student of French, "my standing was very low." Not until 1859, long after Grant left West Point, was Jomini's *Summary of the Art of War* used as a textbook in tactics at the military academy, and then only in translation. There may have been books by Jomini in the West Point library when Grant was a cadet, but there is no evidence that he looked at any of them. Most of the books Grant read at the academy were, he guiltily confessed, novels.

It is true that Grant was exposed to Mahan's views in class, but there is no real evidence that he either fully understood or was affected by them. Unlike his friend William T. Sherman—who announced in 1862, "Should any officer high or low . . . be ignorant of his tactics, regulations, or . . . of the principles of the Art of War (Mahan and Jomini), it would be a lasting disgrace"—Grant never mentioned his old professor in letters or reminiscences. Mahan recalled years later that Cadet Grant had quiet manners and a boyish face but that he was not an outstanding student.

There are several reasons why Grant learned little about the art of war at West Point. None of his instructors, including Mahan, excited him. His earliest hero was not a professor, but Gen. Winfield Scott. "During my first year's encampment," recalled Grant, "General Scott visited West Point, and reviewed the cadets. With his commanding figure, his colossal size and showy uniform, I thought him the finest specimen of manhood my eyes had ever beheld, and the most to be envied. I could never resemble him in appearance, but I believe I did have a presentiment for a moment that some day I should occupy his place on review."

Grant may have been a lackadaisical student because he was shy and could not bear to be laughed at. He was far more concerned about his appearance than about his knowledge of warfare. "If I were to come home now with my uniform on," he wrote in 1839, "you would laugh at my appearance. . . . My pants sit as tight to my skin as the bark to a tree and if I do not walk *military,* that is if I bend over quickly or run, they are very apt to crack with a report as loud as a pistol. . . . If you were to see me at a distance, the first question you would ask would be, 'is that a Fish or an animal?' . . . When I come home in two years (if I live) . . . I shall astonish you *natives.* . . . I hope you wont take me for a Babboon."

Any desire he may have had to be conspicuous—to copy even in a modest way his first hero's ornate dress—vanished soon after he left West Point. "I was impatient to get on my uniform and see how it looked, and probably wanted my old schoolmates, particularly the girls, to see me in it," Grant remembered. But the "conceit was knocked out of me by two little circumstances . . . which gave me a distaste for military uniform that I never recovered from." The first incident occurred while Grant was riding down a street in his uniform, "imagining that every one was looking" at him: "a little urchin, barefooted, and dirty and ragged pants," said to Grant, "Soldier! will you work? No, sir-ee; I'll sell my shirt first!!" Grant was even more embarrassed when he returned home to find a "rather dissipated" stableman parading about in a pair of sky-blue pantaloons that were just the color of Grant's own uniform trousers. "The joke was a huge one in the mind of many . . . people, and was much enjoyed by them," he admitted, "but I did not appreciate it so highly."

Still another reason why Grant, as well as other cadets, learned little about the art of war at West Point was because too little time was devoted to the subject. Mahan mixed lessons on strategy and tactics into his engineering course for fourth-year students. "But few lectures [on the art of war] were given by Professor Mahan," recalled a former cadet, "and these were restricted almost entirely to short descriptions of campaigns and battles, with criticisms upon the tactical positions involved." An officer told a commission that was investigating instruction at the academy in 1860: "I do not think enough importance is attached to the study or standing in the several branches of tactics. These are not taught sufficiently." Most of the officers questioned by the commission agreed that cadets received inadequate instruction in strategy and tactics. "At present," complained a major, "even the infantry tactics is taught by officers of other corps, . . . taken almost hap-hazard, and who . . . have neither the antecedents nor position necessary to inculcate in the cadets a proper appreciation of its merits." A lieutenant who taught a section of "the theory of strategy and grand tactics" at West Point stated that the time allotted to his course "permits little more than the learning of principles." Another instructor proclaimed: "The time given to strategy is entirely too little. The subject is one of the very gravest importance, and in no other branch of the military art is 'a little learning' so dangerous a thing." Yet the superintendent of the academy warned that "it would not be well to have the [academic] standard . . . for graduating made too high. The demands of our service," he insisted, "do not require it."

It was easy enough for young cadets, studying in an environment where academic standards were not exceptionally high and most learning was done by rote, to misinterpret, oversimplify, or simply forget much of what Mahan taught. Grant and most other cadets apparently learned just enough to satisfy their examiners, but once they had passed the course—like so many students before and after them—they quickly forgot what they had been taught. That was not difficult. Mahan's views were neither unequivocal nor always precisely stated.

Nor was much done at West Point or at army posts to stimulate officers to further study. Regulations sometimes discouraged cadets from using the library, and some did not check out a single volume during their four years at the academy. "One of the important objects of education is to give habits of judicious reading," noted Gen. Joseph E. Johnston in 1860. "The present academic course [at West Point] is not calculated to do so. The abstruse sciences, to which the time of the cadet is mainly devoted, can, in after life, interest none whose pursuits require their frequent application, and therefore officers of the Army generally do not retain their school habits." An instructor at the academy testified, "I have never known of a single instance of an officer studying theoretically his profession (when away from West Point) after graduating." Lt. John M. Schofield of the 1st Artillery wrote: "It would be well if artillery officers could study after graduating, but my experience has been that they have no time. Without much subsequent study the elementary instruction is in a great measure lost." And another officer pointed out that the army offered "no incentive to exertion and study beyond the personal satisfaction each officer must feel who has a consciousness of having done his duty. The careless and ignorant officer is promoted, in his turn, with as much certainty as the accomplished and conscientious one."

There is nothing in either his letters or reminiscences to suggest that Grant spent any time studying his profession after he left West Point. Perhaps that is why he could write, "Soldiering is a very pleasant occupation generally." Years later he recalled that except for one instance, "I . . . never looked at a copy of tactics from the time of my graduation [from West Point]." That exception occurred when he received his first Civil War command. "I got a copy of [Hardee's] tactics and studied one lesson," Grant admitted. "I perceived at once, however, that

Hardee's tactics—a mere translation from the French with Hardee's name attached—was nothing more than common sense. . . . I found no trouble in giving commands that would take my regiment where I wanted it to go. . . . I do not believe that the officers of the regiment ever discovered that I had never studied the tactics that I used."

His writings indicate that Grant knew something of Napoleon Bonaparte's campaigns, but references to the Corsican are brief and suggest no more than what Grant might have remembered from his studies at West Point. For example, in 1845 Grant teasingly told his fiancée, Julia Dent, that her brother would have time "to prove himself a second Napoleon as you always said he would." Later, in describing the American flanking movement at Cerro Gordo, Grant suggested that the "Undertaking [was] almost equal to Bonaparte's Crossing the Alps." And finally, in his *Memoirs,* Grant wrote, "I never admired the character of the first Napoleon; but I recognize his great genius."

Most of what Grant knew about war in 1861 he had learned not from lectures or from books but from his own combat experience in Mexico. In his early actions at Palo Alto and Resaca de la Palma, he discovered something significant about himself. Combat was not as upsetting as he had supposed it would be: under fire he had been steady and calm. "Although the balls were whiz[z]ing thick and fast about me," he wrote Julia, whom he later married, "I did not feel a sensation of fear until nearly the close of the firing [when] a ball struck close by me killing one man instantly, it nocked Capt. Page's under Jaw entirely off and broke in the roof of his mouth, and nocked Lt. Wallen and one Sergeant down besides." To a friend, Grant explained: "You want to know what my feelings were on the field of battle! I do not know that I felt any peculiar sensation. War seems much less horrible to persons engaged in it than to those who read of the battles."

These and subsequent engagements strongly influenced Grant in other ways. He learned the value of regular troops and

rigid discipline. Anyone who believes that Grant had an unprofessional approach to war should look carefully at the general's
own words. "The victories in Mexico were, in every instance,
over vastly superior numbers," Grant wrote.

> There were two reasons for this. Both General Scott and
> General Taylor had such armies as are not often got
> together. At the battles of Palo Alto and Resaca de la
> Palma, General Taylor had a small army, but it was com-
> posed exclusively of regular troops, under the best of drill
> and discipline. Every officer, from the highest to the low-
> est, was educated in his profession, not at West Point nec-
> essarily, but in the camp, in garrison, and many of them in
> Indian wars. The rank and file were probably inferior, as
> material out of which to make an army, to the volunteers
> that participated in all the later battles of the war; but
> they were brave men, and then drill and discipline
> brought out all there was in them. A better army, man for
> man, probably never faced an enemy than the one com-
> manded by General Taylor in the earliest engagements of
> the Mexican war. The volunteers who followed were of
> better material, but without drill or discipline at the start.
> They were associated with so many disciplined men and
> professionally educated officers, that when they went into
> engagements it was with a confidence they would not
> have felt otherwise. They became soldiers themselves
> almost at once.

The campaigns of Taylor and Scott were the highlights of
Grant's pre–Civil War military education. From them Grant
learned strategies and tactics he would use in the Civil War.

For example, his Vicksburg campaign was similar to Scott's
bold march to Mexico City. Grant's account in his *Memoirs* of
Scott's campaign could have been, with only a few changes, a
fair description of his own brilliant moves that culminated in the

capture of Vicksburg. "He invaded a populous country, pene-
trating . . . into the interior," noted Grant, "he was without a
base; the enemy was always intrenched, always on the defensive; yet he won every battle."

Grant also saw Taylor's and Scott's forces attack and drive
the Mexicans from both open fields and fortified positions. He
reported with some amazement to Julia after the battle of Resaca
de la Palma: "Grape shot and musket balls were let fly from
both sides making dreadful havoc. Our men [con]tinued to
advance . . . in sp[ite] of [Mexican] shots, to the very mouths of
the cannon an[d] killed and took prisoner the Mexicans . . . taking cannon ammunition and all." After the Americans had successfully stormed Monterey, Grant wrote: "The city is built
almost entirely of stone and with very thick walls. We found all
their streets bar[r]icaded and the whole place well defended
with artillery, and taking together the strength of the place and
the means the Mexicans had of defending it is almost incredible
that the American army now are in possession here."

At first the young officer considered American attacks as
"incredible" and likely to fail, but ultimately he accepted them
as standard tactics. Why not? They always succeeded; U.S.
forces seemed invincible. Not only had they won every battle,
but also, when they attacked, they inflicted heavier casualties
than they suffered. By the spring of 1847, Grant would write of
the American attack at Cerro Gordo, which he witnessed, "As
our men finally swept over and into the [Mexican] works, my
heart was sad at the fate that held me from sharing in this brave
and brilliant assault."

Grant never forgot those assault tactics that had been so successful in Mexico. He used them in the Civil War, often to his
own detriment. They never worked as well for him as they had
for Scott and Taylor. The reason was simple: the standard
infantry weapon of the Mexican War, the smoothbore musket,
had been replaced by a superior rifled musket. The single-shot,
rifled muzzleloader could be fired two or three times a minute;

it could stop an attack at up to four hundred yards, and it could kill at a distance of one thousand yards. This weapon became the great killer of the Civil War. Because of the rifle's increased range and accuracy, Civil War infantry assaults were bloody, sometimes suicidal, affairs. For the first time in more than a century defenders gained the advantage in warfare. A few entrenched men armed with rifles could hold a position against great odds. In May 1864 a Federal soldier fighting in Virginia along the North Anna River wrote, "I discovered that our infantry were tired of charging earthworks; a good man behind an earthwork was equal to three good men outside it."

Yet Grant seemed reluctant to admit to himself that what he had learned in Mexico during the 1840s would not work as well in the United States during the 1860s. Finally, in June 1864, after losing more than seven thousand men in a frontal attack at Cold Harbor, Grant confessed: "I regret this assault more than any one I have ever ordered. I regarded it as a stern necessity, and believed that it would bring compensating results; but, as it proved, no advantages have been gained sufficient to justify the heavy losses suffered."

Some lessons are difficult to unlearn, especially those taught to young people by respected instructors. Taylor and Scott were not merely Grant's commanders; they were his heroes. It is understandable that their tactics and strategies had a lasting influence upon him. "I never thought at the time to doubt the infallibility of these two generals," Grant admitted. Nevertheless, there are two questionable letters that show—if they were written by Grant—that he did have his doubts. Still, Grant insisted that "the opinion of a lieutenant, where it differs from that of his commanding General, *must* be founded on *ignorance.*"

Though he admired and learned from both Taylor and Scott, Grant left no doubt which man influenced him the most. "Both were pleasant to serve under—Taylor was pleasant to serve with," admitted Grant, who announced after the Mexican War's opening battles, "history will count the victory just achieved [by

General Taylor] one of the greatest on record." And he later informed his fiancée that he had so much confidence in Taylor's military skill that "I do not feel my Dear Julia the slightest apprehension as to our suc[c]ess in ev[e]ry large battle that we may have with the enemy no matter how superior they may be to us in numbers."

What Grant later recalled in his *Memoirs* about Taylor is especially significant because it reveals not only what Grant admired in his old general but also how many of Taylor's characteristics and military practices he adopted. Taylor "was opposed to anything like plundering by the troops." So was Grant. "Taylor was not an officer to trouble the administration much with his demands, but was inclined to do the best he could with the means given him." So was Grant. "Taylor never made any great show or parade, either of uniform or retinue." Neither did Grant. Taylor "moved about the field in which he was operating to see through his own eyes the situation." So did Grant. Taylor was not a conversationalist. Neither was Grant. But on paper Taylor "could put his meaning so plainly that there could be no mistaking it. He knew how to express what he wanted to say in the fewest well-chosen words." So could Grant. And finally Grant said of Taylor what so many writers have said of Grant: "No soldier could face either danger or responsibility more calmly than he. These are qualities more rarely found than genius or physical courage."

The similarities between Taylor and Grant are too great to be accounted for by coincidence. At the outset of the Mexican War, Grant doubtless admired Taylor partly because Grant, even as a young soldier, was already much like the old general. But it also seems clear that Taylor, to a greater extent than has been realized, became Grant's military model. No other man so profoundly influenced Grant's pre–Civil War military education. "The art of war is simple enough," Grant once remarked. "Find out where your enemy is. Get at him as soon as you can. Strike him as hard as you can, and keep moving on." Zachary Taylor himself could not have given a better definition of how to fight.

It is ironic that a Southerner and a slaveholder had such a strong influence upon the Civil War's most successful Union general.

CHAPTER FIVE
Jefferson Davis and the Art of War

The president of the Confederacy remains controversial. Historians disagree over just how capable he was as commander in chief and what or who most influenced his military decisions during the Civil War. Almost a century ago, two scholars suggested that Jefferson Davis failed as a war leader because he thought he knew more about the art of war than he actually did. Hamilton J. Eckenrode hinted that the Confederacy may have been doomed to defeat as early as 1847, when Jefferson Davis formed his regiment of Mississippians into an obtuse angle and halted the attacking Mexicans at Buena Vista with converging rifle fire. "The applause [for this spectacular feat] was so great that he was deceived himself," notes Eckenrode. "He was looked on in the South as a great soldier and he was firmly convinced of his own military talents. His war service was destined to be decisive of his future. It put him in the Senate and made him President of the Confederacy. When the Richmond *Examiner* near the close of the Civil War said, "'If we are to perish, the verdict of posterity will be, Died of a V,' it was commenting bitterly on the consequences that had flowed from the famous obtuse angle of Buena Vista."

Maj. Gen. Sir Frederick Maurice, a British military expert, was even more specific. He claimed that Davis failed "in the general direction of [Civil War] military operations . . . because he had never worked out in his mind a system for the conduct of war." His knowledge of strategy "was insufficient to enable him to appreciate the difficulties of and the need for unity of direction of forces scattered over a wide area. Here," insisted Maurice, was "one more example of the danger of a little knowledge." Davis had "a tendency to rely too much on his small military experience, which caused him to concern himself with minor details." He simply "did not realize that the command of a battalion in the field might be an inadequate schooling for the direction of a great war."

In 1956 David Herbert Donald presented a provocative new thesis. He argued that the rigidity of Davis and his generals contributed to Confederate defeat. But it was not the Mexican War that had fossilized them, it was their devotion to the outmoded military ideas of Baron Henri Jomini. Northerners innovated and won; Southerners remained inflexible and lost. Donald claimed that Davis—a "military martinet, stiff and unbending," who "was constitutionally incapable of experimenting"— "retained to the end [his] . . . faith in Jomini's maxims."

Since the Donald essay appeared, Jomini has been mentioned in the texts and notes of most serious studies of Davis and other Confederate military leaders. But there is no agreement on either the nature or the extent of Jomini's influence on these men. T. Harry Williams thought it was strong and detrimental to Confederate generals, especially Robert E. Lee, but Williams makes no claim that Jomini's ideas shaped Davis's policy. Even so, Williams calls Davis's defensive strategy "the worst strategy for the South." Frank E. Vandiver admits that Jomini's maxims probably influenced Davis, who "had studied principles of war at West Point," but he insists that the Confederate president developed his own "bold and original war policy, which he called the 'offensive-defensive.'" More recent writers emphasize "Confederate strategy's strong conformity to the teachings of Jomini and Napoleon, and the prominent role of [Gen. P.G.T.] Beauregard in securing this conformity." Two other historians, Thomas L. Connelly and Archer Jones, argue that Davis favored a defensive or a counteroffensive strategy until he was won over in 1863 to the Jominian concept of "a surprise offensive concentration on an enemy weak point." This was precisely the strategy preached by Beauregard. Indeed, Connelly and Jones conclude that the "story of Confederate strategy can be perceived as a belated triumph for the western concentration bloc and for Beauregard's ideas."

All of these writers agree that, to some extent, Jomini shaped Confederate military thinking, but they disagree on just how strongly Davis was influenced and in what way. Donald argues that Davis consciously followed a Jominian strategy; Vandiver claims that Davis, though schooled in Jominian principles, adopted an "original war policy"; and Connelly and Jones insist that Beauregard's ideas, which came from Jomini and Napoleon, ultimately dominated Davis and Confederate strategy.

It is not my purpose here to challenge or to choose between these various theses, only to offer a mild demurrer. It seems that these distinguished scholars have presented conclusions based more on logic than on evidence. Dennis Hart Mahan taught Jomini's ideas at the U.S. Military Academy, which Davis and most high-ranking Confederate generals attended; Jomini's works were available in antebellum America either in French or in translation; consequently, it appears reasonable that West Point graduates, who had studied French and had taken courses in military science, were thoroughly familiar with the writings and maxims of Jomini.

But were they? Almost none of the letters by Confederate generals that I have examined mentioned Jomini. In 1860 Gen. Joseph E. Johnston recommended that Jomini's *Art of War* be dropped as a textbook at West Point because he considered Decker's *Tactics* and "three little works by Frederick the Great" more "instructive." Gen. Ulysses S. Grant, who graduated from the academy in 1843, claimed that he never read any of Jomini's works. It is sometimes overlooked that none of Jomini's books was used as a text while Jefferson Davis was at West Point. An English translation of Guy de Vernon's *Treatise on the Science of War and Fortification* was the text for a course on engineering and the art of war. One of Davis's worst subjects (he ranked twenty-fifth in a class of thirty-four), it was taught not by Dennis Hart Mahan but by David B. Douglass, an 1813 graduate of West Point. Of course, Davis may have studied Jomini's works after he left the military academy, but I have found no evidence that he did. Connelly and Jones also admit that neither Davis nor Lee "enunciated their [strategic] principles clearly nor showed to whom, if anyone, they were indebted."

If Davis got his Jomini indirectly from Beauregard, as Connelly and Jones claim, the Confederate president must have done so unconsciously, for he and Beauregard hated each other.

"My plan of campaign at Drewry's Bluff [in 1864] would have given us a glorious triumph . . . and probably peace and independence," boasted Beauregard, "but that obstinate and obstructive man who was at the head of our affairs ruined everything! He was no more fit to comprehend a bold and important military operation than a Benedek!" (Ludwig von Benedek was an Austrian general who was disastrously defeated at Sadowa in 1866.) Later, Beauregard wrote his friend Thomas Jordan: "Do you recollect what I used to say sometimes at Charleston, to-wit: 'That if Alexander, Caesar, Frederick the Great and Napoleon had been surrounded by such men as Mr. Davis had selected to be members of his cabinet and of the Government Bureaux and command some of his armies the names of those Great Emperors would hardly have been heard of in history except through their errors & defeats.'"

More important to the argument presented by Connelly and Jones is whether Beauregard was a Jominian. Such a question may seem absurd. He must have been, this "Napoleon in Gray" (as his biographer called him), this dapper Creole who reminded people of "Paris and Napoleon and Austerlitz and French legions." Jomini's overwhelming influence upon such a man's military ideas would appear as certain as Beauregard's supposed admiration for all things Gallic. But concrete evidence is scarce. I have been unable to find any place where Beauregard acknowledged Jomini's influence upon him. On the contrary, what I have discovered are tantalizing bits and pieces of evidence that are in no way conclusive but together raise some doubts about Beauregard's admiration for Jomini. For example, it was not Jomini that Beauregard recommended to his brother-

Jefferson Davis

in-law, Charles Villere, in 1862. "I did not take up my pen to give you a lecture on the 'Art of War,'" Beauregard wrote, "if you wish to learn something on that important subject, study 'The Theory of War' by Lt. Col. P.L. MacDougall—1 vol. London, & look particularly at from page 51 to 169. It is the best 'Field Book' I have yet read on that subject."

Again in 1862, in a letter to Gen. Braxton Bragg, Beauregard recalled not the lessons taught by Jomini or his interpreter at West Point, Dennis Hart Mahan, but rather those of the natural and experimental philosophy professor, William H. C. Bartlett. "In *tactics* as in *statics*," wrote Beauregard, "the force is equal to the mass multiplied by the square of the velocity, as Professor Bartlett used to teach us at West Point. We must profit by his lessons to put to rout those abolition hordes."

Beauregard admitted to a friend in 1867 that he did not own Jomini's works, but even more startling perhaps is his criticism of French tactics. "You are aware that the French &, generally, Latin races, generally attack in *columns* of Regts, Brigades or Divs," Beauregard wrote, "whereas the Anglo-Saxon races, Americans &c, always attack in *line* of battle. I prefer definitely the latter which gives a much greater development of fire— which after all decides the fight." That Beauregard always signed his letters "G.T." or "Gus," never "Pierre," may tell us more than we thought about his cultural identification.

It must be obvious by now that anyone bold, or foolish, enough to attempt further analysis of the Confederate president must somehow resolve a number of disagreements and some complex problems. Perhaps the best way to supplement what has already been done is first to examine the military ideas that Davis expressed before the Civil War.

By 1861, Davis had developed some clear views on military affairs. He believed that wars were justified to protect the honor or the security of a people. The Kansas civil war of the 1850s shocked him, for he abhorred the killing of civilians during any hostilities. He believed that war should consist solely of combat between organized armies. Years later, when General Grant was dying of cancer, Davis wrote, "I . . . have felt a human sympathy with him in his suffering, the more so because I think him so much better than the pillaging, house-burning, women persecuting Sherman & Sheridan."

Though war could be horrible, Davis thought that it could be glorious and just. "I hold that in a just war we conquered a large portion of Mexico," he argued before the Senate in 1848, "and that to it we have a title which has been regarded as valid ever since men existed in a social condition—the title of conquest." And to Sen. John C. Calhoun's charge that the Mexican War was "odious," Davis replied:

Odious for what? On account of the skill and gallantry with which it has been conducted? Or is it because of the humanity, the morality, the magnanimous clemency which has marked its execution? Where is the odium? What portion of our population is infected with it? From what cause does it arise? It cannot be on account of the origin of the war, the extraordinary unanimity with which it was declared by both Houses of Congress, [or] the eagerness with which our citizens pressed to the service. . . . We have cause to be proud of the record this war will leave behind . . . . We the actors of to-day, must soon crumble to dust . . . , but the events of this war will live in the history of our country and our race, affording, in all ages to come, proof of the high state of civilization amongst the people who conducted it.

The mention of race in the debate with Calhoun was no accident of oratory. Davis was certain that white Americans, and especially white Southerners, were a martial people generally superior to those around them. While a cadet a West Point in 1825, Davis admitted to his brother, *"The Yankee part of the corps . . . are not such as I formed an acquaintance with."*

But Davis did not believe Northerners were cowards. Early in the Civil War, he told a lady that "only fools doubted the courage of the Yankees, or their willingness to fight when they saw fit. And now that we have stung their pride, we have roused them till they will fight like devils."

In 1861 Davis told the famous English reporter William H. Russell: "In Europe they laugh at us because of our fondness for military titles and displays. All your travellers . . . have commented on the number of generals, and colonels, and majors all over the [South]. . . . But the fact is, we are a military people . . . . We are not less military because we have had no great standing armies. But perhaps we are the only people in the world where gentlemen go to a military academy who do not intend to follow the profession of arms."

The superiority of whites, Davis admitted, was often established and maintained by force. But this was as it should be. Slavery, he insisted, restrained blacks "from the vicious indulgences to which their inferior nature inclines them." Mexicans too were inferior to the white race because their blood was mixed with that of Indians, who were "cruel and thieving, a race of men utterly below . . . the white man, and never capable of rising to his level."

The Mississippian's proposal to the Senate in 1850 that cavalry should be assigned to protect the frontier contained a strong racist argument. "These men," he explained, "equipped and mounted, can . . . tame the terror of those predatory Indians which infest the borders of Texas. Our race is superior to theirs; our horses are superior to theirs; we are their superiors in every way. As to the skill and horsemanship of the wild men on their little grass-bred horses, it is nothing when brought face to face with our own race, riding our own horses and bearing the weapons which a skilful ordnance corps furnish to our troops."

While he was either a member of Congress or secretary of war, Davis revealed many of his military concepts during the 1850s. He directed his efforts mainly toward protecting the west-

ern frontier and the seacoasts and improving army weapons and
efficiency. He boasted that his "acts of public interest" as secretary of war included improved coastal and frontier defenses, the
adoption of the rifled musket and the "Minnie ball" or bullet,
and extensive geographical surveys and explorations across the
continent to discover the best railroad route to the Pacific Coast.
Davis, who appears to have recognized the strategic value of
railroads, wrote, "one of the most effectual elements of military
power must be railroads leading from the seat of population and
supply to all possible points on our frontier."

One reason why Davis worked to strengthen coastal defenses
and to find a rail route to the West Coast was because he had little confidence in the navy's ability to protect the country from
invasion. Though he often praised the navy's past exploits, he
believed that its true role was to support the army. The nation
should not "bear the useless expense of a naval establishment
larger than was necessary for its proper uses in a time of peace,"
Davis insisted. The cost of maintaining a fleet large enough to
challenge any great maritime power, or even to keep communication lines open to the Pacific in time of war, would be prohibi-
tive. The country could best be defended by fortified harbors
and a railroad system that connected the interior of the country
and the coasts. Like many Southerners, Davis tended to associ-
ate the navy with the interests of the Northeast and to minimize
its importance in warfare.

If Davis underestimated the navy's importance in war, no
such charge can be made against him regarding the army. The
improvement of that service, especially the training of officers,
always had his support. He favored extending the time devoted
to the martial arts at West Point as well as increasing the pay of
professors. He also insisted that the West Point commandant be
"a soldier of such character and experience as to enable him to
teach the strategy of war with advantage. . . . To effect this, it is
essential that he should be a soldier tried in war." Such a statement was a direct criticism of the interpreter of Jomini, Prof.

Dennis Mahan, who had no combat experience.

In 1850 Davis advocated raising the pay of West Point professors from $1,792 to $2,000 per year. Ten years later he headed a commission that recommended annual salaries of $2,200 plus rations for all professors at West Point. It would be "poor economy to strike at the source of the army's glorious reputation by parsimony in the salary of the professors," Davis argued, "instruction at this institution is peculiar"—"the science of war and of military engineering is taught in no other institution of the country. Therefore these chairs must necessarily be filled by officers drawn from the army, and must be men of the highest attainment in their profession."

To ensure what he considered adequate instruction, Davis favored 60 days of lessons in the science of war and an increase in the number of days devoted to tactics (from 62 to 84) and to riding (from 105 to 115).

Character and experience were essential not just in a commander of cadets; these were qualifications that Davis believed he—and all great soldiers—innately possessed. Though he owed much of his own political success to the military reputation he had acquired in Mexico, Davis disliked political generals because he thought they too often lacked character and military experience. "We have too many new generals, seeking a reputation for other (political) spheres," he announced in 1846. And later, when Pres. James K. Polk offered him promotion to general and command of a brigade of volunteers, Davis refused—not because he considered himself unqualified but because it seemed to him an inappropriate political appointment.

Many of Davis's ideas on military leadership and strategy were formed in Mexico, where Zachary Taylor became his military model; he also was the only army commander under whom Davis ever served. Taylor was the "great captain of the age," Davis avowed, "the world held not a soldier better qualified." A great commander, Davis informed Beauregard in 1861, was a man of moral strength, dauntless courage, and the "power that moves and controls the mass. This is not an ideal," insisted the Confederate president, "but a sketch of Taylor when general of the little army, many of whom would, no sooner have questioned his decisions, or have shrunk from him in the hour of danger than if" he had been their father.

This assertion was not just hindsight; Davis had demonstrated his loyalty to Taylor before either of them became Buena Vista heroes. "The desire to be in every battle fought during my term of service is strong," Davis wrote in January 1847, "but I could not in the present condition of Gen. Taylor ask to leave him." At that time most of Taylor's veterans had been transferred to Gen. Winfield Scott's army at Veracruz. Besides, Davis bluntly concluded, "I have no confidence in Genl. Scott."

Davis admired Taylor so much that he romanticized his old commander into something he was not—a soldier skilled in "military science." But it was Taylor's "manly courage" that Davis most appreciated. Of the first Mexican War battles, he wrote, Taylor "paused for no regular approaches, but . . . dashed with sword and bayonet on the foe."

It is not surprising that Davis believed that this was how war should be fought. At Monterey he impatiently led his regiment against a Mexican redoubt. "Now is the time," he reportedly shouted as his troops slowed their advance. "Great God, if I had fifty men with knives I could take the fort." The Americans, with Davis in front, rushed forward and drove the Mexicans from their strong position. The Mississippian's "power" and "courage" inspired a young soldier to write: "I verily believe that if he should tell his men to jump into a cannon's mouth they would think it all right, and would all say, 'Colonel Jeff . . . knows best, so hurrah, boys, let's go ahead.' He is always in front of his men, and ready to be the first to expose himself. I never wish to be commanded by a truer soldier than Colonel Davis."

As president of the Confederacy, Davis would be guided in his military appointments by the concepts of leadership that he had formed before the Civil War. He especially admired courage, modesty, boldness, and experience, and he found these characteristics in Albert Sidney Johnston, Robert E. Lee, and Samuel Cooper—the three highest-ranking Confederate generals. Of them Davis wrote: "It is a noteworthy fact that the three highest officers in rank, and whose fame stands unchallenged either for efficiency or zeal, were all so indifferent to any question of personal interest, that they had received their appointment before they were aware it was to be conferred. Each brought from the Army of the United States an enviable reputation, such as would have secured to him, had he chosen to remain in it, after the war commenced, any position his ambition could have coveted." Davis also found, at least to his own satisfaction, these same admired qualities in less likely individuals. Many of the men he appointed to high military rank had no better qualifications than that Davis had known and liked them at West Point, in the "old army," or in Mexico.

If the president appointed and retained men who seemed to him to possess those personal traits that he considered essential in military leaders, he also denounced and sometimes removed others who did not. From the war's outset, Davis tended to personalize disagreements. The two most famous examples of this are Joseph E. Johnston and P.G.T. Beauregard. Part of the problem appears to have been the generals' refusal to acknowledge that Davis knew as much about the art of war as they did. The president quickly concluded that they were too contentious and too jealous of their prerogatives and reputations; ultimately, he decided that they were untrustworthy.

After Davis and Johnston had a dispute over rank early in the war, they never trusted each other, but in 1862, after Johnston was wounded, Davis spoke well of his generalship. By 1863, one observer noted that "the President detests Joe Johnston . . . and General Joe returns the compliment with compound interest." As the Confederacy collapsed in April 1865, Davis complained to his wife: "J.E. Johnston and Beauregard were hopeless. . . . Their only idea was to retreat." And after the war Davis frequently denounced Johnston for his bad character, "selfishness," "convenient" memory, and "malignity and suppression of the truth."

As early as January 1862, it was clear to observers in Richmond that the president disliked Beauregard. "In speaking of the . . . Generals, their qualities & c., he . . . never names Beauregard," noted a cabinet member, "he does not like him or think much of him." Davis revealed his contempt for the Creole as well as his conviction that the man was not resolute when he wrote in October 1862, "Beauregard was tried as Commander of the Army of the West and left it without leave, when the troops were demoralized and the country he was sent to protect was threatened with conquest." And he replied when a delegation of Tennesseans asked him to restore Beauregard to command that he would refuse even if the whole world requested it.

Davis not only judged men by the standards that he had adopted before 1861, he also brought with him to the presidency a number of other views and prejudices on the art of war that would shape Confederate military affairs and strategy. His belief that what could be both just and glorious—as expressed in his debate with Calhoun—helped give Davis the confidence he needed to initiate hostilities in 1861.

He considered Southerners a martial people who would fight magnificently, or as he told a lady in 1861, "we will do all that can be done by pluck and muscle, endurance, and dogged courage, dash, and red-hot patriotism." His own fondness for combat caused him to favor bold—indeed, sometimes reckless—generals. He had some understanding of the strategic value of railroads, but his bias against the navy caused him to neglect that vital service.

His concept that wars should be fought only between organized armies prevented him from encouraging extensive espionage, sabotage, or guerilla warfare. His strong racial prejudices kept him from supporting the use of slaves as soldiers in the Confederate army until it was too late for them to help the

South. The standards by which Davis evaluated men aroused much criticism. Though he disliked political generals, he appointed enough of them to irritate professional soldiers but not enough to satisfy the politicians. By early 1862, Howell Cobb of Georgia complained that the president preferred "drunken West Point men . . . to worthy and accomplished men from private life." And in 1863 the head of the Bureau of War claimed that even "Mr. Davis's friends say that he is . . . the worst judge of men in the world, apt to take up with a man of feeble intellect or character, and when he had once done so, holds on with unreasoning tenacity."

Of all the military influences upon Davis before 1861, those from the Mexican War unquestionably were the most profound. The Confederacy's defeat may not have been ensured, as Bernard DeVoto flippantly remarked, by what Jefferson Davis learned "in exactly five days of action" in Mexico, but those months with Taylor's army stocked the future president with a reservoir of military experiences from which he continually drew lessons and judgments. After the Civil War, in a dispute over some military matter, Davis insisted that he knew a point he had made was correct. How did he know? His "experience as a commander of volunteers" in Mexico convinced him that he was right.

Objective evaluation of men or conditions was difficult for a romantic who considered organized combat in behalf of a just cause both noble and heroic—the ultimate test of a courageous gentleman. Davis not only favored loyal mediocrities over more able but contentious men, but he also believed that patriotism, prayer, and determination were enough to ensure victory. Along with his unwavering faith in himself and his cause, the Confederacy's president had the remarkable ability to ignore unpleasant realities. He often substituted the mere will to win for careful planning, frequently underestimated the extent of Confederate military disasters, and asked more of his generals than their means allowed. Jefferson Davis was a military mystic who romanticized and idealized warfare and the cause he led.

CHAPTER SIX
A Mexican War Hero

Braxton Bragg was a major participant in the Mexican War; indeed, the war made him famous, led directly to his marrying a rich woman, and indirectly to his becoming a Confederate full general. He returned to the United States from Mexico a national hero, the man who had stopped the enemy at Buena Vista with "a little more grape." There were rumors that he might be nominated for public office. Nothing came of this, but the army named a military post in his honor—not the modern base at Fort Bragg, North Carolina, established much later, but an earlier Fort Bragg on the northern coast of California.

Before the war with Mexico, Bragg had devoted too much of his military career to disputes with high-ranking superiors—including his regimental commander and the army's top general, Winfield Scott. Bragg had been court-martialed and convicted, censured by the secretary of war, the adjutant general, and the commander of the army's Eastern Division. No other junior officer could boast of so many high-ranking enemies. As the most cantankerous man in the army, Bragg seemed at this point to have an uncertain military future.

Yet, ironically, he received the greatest boost to his career only a few months after his most recent quarrel with his superiors. On June 18, 1845, he was ordered to join Brig. Gen. Zachary Taylor's army for the defense of Texas against Mexico.

At his initial base at Corpus Christi, Bragg drilled his men regularly, and agreed with a reporter who noted, "very few soldiers are fit for the light artillery—it requires bold and expert horsemen," troopers skilled in gunnery as well as "in using the sabare." A 4th Infantry officer considered the movements of Bragg's battery almost perfect. The men and horses responded instantly as their captain, a tall, thin man with "large black eyes and heavy brows," gave commands in "a nervous, tremulous voice." What impressed this observer most was Bragg's "industry, attention to duty, and strict regard for discipline."

After marching from Corpus Christi to the Rio Grande, Taylor constructed a fort on the north bank of the river. Believing

A Mexican warrior *(Braxton Bragg)*

this fortification to be "in a good state of defense," Taylor left with most of the army to visit his supply base on the Gulf. Bragg's battery was among the units left behind to guard the fort.

Two days after Taylor departed, the siege of Fort Texas began. A newsman reported that "the Mexicans opened their batteries on our fort, or rather our grand entrenchments, from that moment it was right hot work." After several hours both sides had to cease-fire until their guns cooled. The exchange of gunfire lasted for several days, by which time several of Bragg's horses had been killed and the Mexicans had surrounded his position. To their demand that the Americans surrender, a council of officers refused.

Taylor returned on May 9, having won victories at Palo Alto and Resaca de la Palma, and the Mexicans retreated across the Rio Grande. They had fired some 2,700 shells into Fort Texas, but only fifteen Americans had been killed or wounded. Even so, an officer who had been with Taylor admitted: "I would have rather fought twenty battles than have passed the bombardment."

Neither the artillerymen nor any other troops saw action again for several months. Following the occupation of Matamoros, Bragg spent much of his time directing the defense of Capt. Seth Thornton, whose ambush and capture had been the immediate cause of hostilities. Having been released by the Mexicans, Thornton, arrested and charged with cowardice by U.S. authorities, selected as his lawyers Bragg and Maj. Philip Barbour of the 3d Infantry. Bragg's experiences with courts-martial may have recommended him to Thornton. At the trial, which lasted a week, Bragg presented an elaborate defense. "It was a strong one," reported Barbour. The court acquitted Thornton.

Bragg turned from law to war again in early August when the army, augmented by volunteer units and supplies, moved to Monterey, some 250 miles southwest of Matamoros. Throughout the march Bragg maintained strict discipline, and he used the army's short stops to practice combat formations. "We paused in our walk to witness the morning drill of Captain Bragg's excellent company of artillery," wrote an officer. "The horses, as well as men, seemed to understand their business perfectly; they whirled the guns and caissons over the plain with wonderful rapidity and ease." This observer also believed that light field batteries were "the most formidable auxiliaries that science has ever given to war," and he reported that "Bragg, a skillful and courageous officer, is distinguished for his attention to the minutiae of his profession, a merit to be esteemed no less than heroic daring."'

Bragg's battery was primed for battle when it arrived outside Monterey. So was Taylor, who intended to take the city. Protected by strong forts, an army larger than Taylor's, and mountains on three sides, Monterey seemed impregnable. The Americans numbered slightly more than six thousand men, divided into two divisions of regulars and two divisions of volunteers. Their artillery consisted of four field batteries, a pair of 24-pounder howitzers, and a 10-pounder mortar. Taylor assigned the light guns to the regular divisions and divided his army, sending some volunteers and a division of regulars commanded by Brig. Gen. William J. Worth to flank the forts at the western edge of the city and to close the highway to Saltillo.

To divert attention from Worth's movements, Taylor gathered the remainder of his army on the plains to the east of Monterey. "We presented quite an imposing appearance," observed an infantry officer, but no action took place.

The next morning, while Worth's men cut the Mexican supply line and blocked any retreat from the city by occupying the road to Saltillo, Taylor's troops attacked Monterey's eastern defenses. The infantry, supported by Bragg's and another light battery, led the way. As they advanced, Taylor noticed some Mexican cavalry on his flank. He later wrote, "Captain Bragg, who was at hand, immediately galloped with his battery to a suitable position, from which a few discharges effectually dispersed the enemy."

Inside the city the Mexicans were more difficult to dislodge. With more courage than discretion, the Americans charged down barricaded streets and into a pointblank Mexican fire that halted their advance. One officer recalled, "Captain Bragg's battery was under a destructive fire, which killed and disabled several of his men and horses."

Ordered to withdraw, Bragg did so with difficulty. His gunners, temporarily blinded by dust from Mexican shells hitting adobe and stone buildings, had been unable to fire a shot. To retreat, he had to unlimber his gun carriages and reverse them; the narrow streets prevented an easy turn about. Before the battery reached the city's outskirts, two of its horses had been killed. Bragg halted the retreat and ordered Lieutenants John F. Reynolds and Samuel G. French to cut their harnesses and push the dead animals off the road. By the time this had been done, two more horses had been hit. They were released, wrote French, "and with their entrails dragging commenced eating grass." An officer who passed Bragg's battery at this point pronounced it "a perfect wreck." He reported, "a number of artillerymen, and more than a dozen horses, were down in the same spot; the ground about the guns [was] slippery with foam and blood," but Bragg and his men, still "exposed to a galling fire, were deliberately stripping the harness from the dead and disabled animals, determined that not a buckle or strap should be lost upon the field."

Bragg began to make repairs as soon as his battery got beyond the range of the Mexican guns. His heavy losses troubled him, for he knew that his ability to fight—indeed the success of the campaign—depended upon sufficient men, horses, and equipment. Since he could count on no replacements, he resolved to salvage everything possible; indeed, he sent French back to the outskirts of Monterey to retrieve any equipment left with the dead horses. French went reluctantly. On the way he met General Taylor, who told him to forget about lost equipment. French had some anxious moments on his ride back to camp as he dodged Mexican shots, and he "never forgave Bragg for the picayune order."

For a second time that same day, Bragg's battery returned to Monterey, this time in support of Brig. Gen. William O. Butler's Volunteer Division, but the city's narrow streets prevented his gunners from accomplishing much.

Fortunately for the Americans, General Worth had achieved a number of tactical successes that more than compensated for Taylor's limited gains. By nightfall on September 21, Worth had captured all but one of the forts that protected the rear and western flank of Monterey. The following day, while Taylor's men remained inactive, Worth took the works on Independence Hill and trapped the Mexican army in the city.

Taylor's entire army advanced at daybreak on September 23. Bragg's battery crossed the plain within range of the citadel's guns and rushed into Monterey at full gallop. "The fighting was very severe, but nothing compared to that on the 21st," explained an infantry officer, "except at one street running directly from the Cathedral." There the Mexicans, protected by a barricade and stone houses, poured a "shower of bullets" down the street and stopped the American advance. The 3d Infantry was still pinned down when Bragg arrived to support them. He immediately moved one of his guns into the open and fired "up the street [but] with very little effect, as the weight of the metal was entirely too light." Nevertheless, Bragg's action allowed the infantry to maneuver. An officer recalled that when the gun was pointed at the Mexicans, they "would fall behind their barricade, and at that time we could cross without a certainty of being shot." The artillerymen suffered heavy losses; among the men killed was Bragg's first sergeant, who "was shot through the heart while aiming his gun."

When ammunition ran low in the afternoon, Taylor broke off the engagement. The fighting in Monterey had been a field artilleryman's nightmare; aside from a body of lancers, which Bragg easily dispersed, he had been unable to find a good target.

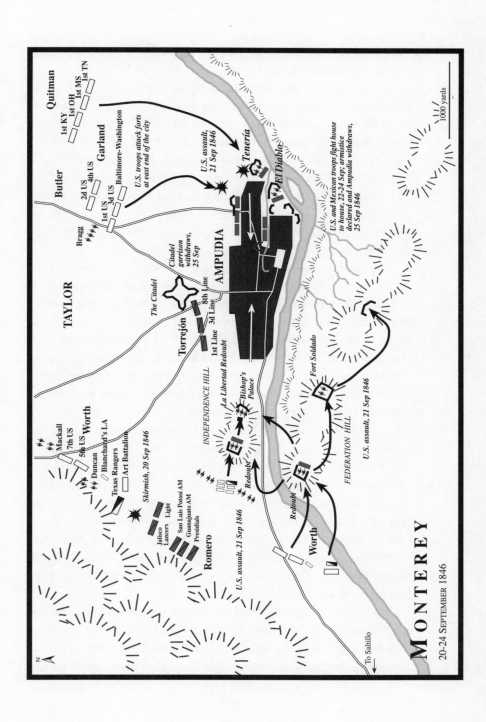

MONTEREY

20-24 SEPTEMBER 1846

1000 yards

TAYLOR

Quitman

1st KY
1st OH
1st MS
1st TN

Butler

Garland

2d US
4th US
1st US
3d US

Baltimore-Washington

U.S. troops attack forts at east end of the city

Bragg

Teneria

U.S. assault, 21 Sep 1846

El Diablo

AMPUDIA

Citadel garrison withdraws, 25 Sep

The Citadel

Torrejón

8th Line
3d Line
1st Line

La Libertad Redoubt

Bishop's Palace

INDEPENDENCE HILL

U.S. and Mexican troops fight house to house, 22-24 Sep; armistice declared and Ampudia withdraws, 25 Sep 1846

Fort Soldado

Redoubt

FEDERATION HILL

U.S. assault, 21 Sep 1846

Worth

Mackall
7th US
5th US Worth
Duncan
Blanchad's LA
Texas Rangers
Art Battalion

Skirmish, 20 Sep 1846

Jalisco Lancers
San Luis Potosí AM
Guanajuato AM Light
Presidials

Romero

U.S. assault, 21 Sep 1846

Redoubt

Redoubt

To Saltillo

N

But before his battery could withdraw from Monterey, Reynolds had to call on volunteers to help dislodge a gun carriage from the narrow street. During the dislodgement, several additional artillerymen were killed. When a horse driver fell dead from his saddle, Bragg ordered a halt and directed French "to dismount and take off the man's sword." "I did so," recalled French, "and took from his pocket a knife, for I thought I might be sent back if I did not save that too." But Bragg refused to take the knife because "it was not public property." French explained, "I write down these little things, for they give instances of the observance of details, characteristic of this officer, not obtained from history."

The American assaults were over; the next day Mexican officers rode into the American lines under a flag of truce to negotiate their surrender. Taylor's terms were almost as generous as his praise of his men's bravery and determination. He praised especially the artillerymen's conduct: "Captains Bragg and [Randolph] Ridgely served with their batteries during the operation under my own observation, and in part under my immediate orders, and exhibited distinguished skill and gallantry." Another high-ranking general insisted that Bragg, Ridgely, "and their subalterns deserve the highest praise for their skill and good conduct under the heaviest fire."

Unfortunately, no amount of commendation could offset the false lesson Bragg learned at Monterey. "You will perceive that our loss has been severe," Taylor admitted to a friend, "but when the superior numbers of the enemy, and his strongly fortified position are taken into consideration, I think we may congratulate ourselves that [our losses] were not greater. A great destruction of life must, at best, generally attend an attack upon an enemy in a fortified position."

Taylor was right; he had been lucky indeed to capture a stronghold by assault with the relatively light losses of approximately eight hundred casualties. But such impressionable young officers as Bragg missed the point. They discounted the hazards of such assaults and even minimized Taylor's misuse of artillery. What seemed important to them was Taylor's success; he had proved that a determined attack could overcome the strongest defense. After Monterey, if not before, Taylor became Bragg's military ideal and mentor.

While the army rested at Monterey during the armistice, Bragg received official notice of his promotion to captain and his assignment to a new command. For months, Congressman George S. Houston of Alabama, probably at the insistence of Bragg's brother John, had demanded that Bragg be given command of the fully equipped light battery, formerly commanded by the late Maj. Samuel Ringgold.

Bragg's right to command Company C was challenged by Capt. Thomas W. Sherman, who informed the War Department that he deserved the appointment. General Scott refused to decide the issue; rather, he authorized Taylor to transfer Bragg and Sherman out of his army if such action seemed "essential to the good of the service." Taylor opposed the transfer of either man; he needed and hoped to retain both, but he definitely intended to keep Bragg. "It is vitally important, for the good of the service, that a permanent and efficient captain, experienced in the field service of artillery be attached to Company C which is greatly in want of administrative care and management," Taylor informed Scott. "I deem Captain Bragg eminently qualified in all respects for this command; the battery which he leaves has by his care been brought into such good condition, and is withal so well officered, that it may suffer a change of commanders without material injury." Taylor's strong letter settled the question. Bragg assumed command of Company C and Sherman got Bragg's old battery.

To his new command, Bragg brought his usual high standards of drill, discipline, and efficiency. Company C, though still the best-equipped battery in the army, had lost heavily in horses and material during the recent campaign. To recoup these losses, Bragg swept the area around Monterey for leather, metal, and horses. When he could find any of these items, he bought them with company money. His attitude was wholly pragmatic; so much so, in fact, that he purchased animals that belonged to other American units. The bereft colonel of a Tennessee volunteer cavalry regiment complained acidly to Brig. Gen. Gideon J. Pillow, "I am under the disagreeable necessity of reporting to you the fact that some five soldiers in the cavalry regiment have sold their horses to Capt. Bragg of the 3rd Artillery." When Bragg could not buy horses, he borrowed them.

He soon had Company C in excellent repair. An officer who joined the company shortly after Bragg took command considered it "in the highest state of efficiency, discipline, and drill of any organization, of any arm, that I have ever seen." Six horse teams pulled the battery's four guns, each "served by a detachment of twelve men mounted on high-mettled and well-trained horses over the plain of exercise like a whirlwind."

When the truce ended, Bragg was ready for action, but on January 14, 1847, Taylor received a letter from General Scott, who was on his way to capture Veracruz and conquer Mexico. "I am not coming, my dear General, to supersede you in command," wrote Scott. "But, my dear General, I shall be obliged to take from you most of the gallant officers and men whom you have so long and so nobly commanded."

Taylor, who had presaged such developments, was apoplectic. He knew the administration had condemned him for the liberal terms granted the Mexicans at Monterey. But Taylor had no conception of the depth of Pres. James K. Polk's dislike. Taylor had counted on his own popularity and on General Scott for protection against the president, but now the beleaguered general suspected a plot. "The course which [Scott pursues] cannot be misunderstood," Taylor informed his brother, "it is to break me down, to strip me of my command."

Bragg, who was too emotionally committed to do otherwise, shared his chieftain's views. In his ambivalent attitude toward authority, superiors were either heroes with whom Bragg could identify or villains and fools. He denounced Scott and the administration, calling that general's developing campaign a "d——d expedition [that] has carried off everything." Bragg happily informed a friend that Taylor no longer intended to remain on the defensive in northern Mexico. "He has received new lights on the subject; I heard him most emphatically express his opinions, and candidly confess that he had changed his mind completely." Taylor wanted a fight. "I shall in a day or two have near 5,000 men; the greater portion of them will be volunteers yet I have no fears but we will give a satisfactory account," Taylor boasted.

Hatred of Scott overcame reason in both Taylor and Bragg. To advance deeper into Mexico with only five thousand soldiers, mostly inexperienced volunteers, was rash indeed. The only veteran regulars that remained from Taylor's original army were four companies of dragoons and Bragg's and Thomas Sherman's undermanned batteries, which had been virtually stripped of experienced men. Instead of its full complement of five officers and seventy enlisted men, Bragg's company consisted of three officers and thirty men, nearly all of them raw recruits. To supplement his veterans, Taylor had merely Gen. John E. Wool's and Maj. John M. Washington's untried eight-gun battery; these were the only regulars the government allowed Taylor to retain from a division that arrived in December. And the country over which the army would advance was not favorable for invaders.

Regardless of handicaps, Taylor moved south from Monterey early in February. He marched seventy miles to Saltillo, left a detachment, and then recklessly proceeded eighteen miles farther south. There reports of the approach of a large Mexican army cooled Taylor's offensive ardor, and on February 21 the Americans retreated to Saltillo, where Taylor divided Bragg's battery, sending one gun to defend the town and another to guard the army's supply wagons. Bragg, without officers and with only two guns under his control, went along with Col. William R. McKee's regiment of Kentucky volunteers to hold the extreme right of the Buena Vista defensive line.

When Bragg reached his assigned location, he unlimbered his two guns, threw up a "slight breastwork," and waited. From his location on the right flank, he could view the entire American position, which extended some three miles east across the Saltillo Road to a mountain pass. Bragg's battery and McKee's Kentuckians were separated from the other American units by a series of almost impassable gullies, ten and twenty feet deep, which ran southwest from Buena Vista. Beyond these gullies Bragg could see part of Washington's battery and two regiments of volunteers guarding the road. Farther east were other regiments, T. W. Sherman's battery, dragoons, and the remainder of Washington's battery. Near the base of the mountains, far to the east, Bragg could barely distinguish Arkansas and Kentucky cavalry regiments. The American line was thin, and Bragg kept "a vigilant watch" during the night. Sleep was impossible for most of the men anyway. Early in the evening martial music filtering up from the enemy's camp nearby kept them awake; later, it rained and turned cold.

The battle opened the next morning on the extreme left of the American line. "From my position," wrote Bragg, "I could clearly observe the enemy's movements, and perceived that unless I recrossed the ravine, I should be excluded from the action." He secured permission to move from Taylor's chief engineer and started toward the fighting. Before he had gone far, Bragg noticed a heavy cloud of dust on the Saltillo Road. Alarmed that this might indicate Mexican cavalry in the American rear, he hastened to investigate, only to discover that Taylor and his escort had raised the dust as they hurried to the front.

Bragg then followed the action to the left-center of the American line, halted near a squadron of the 1st Dragoons, and opened fire with what he called "marked effect on masses of the enemy's infantry. Here I remained," he noted, "and kept up my fire until I observed our left flank turned, and the enemy rapidly gaining our rear." The Americans there were in full retreat. "Two

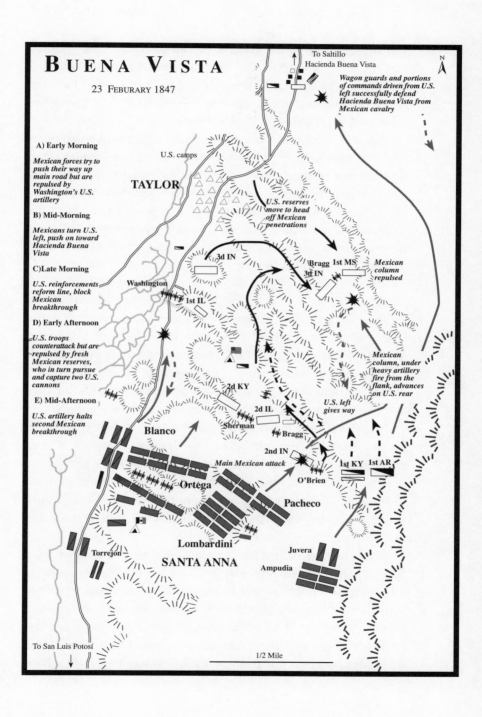

BUENA VISTA

23 FEBURARY 1847

N

To Saltillo
Hacienda Buena Vista

*Wagon guards and portions
of commands driven from U.S.
left successfully defend
Hacienda Buena Vista from
Mexican cavalry*

A) Early Morning

*Mexican forces try to
push their way up
main road but are
repulsed by
Washington's U.S.
artillery*

B) Mid-Morning

*Mexicans turn U.S.
left, push on toward
Hacienda Buena
Vista*

C) Late Morning

*U.S. reinforcements
reform line, block
Mexican
breakthrough*

D) Early Afternoon

*U.S. troops
counterattack but are
repulsed by fresh
Mexican reserves,
who in turn pursue
and capture two U.S.
cannons*

E) Mid-Afternoon

*U.S. artillery halts
second Mexican
breakthrough*

U.S. camps

TAYLOR

*U.S. reserves
move to head
off Mexican
penetrations*

3d IN

Washington

1st IL

2d KY

2d IL

Sherman

Bragg

Blanco

Ortega

2nd IN

O'Brien

Main Mexican attack

Pacheco

Bragg 1st MS
3d IN

*Mexican
column
repulsed*

*Mexican
column, under
heavy artillery
fire from the
flank, advances
on U.S. rear*

*U.S. left
gives way*

1st KY 1st AR

Lombardini

Torrejón

SANTA ANNA

Ampudia

Juvera

To San Luis Potosí

1/2 Mile

whole regiments [of] Indiana & Arkansas [troops] ran [at] the first fire and none returned," Bragg informed a friend. And several years after the battle, Bragg wrote his brother that the Kentucky cavalry under Col. Humphrey Marshall "did some fine running & no fighting [at Buena Vista]."

When he saw the Americans retreat, Bragg moved to intercept the Mexicans. "The enemy was now pouring masses of infantry and cavalry along the base of the mountain on our left, and was gaining our rear in great force," reported General Taylor. "The 2d Kentucky regiment and a section of artillery under Captain Bragg arrived at a most opportune moment." A deep ravine prevented Bragg's or Sherman's battery, which soon arrived, from unlimbering directly in front of the enemy's columns, but their rapid and sustained fire on the attacker's flank disrupted the assault. "So destructive was our fire," claimed Bragg, "that the enemy's column was divided, and a large portion of it retreated, leaving those in front totally cut off.." Supported by Col. John J. Hardin's regiment of Illinois volunteers, Bragg pursued the retreating Mexicans close to their own lines, where his guns "played upon the enemy's infantry and cavalry" until driven back by the fire of a heavy battery.

Bragg was only temporarily out of action. As he explained in his report, "My ammunition, by this time, was exhausted from my limberboxes; my old cannoneers could not leave their guns; and my recruits—for the first time under fire—I found unequal to the task of replenishing my supply." He halted the battery under the cover of a ravine and personally supervised the transfer of ammunition to the forward boxes.

While he replenished his ammunition, Bragg heard increased firing; the Mexicans, heavily reinforced, had renewed their attack on the American left flank. As Bragg returned to action, he could see that only Sherman, with one gun, and Col. Jefferson Davis's red-shirted Mississippi regiment stood between the enemy and the rear of the American army. The outnumbered Mississippians had just been overwhelmed and were in retreat as Bragg arrived. "I am happy to believe," he wrote, "that my rapid fire, opened just at this time, held the enemy in check until Colonel Davis could gain a position, and assume a stand." General Wool reported, "This was the hottest as well as the most critical part of the action; and at the moment when our troops were about giving way the batteries of Captains Sherman and Bragg by a well directed fire checked and drove back with great loss the enemy who had come close upon the muzzles of their pieces." One of Bragg's detached guns had rejoined the battery, and he used it to pound the Mexicans. As they withdrew, the artillery advanced several hundred yards. "From this point I several times fell back, and as often advanced," Bragg explained, "regulating my movements by those of the enemy, my support being weak and uncertain." Wool ordered cavalry forward at the captain's request, and when the Americans counterattacked, Bragg advanced to within canister range of the Mexican masses, confident that he could "inflict a loss upon the enemy from which he could not possibly recover."

But at this juncture an unusual event prevented the enemy's annihilation. Bragg's unrelenting fire, which "frequently threw whole columns into disorder," panicked the Mexican troops; several of their officers galloped into the American lines and asked, in the name of the Mexican commander, what peace terms Taylor would accept. General Wool, the senior American officer in the area, had no idea, but the question so confounded him that he halted the action to discuss the matter. The Mexicans, whom Bragg thought were trapped, escaped as the American barrage ceased. Only when the enemy opened fire, as Wool rode toward them with a white flag, did the general realize he had been tricked.

The American left flank now seemed secure, but Bragg feared the Mexicans would next attack the center. Consequently, he moved his guns in that direction. It was now past noon. The battery had been in action since early morning. The men were tired, and the horses, Bragg recalled, "were so exhausted that a walk was all that could be forced from them by both whip and spur." Several deep ravines blocked his path, so Bragg took a circuitous route. Before he reached the front, however, he heard "an awful roar of musketry." Certain that Taylor needed more guns, Bragg left some of his "heaviest carriages [and] caissons, and pushed on with such as could move most rapidly."

It was fortunate that he did, for as Taylor confessed: "The moment was most critical. Captain [John Paul Jones] O'Brien was finally obliged to leave his guns on the field—his infantry support being entirely routed." Mexican forces advanced unopposed as Bragg's exhausted battery reached the front. While his gunners unlimbered and loaded canister, Bragg asked Taylor, who was nearby, for infantry support. None was available; his battery alone stood between the Mexicans and victory. "Now, for the first time," recalled Bragg, "I felt the imminent peril in which we stood." He returned to his guns, steadied his men with a few words, and directed them to fire as rapidly as they could load. Col. Jefferson Davis, some distance away, "saw the enemy's infantry advancing in three lines upon Captain Bragg's battery, which though entirely unsupported, resolutely held its position." Bragg withheld his fire until the Mexicans were but a few yards away. "The first discharge of canister caused the enemy to hesitate," reported Taylor, "the second and third drove him back in disorder, and saved the day."

The battered American line held. "When the day closed we could not have mustered 2500 men," Bragg wrote William T. "Cump" Sherman in California. But numbers were unimportant; what mattered was that Taylor's men had stopped the Mexicans. Both armies were exhausted, but Bragg was too tense to relax. That night he remained at the front with guards posted and horses in harness. The anticipated Mexican attack never came. At daylight the Americans discovered that the enemy had deserted the field. Taylor wanted to pursue and harass the Mexicans but "found it impossible to accomplish anything of importance without rest."

Afterward, Bragg called Buena Vista "an awful fight" that the Americans had been fortunate to win. "Nothing under Heaven saved us but the prestige of old Zach," insisted Bragg. "Wool was whipped when Gen'l Taylor reached the ground." Wool had ordered Washington's artillery to retreat, but Taylor countermanded the order and thus saved the army. Taylor, Bragg told a reporter, "did what no other general ever did—he rallied the beaten forces, a large portion of whom had never stood under fire before, and brought them back upon the field." "This [rout of the volunteers] is all denied now with solemnity and indignation, but it's still true," Bragg informed Cump Sherman scarcely a week after the battle. "Old Z. has said so, and officers who heard the order still repeat it. Indeed, Cump, to go to the merits of the case, no man deserved so little credit at Buena Vista as Genl Wool."

Only the volunteer troops, Bragg believed, matched Wool's incompetence. "For the details of the military operations on this line," Bragg wrote, "I refer you to Genl Taylor's despatches. They are generously full so far as good conduct went, but rather silent on the subject of volunteers running &c &c." If the Americans had had "anyone of our old regular Infantry regiments," contended Bragg, "we would have carried the enemy's artillery and destroyed his army." With two thousand regulars, he believed, the entire Mexican army could have been captured. In these views, Bragg echoed Taylor, who boasted, "Had [Scott and Polk] left me 1000, or even 500 regulars I feel satisfied the Mexican Army would have been completely broken down, & the whole of its artillery, & baggage captured or destroyed." But an army of volunteers had been unequal to the task. Three entire regiments scattered at the first shot, and only nine men out of five companies of the Baltimore Volunteer Battalion "remained on the field," claimed Bragg. "With the exception of the Miss. regiment under Col Davis, a graduate [of West Point], you may say ditto of almost all who were here." "It is a fact," asserted Bragg, "that the wounded in the hospitals were trampled to death by refugees endeavoring to hide and pass for sick and wounded. And yet, that was a volunteer victory!! If any action in the whole war, Cump, proves the inefficiency of Vols. that is the one."

Bragg, of course, had always been frank and critical. Tolerance of those he disliked was impossible. He passed moral judgments quickly and constantly sought to justify his own and his heroes' prejudices. He rarely saw more than one side to any question. Things were either right or wrong; people were either good or bad, friends or enemies. Bragg invariably denounced those he disliked openly and in the most sarcastic manner; he learned neither tact nor restraint in Mexico.

Discretion seemed too pale a virtue after Buena Vista. Neither the march from Monterey nor the stand against the Mexicans had been discreet. Boldness, bravery, and independent action had characterized the campaign. These were the traits both Bragg and his military ideal, Zachary Taylor, had demonstrated at Buena Vista; these were also the military characteristics, sanctioned by Napoleon, that Bragg admired most at the outbreak of the Civil War.

Bragg learned little from either Taylor—whose strategy and tactics were essentially reckless attacks or stubborn defenses—or from the war itself. What Bragg appears to have missed, the real lesson of Buena Vista, was the great advantage defenders with sufficient mobile firepower enjoyed over attackers. This failure to understand what had happened and how it could be applied in later battles is both significant and curious. It is significant because of Bragg's command responsibilities in the 1860s; it is curious because a close examination of the Buena Vista battlefield convinced Bragg that artillery had accounted for "nine-tenths of the [enemy's] killed and wounded." He proudly informed a friend, "Old Zach accords the whole credit of the day to the artillery."

Taylor was even more specific; he officially reported that "Captain Bragg saved the day." Later, Maj. Gen. Joseph Hooker would call Taylor's statement "the highest praise ever awarded an officer of [Bragg's] rank on the battlefield."

No doubt Bragg deserved Taylor's praise. He had been fortunate enough to be in the right place at the propitious moment, but he had helped make his own luck. From the outset, he had followed the fight and sought to put his guns where they would do the most damage to the Mexicans. He, in turn, commended his subordinate officers and men, who had "fully sustained the distinguished reputation" they had already established. They were well drilled and disciplined because Bragg had given that meticulous attention to detail that Samuel French thought ridiculous but Maj. Luther Giddings correctly considered "a merit to be esteemed no less than heroic daring." Though Bragg's firepower at Buena Vista was hampered by inept recruits and the detachment of two of his guns, his battery nevertheless established an unparalleled record for muzzle-loading cannon—each gun fired an average of 250 rounds of ammunition.

After Buena Vista, Bragg married a Louisiana lady, Eliza Brooks Ellis of Thibodaux; late in 1855, he resigned his commission as a brevet lieutenant colonel and on February 8, 1856, committed himself to a new career. He purchased a sugar plantation three miles north of Thibodaux for $152,000. It included sixteen hundred acres of land, "buildings, dwelling houses, sugar house mill, engine, and the stock of cane and seed cane, horses, mules, cattle, hogs, sheep, farm utensils, agricultural implements," and 105 slaves.

For this estate, which Bragg named Bivouac, he paid nearly $25,000 in cash, agreed to pay another $30,000 before May 1, 1857, and the remainder in eight yearly installments bearing 6 percent interest. The down payment, he admitted after the war, was made with his wife's money, but Bragg was listed as the sole owner. Soon after acquiring Bivouac, Bragg predicted, with characteristic pessimism, "The high price [of sugar] alone can save us."

But not even the high price of sugar would save Bivouac for the Braggs. During the Civil War, the Federals "liberated" the property; eventually, the estate was auctioned off for unpaid taxes. The Braggs, whose future seemed so promising following the Mexican War, never recovered what the next war cost them. Mrs. Bragg never regained her Louisiana home, and Braxton Bragg never regained the heroic battlefield reputation he had won at Buena Vista.

CHAPTER SEVEN
A Tactical Revolution

Sometime after the Civil War, an unreconstructed Rebel, Robert Toombs, was arguing with a Federal army officer over the relative fighting qualities of Union and Confederate soldiers. "Well, we whipped you," the exasperated officer finally told Toombs. "No," Toombs retorted, "we just wore ourselves out whipping you."

As a general, Toombs left a great deal to be desired, but he was a perceptive military analyst. His statement that the Confederacy beat itself may have been intended as a joke, but as an appraisal of how the South lost the Civil War, it was surprisingly accurate.

More than 600,000 Americans died in the Civil War, a greater American mortality than in the two world wars and the Korean War combined. The charge of the British Light Brigade at Balaclava (almost 40 percent of its men were shot in the "Valley of Death") has symbolized needless sacrifice, but heavier losses were common during the Civil War. Some 60 Union regiments lost more than half their men in a single engagement, and at least 120 others sustained losses equal to the Light Brigade's. In eleven different campaigns, the Union suffered 10,000 casualties; over 1,000 men were killed or wounded in fifty-six different actions. At Gettysburg one of every five Federal soldiers present was hit, and a Minnesota regiment was decimated, losing 82 percent of its men.

Proportionally, Confederate losses were even greater. More than 80,000 Confederate soldiers fell in only five battles. At Gettysburg three of every ten Southerners present were hit; one North Carolina regiment lost 85 percent of its strength, and every man in one company was killed or wounded. In the first twenty-seven months of combat, the South lost 175,000 men. This number exceeded the entire Confederate military service in July 1861 and the strength of any army Robert E. Lee ever commanded.

Losses were so staggering because officers on both sides fought by the books, and the books were wrong. All the official and unofficial tactical manuals insisted that bayonets would

Line of battle

decide the outcome of battles and that troops should assault either in long lines or in massed columns. Such assumptions were tragically in error, for by 1861, bayonets were obsolete weapons and played no significant role in the outcome of the Civil War. During the Virginia campaign of 1864, when there was more close combat than usual, 33,292 Federal soldiers were treated for bullet wounds but only 37 for bayonet wounds.

Before the Civil War, bayonet attacks had been justifiable because the basic infantry firearm, the smoothbore musket, was highly inaccurate. A soldier might fire a smoothbore musket at a man all day from a distance of a few hundred yards and never hit him. Nevertheless, field commanders of the early 1800s favored smoothbores over rifles for general infantry use. Rifles required too much time and effort to load because each bullet had to be slightly larger than the bore; otherwise, when the weapon was fired, the bullet would fail to spin through the barrel along the rifled grooves. These grooves gave the rifle both its name and its superiority in range and accuracy over the smoothbore. Usually, only special units such as the British sharpshooters at Waterloo were equipped with rifles, and then the men were also issued ramrods and mallets with which to hammer in their shots. Loading took two minutes.

Tactics during the first half of the nineteenth century were designed to compensate for the smoothbore's inaccuracy and short range. Armies learned to perform series of maneuvers and sometimes prepared for battle within a few hundred yards of each other. Soldiers fought in tight formations and fired in volleys. The usual battle alignment was two or three lines of infantry, armed with smoothbores and long bayonets, supported in the rear by artillery and on the flanks by cavalry. After the infantrymen had fired a volley, they advanced, elbow to elbow, at a trot. The defenders, who had time to fire only one or two volleys before the attackers reached their line, either repulsed the assault or retreated to reform and counterattack. Success in battle usually depended upon strict discipline and precise

movements. If the infantrymen on either side broke, enemy cavalry dashed in from the flanks to slash at their retreating foe
with sabers. Most infantry attacks were checked by artillery firing scattershot. Although an army might advance and retreat
several times during a battle, it rarely suffered heavy losses.

Americans had used these conventional tactics successfully
during the Mexican War. At Palo Alto in 1846, Zachary Taylor
formed his three-thousand-man army in one long line. "The
Mexicans immediately opened fire upon us, first with artillery
and then with infantry," wrote an American officer. "At first
their shots did not reach us, and the advance . . . continued. As
we got nearer, the cannon balls commenced going through the
ranks. They hurt no one, however, . . . because they would strike
the ground long before they reached our line, and ricochetted
through the tall grass so slowly that the men would see them
and open ranks and let them pass. When we got to a point
where the artillery could be used with effect, a halt was called,
and the battle opened on both sides." The Americans attacked;
the Mexicans retreated, and by nightfall Taylor's men occupied
the Mexican position. American losses were only nine killed and
forty-seven wounded.

Bayonet assaults in the 1860s were far more costly than ever
before because the smoothbore musket had been replaced by a
better weapon. The technological innovation that finished the
smoothbore as the standard infantry arm was the development
in the 1850s of the Minié "ball." Neither Captain Minié's inven-
tion nor a ball, the projectile actually was an elongated bullet
with a hollow base; it was small enough to fit easily into the
rifle's bore but would expand automatically when fired and fit
snugly into the rifled grooves. The Minié bullet made the rifled
muzzleloader a practical military weapon.

Both sides used a variety of small arms during the Civil War,
but the basic infantry weapon was the single-shot, rifled muzzleloader, either the Springfield caliber .58 or the British Enfield
caliber .577. The Springfield rifle was fifty-six inches long and

weighed nearly ten pounds when fitted with its eighteen-inch triangular bayonet. All parts were interchangeable.

Between 1861 and 1865, more than 1,600,000 of these rifles were produced in the United States at a cost of $14.93 each. The Enfields, which were more popular in the South, varied considerably in length and bayonet type, but they all fired the same ammunition. Moreover, they were the equal of any Union rifle—so good, in fact, that after the fall of Vicksburg, Maj. Gen. U. S. Grant rearmed some of his Union regiments with captured Enfields.

Compared with pre–Civil War shoulder weapons, the rifled muzzleloader was a firearm of deadly accuracy. It could be fired two or three times a minute, could stop an attack at up to four hundred yards, and could kill at a distance of one thousand yards. In October 1861 a Union soldier wrote his parents: "We went out the other day to try [our rifles]. We fired [from a distance of] 600 yards and we put 360 balls into a mark the size of old Jeff [Davis]." In contrast, some Illinois soldiers armed with smoothbore muskets fired 160 shots at a flour barrel 180 yards away. It was hit only four times.

The rifle became the great killer of the Civil War. It inflicted 80 percent of all wounds and revolutionized tactics. Because of the rifle's range and accuracy, Civil War infantry assaults were always costly. For the first time in over a century, defenders had the advantage in warfare. "One rifle in the trench was worth five in front of it," wrote Maj. Gen. J.D. Cox. Perhaps he exaggerated a bit, but a few entrenched men armed with rifles could hold a position against great odds. The rifle and the spade had made defense at least three times as strong as offense.

But no one knew this at the beginning of the Civil War. Shortly before, the army had decided to modify infantry tactics because officers believed they could offset the rifle's range and accuracy simply by teaching soldiers to move more quickly in battle. "They are introducing the light infantry tactics this spring, a new thing," wrote Cadet Henry A. du Pont from West Point on

March 28, 1857. "There are a great many very rapid movements in it, and many of them are performed in double quick time, that is running. Within the last week [Col. William J.] Hardee [commandant of cadets and author of the new tactics book] has had the whole battalion going at double quick with the band. . . . It will take time for everyone to learn to keep step. I expect that they will almost run us to death when the board of visitors come." Two months later du Pont admitted that the new tactics were "no doubt better in some respects, that is to say that troops drilled to them would be more efficient, but they do not look so well, for it is impossible to attain . . . the same precision and accuracy with all this running and quick movements, as was possible under the old system, and besides it is much harder work."

If the new tactics could have stressed dispersal as well as speed, then attackers might have had a chance to overcome the advantage rifles had given defenders, but dispersal of forces was impracticable in the 1860s. In some ways the Civil War was a modern struggle: in minutes generals communicated with each other by telegraph over thousands of miles, and trains quickly carried large armies great distances and piled mountains of supplies at railheads. But in other ways the war was strikingly antiquated: men walked or rode horses into battle, and their supplies followed in wagons. No telephone lines connected combat units with each other or with field headquarters; all messages went by courier on horseback. This traditional system of battlefield communication bound Civil War generals to close-order formations. They had no choice; the dispersal of forces to avoid the rifle's firepower and accuracy would have made communication even more difficult and further weakened an officer's control of his men in battle. Even though they usually kept their troops in tight formations, Civil War commanders never completely solved the problems of battlefield communication and management. In the Wilderness in 1864, both Lee and Grant lost effective control of their armies after the action began.

Except for the quicker movements required of troops, the

new tactics were much like the old ones. Both emphasized close-order formations and taught men to rely on the shock effect of bayonet assaults. A Prussian officer who visited the South in 1863 recalled that "there was diligent drilling in the camps according to an old French drill manual that had been revised by Hardee, and I observed on the drill field only linear formations, wheeling out into open columns, wheeling in and marching up into line, marching in line, open column marching, marching by sections, and marching in file. The tactical unit in battle seemed to be the brigade. The drilling, according to my observation, seemed to be somewhat awkward. The cavalry drilled in a manner similar to ours, and the main emphasis was on a good jog, with loud yelling and shouting. The infantry also used this sound, the famous rebel yell, in bayonet attacks."

The Confederate yell was intended to help control fear. As one soldier explained: "I always said if I ever went into a charge, I wouldn't holler! But the very first time I fired off my gun I hollered as loud as I could, and I hollered every breath till we stopped." Jubal Early once told some troops who hesitated to charge because they were out of ammunition, "Damn it, holler them across."

Union soldiers studied the same manuals and practiced the same drills as the Confederates. "Every night I recite with the other 1st Sergts and 2nd Lieutenants," wrote a Union sergeant in 1862. "We shall finish Hardee's Tactics and then study the 'Army Regulations.' Theory as well as practice are necessary to make the perfect soldier." In 1863 a Union corporal explained that the noncommissioned officers of his company "have lessons in tactics every night at the Captains quarters to fit them to drill the privates in squads according to the book." Union general Marsena R. Patrick, a graduate of West Point, wrote on March 30, 1862, "Although this is the Sabbath, I have been obliged to look over Tactics, Regulations etc. etc." The next day he described how he drilled his troops for combat: "Formed [them] in Mass—then in Column—then deployed by Battalion—in 4 lines . . . and then handled them in masses almost exclusively." On April 1 he drilled his men "in Mass Movements some 2 or 3 hours," and on July 18 he wrote, "The Drills, for some time back, have been very interesting, as the men are beginning to see the value of them."

After the war Union general William B. Hazen admitted that most Civil War battles were merely the formation of troops into lines to attack or to repel attacks. Almost any battle can serve as an example. "I saw our infantry make a charge [at Murfrees-boro]," wrote a Confederate, "they got [with]in fifty yards [before the Federals] fired a shot, when they poured the heaviest volley into them that I ever saw or heard." A Louisiana soldier wrote of the fight at Perryville, "The men stood right straight up on the open field, loaded and fired, charged and fell back as deliberately as if on drill." At Shiloh the Confederates attacked by corps in four lines across a three-mile front. Such an arrange-ment of forces could result only in disorder and confusion, and within a few minutes after their first contact with the enemy, the Southerners became hopelessly tangled, with corps, divisions, and brigades pell-mell in one battle line.

During the encounter at Winchester in the spring of 1862, Richard Taylor's brigade attacked in long lines with the men elbow to elbow. As they advanced many fell and others wavered. "What the hell are you dodging for?" screamed Taylor. "If there is any more of it, you will be halted under fire for an hour." With Taylor leading the way, the brigade marched to within fifty yards of the enemy "in perfect order, not firing a shot." Taylor proudly reported that his men closed "the many gaps made by the [enemy's] fierce fire" and preserved "an align-ment that would have been creditable on parade." Two weeks later Taylor used a similar attack formation at Port Republic. These two battles cost him five hundred casualties and taught him nothing.

Besides Taylor, many generals favored traditional weapons and tactics. Stonewall Jackson, often praised as a military innovator, was partial to bayonet assaults. Alexander R. Lawton claimed that Jackson "did not value human life. . . . He could order men to their death as a matter of course. Napoleon's French conscription could not have kept him supplied with men, he used up his command so rapidly." In little less than six months in 1862, Jackson's tactics cost the South over twenty thousand casualties—the equivalent of one entire army corps— or almost twice the number of men under Jackson's command when the campaign began. Jackson was so committed to conventional offensive tactics that he once actually requested that some of his troops be equipped with pikes instead of muskets. Pikes, he explained, should be "6 or more inches longer than the musket with the bayonet on, so that when we teach our troops to rely upon the bayonet they may feel that they have the superiority of arm resulting from its length." Apparently, Lee saw nothing wrong with such a request; he approved it and ordered Josiah Gorgas, chief of ordnance, to send pikes to Jackson. Gorgas sent muskets instead.

One Confederate general even considered the bayonet too modern and "inferior to the knife" because Southerners "would require long drilling to become expert with the [bayonet] . . . but they instinctively know how to wield the bowieknife."

Brig. Gen. Henry Wise, a former governor of Virginia, scoffed at both new weapons and new tactics. He insisted that "it was not the improved arm, but the improved man, which would win the day. Let brave men advance with flint locks and old-fashioned bayonets, . . . reckless of the slain, and he would answer for it with his life, that the Yankees would break and run."

Wise's views were extreme, but even the highest-ranking officers failed to recognize the limitations of traditional arms, formations, and services. Winfield Scott predicted at the outset that the war would be won by artillery. He was wrong, of course; only about 10 percent of all Civil War casualties were the results of artillery fire. In February 1862, Joseph E. Johnston, commander of Confederate forces in Virginia, wrote Adjutant

General Samuel Cooper "we should have a much larger cavalry force. The greatest . . . difficulty, in increasing it, is said to be the want of proper arms. This can be easily removed by equipping a large body of lancers." Johnston claimed that lances "would be formidable . . . in the hands of new troops, especially against the enemy's . . . artillery." Cooper wisely ignored Johnston's suggestion; cavalry armed with sabers or lances were no match for artillery or infantry in the 1860s.

No one guessed just how much the rifled musket had diminished the importance of cavalry and artillery. At first, cavalry officers trained their troopers to charge infantry and artillery. A Union private recalled a drill in December 1861 where infantry regiments fired blank shots at each other and "a squadron of cavalry dashed around . . . and charged down on them with the wildest yells." Another Union infantryman wrote in 1862: "We had our first Brigade drill day before yesterday. . . . The Cavalry charged down on us and for the first time I saw something that looked like fighting. . . . It was a beautiful sight, and our officers expressed themselves well satisfied with the drill." One soldier described how his regiment formed a hollow square to repel cavalry charges: "When they charge us with wild yells (some of them get awfully excited, so do the horses), it takes some nerve to stand against them, although it is all a sham. But we have found out one thing—horses cannot be driven onto fixed bayonets and I dont believe we shall be as afraid of the real charge if we ever have to meet one in the future. We are learning a good deal, so are the Cavalry."

But cavalry generals on both sides learned their lessons slowly. "Not until the closing days of the war did we wake up to what our experience . . . ought to have taught us," confessed James H. Wilson. When Philip H. Sheridan took command of the Army of the Potomac's cavalry in 1864, he proposed to concentrate it to fight the enemy's cavalry, but his superior officer objected. Sheridan recalled that "my proposition seemed to stagger General [George] Meade," who "would hardly listen . . . , for he was filled with the prejudices that, from the beginning of the war, had pervaded the army regarding the . . . cavalry." Until his death, Confederate cavalryman J. E. B. Stuart held the archaic and romantic view that the "duty of the cavalry after battle is joined is to cover the flanks to prevent the enemy from turning them. If victorious, it improves the victory by rapid pursuit. If defeated, it covers the rear and makes vigorous charges to delay the advance of the enemy—or in the supreme moment in the crisis of battle . . . the cavalry comes down like an avalanche upon the troops already engaged with splendid effect."

A number of bloody failures often occurred before even the more astute cavalry commander learned he could no longer use pre–Civil War tactics successfully. The charge of the 5th U.S. Cavalry at Gaines's Mill in June 1862 is an excellent example of the frequent misuse of horsemen. This regiment lost 60 percent of its troopers in a saber attack on Confederate infantry and artillery. One of the attackers, Pvt. W.H. Hitchcock, recalled the action: "We dashed forward with a wild cheer, in solid column of squadron front; but our formation was almost instantly broken. . . . I closed in to reform the line, but could find no one at my left, so completely had our line been shattered by the musketry fire in front." At this point, Hitchcock's horse veered off to the rear. "I dropped my saber," he admitted, "and so fiercely tugged at my horse's bit as to cause the blood to flow from her mouth, yet could not check her." Finally, he gained control of his mount, "turned about and started back. . . . The firing of artillery and infantry . . . was terrific," Hitchcock remembered. "None but the dead and wounded were around me. It hardly seemed that I could drive Lee's . . . veterans alone, so I rode . . . off the field." Nearly 250 men had galloped into action; only about 100 returned.

After such tragic experiences, many horsemen and their commanders became so gun-shy that Union general John A. Logan allegedly offered a reward for a dead cavalryman, Federal or Confederate, and one of Sherman's soldiers wrote in 1863: "We have considerable cavalry with us, but they are the laughing stock of the army and the boys poke all kinds of fun at them. I really have as yet to see or hear of their doing anything of much credit to them."

Despite such derision, cavalrymen performed many creditable services: they were excellent courier, scouts, and raiders; when necessary, they dismounted and fought as infantry. But Civil War horsemen were no longer effective as a shock force in assaults. They were too vulnerable to accurate rifle fire.

Some generals attempted to use artillery as an offensive weapon and almost invariably failed. Before Pickett's charge at Gettysburg, 150 Confederate guns pounded the Union line without doing much damage. The Federals merely dug in and waited for the bombardment to end; they suffered very few casualties from artillery fire. In his assault on the Federal left at Murfreesboro, John C. Breckinridge placed his batteries between two lines of infantry and ordered them to join the attack. He ignored a young artillery officer's warning that such an arrangement of guns would cause confusion and misdirection of fire. As the Confederate gunners advanced, sandwiched between the infantry lines and unable to find clear fields of fire, they hit some of the Southern infantrymen. Federal shells disabled several Confederate guns, and three were captured when the attack failed.

Though relatively ineffective as an offensive weapon, artillery was a most important adjunct to the infantry on defense. At Malvern Hill the Federals massed over two hundred guns to stop what could have been a breakthrough; at Gettysburg twenty-five cannon along Plum Run held the Union line without infantry support; at Atlanta only twenty-nine guns checked twelve thousand Confederates; and at Murfreesboro fifty-eight pieces of artillery helped disrupt Breckinridge's assault. Used in defense, artillery was deadliest in precisely those areas offensive artillery could not reach. When infantry assault columns got within four hundred yards, the defenders loaded their guns with scattershot, or canister, that decimated closely bunched infantry.

Attacks on strongly posted batteries rarely succeeded and nearly always penalized the attackers heavily. A Confederate diarist wrote of his brigade's attempt to take some Federal guns at Spotsylvania in 1864: "After being subjected to a heavy artillery fire for some time we were ordered . . . to charge the enemy. We charged them. . . . Our loss [was] heavy. We fell back."

Perhaps Maj. Gen. D.H. Hill left the best description of the Confederate attack on the Union line at Malvern Hill. "I never saw anything more grandly heroic," he wrote. "As each brigade emerged from the woods, from fifty to one hundred guns opened upon it, tearing great gaps in its ranks. . . . Most of them had an open field half a mile wide to cross, under the fire of field artillery . . . and . . . heavy ordnance. It was not war—it was murder."

When the struggle began, neither the North nor the South was prepared for war, much less for murder. There were no strategic plans ready; indeed, it was uncertain which side would be the invader. President Lincoln and Secretary of War Simon Cameron, who had no military experience, gladly relegated the awesome responsibility of strategic planning to Winfield Scott, hero of two previous wars. "General Scott seems to have *carte-blanche*," noted an observer in May 1861. "He is, in fact, the Government."

Yet Scott failed to inspire confidence. He was seventy-five years old and a semi-invalid. State Senator Alexander K. McClure and Gov. Andrew Curtin of Pennsylvania, who saw Scott the morning after Fort Sumter fell, concluded "that the old chieftain had outlived his . . . usefulness, and that he was utterly unequal to the appalling task he had accepted." After the Pennsylvanians had left Scott's office, Curtin threw up his hands and exclaimed, "My God, the country is at the mercy of a dotard."

A few days later, when the governor of Iowa called, Scott dodged any discussion of strategy, reminisced instead about his service in the War of 1812, and then fell asleep in his chair. But Scott may have put on a senile act to disarm nosey politicians, for President Lincoln only half jokingly told a visitor, "Scott will not let us outsiders know anything of his plans."

The old general revealed his scheme in May. He told the president the best way to defeat the Confederacy was to encircle it and then divide it by means of a naval blockade and a drive down the Mississippi River. Such action, Scott believed, would make it possible "to envelop the insurgent States and bring them to terms with less bloodshed than by any other plan." Cut off from the outside world, the Confederacy would slowly strangle and die as if caught in the grip of a giant anaconda.

The "Anaconda" plan proved that Scott could still view military problems realistically, but he misunderstood the nation's temper. He knew the Union was unprepared for an immediate offensive and that no major action should be taken until a large army of regulars and three-year volunteers had been assembled and trained. His mistake was in assuming that the people would wait.

William T. Sherman recalled that "Congress and the people would not permit the slow and methodical preparation desired by General Scott." Northerners demanded action; Scott's policy was too conservative, too cautious. Sherman observed in late June how Scott "seemed vexed with the clamors of the press for immediate action, and the continued interference in [military] details by the President, Secretary of War, and Congress." Secretary of the Navy Gideon Welles admitted that he disapproved of Scott's plan as "purely defensive." Welles wrote in his diary that "instead of halting on the borders, building intrenchments . . . we should penetrate their territory."

The cry "On to Richmond!" soon became too insistent for Lincoln to ignore. He realized that, whatever its military merits, Scott's plan was politically inexpedient. So on June 29, 1861, the president and his cabinet overruled the old general's objections to an immediate offensive. Thence the Union would follow an offensive strategy aimed at the occupation and conquest of the South.

At first the Confederacy planned to fight a defensive war. President Davis explained that "the Confederate Government is waging this war solely for self-defense, . . . it has no design of conquest or any other purpose than to secure peace and the abandonment by the United States of its pretensions to govern a people who have never been their subjects and who prefer self-government to a Union with them."

The South's decision to fight a defensive war was sound; in fact, it was the only tenable military policy the government could have followed. The North had greater resources and a three-to-two military manpower advantage over the South. An offensive strategy would almost certainly exhaust the Confederacy more quickly than the Union, for an invasion takes more men and resources than a defense. As a rule, defense is the most economical form of warfare. Civil War defenders enjoyed even greater advantages than usual because tactics lagged behind military technology. The rifled muzzleloader gave them at least three times the strength of the offense; theoretically, the Confederates could have stayed in entrenchments and killed every man in the Union army before the South exhausted its own human resources.

But the Confederacy flung away its great advantage because Southern sentiment overwhelmingly favored an invasion of the North. Confederate secretary of state Robert Toombs announced in May 1861 that he was for "taking the initiative, and carrying the war into the enemy's country." He opposed any delay. "We must invade or be invaded," he announced. In June 1861 the famous Confederate war clerk John Jones wrote in his diary: "Our policy is to be defensive, and it will be severely criticized, for a vast majority of our people are for 'carrying the war into Africa' without a moment's delay. The sequel will show which is right, the government or the people. At all events, the government will rule."

Jones was wrong; the government did not rule. Just after

First Manassas in July 1861, Davis indicated in a public speech that he was ready to abandon his defensive strategy. "Never heard I more hearty cheering," recorded Jones. "Every one believed our banners would wave in the streets of Washington in a few days; . . . that peace would be consummated on the banks of the Susquehanna or the Schuylkill. The President had pledged himself . . . to carry the war into the enemy's country. . . . Now . . . the people were well pleased with their President."

Although Davis called his new policy "defensive-offensive," it was in fact an offensive strategy, for the president held a view best described by one of today's clichés: the best defense is a good offense. In September 1862 Davis wrote the commanders of the South's two largest armies that "we [must] . . . protect our own country by transferring the seat of war to that of [the] . . . enemy. . . . the sacred right of self defence demands that if such a war is to continue its consequences shall fall on those who persist in their refusal to make peace." Davis concluded his instructions with an order that Confederate armies "occupy the territory of their enemies and . . . make it the theatre of hostilities."

The substitution of an offensive for a defensive strategy early in the war probably doomed the Confederacy. Southern leaders could have enjoyed all the moral and military advantages of remaining defenders. Instead, they chose to be aggressors. Confederate forces attacked in eight of the first twelve big battles of the war, and in these eight assaults, 97,000 Confederates fell— 20,000 more men than the Federals lost in these same battles. President Davis's cult of the military offense bled the South's armies to death in the first three years of combat. After 1863 the Confederates attacked less often. Attrition forced them to defend; they had spent too much of their limited manpower in unsuccessful offensives. Even so, Confederate generals attacked in three of the last ten major campaigns of the war.

A close examination of two battles indicates in some detail how so many men were lost. Both Stones River and Chickamauga are examples of sustained Confederate attacks, and an analysis of regimental losses in each battle reveals a high degree of correlation between assaults and casualties. Because the Federals were on the defense in both engagements, they suffered relatively fewer casualties except in those units that were outflanked or surrounded. It is significant that half of the most battered Union regiments incurred their highest casualties when they attacked or counterattacked. At Stones River the 15th Indiana lost 130 of its 440 men in a single bayonet charge, and the 34th Illinois and the 39th Indiana each sustained 50 percent casualties in a counterattack. In still another attempt to check the Confederate advance, a brigade of regulars charged into a dense cedar grove and lost 500 men in about twenty minutes. The 16th and 18th U.S. Infantry Regiments, which formed the center of this assault group, lost 456 men from a combined total of 910. At Chickamauga the 87th Indiana suffered over 50 percent casualties in one charge across an open field, and three Illinois regiments—the 25th, 35th, and 38th—together with the 26th Ohio tried to dislodge part of Bushrod Johnson's Confederate division from the crest of a hill. The attack failed and cost the Federal regiments 791 of their 1,296 men.

Confederate losses were even more exceptional. Of the eighty-eight Confederate regiments present at Stones River, twenty-three suffered over 40 percent casualties. Moreover, 40 percent of the infantry regimental commanders were killed or wounded, and in several regiments every field officer was lost. Eight of the twenty Confederate brigades that fought at Stones River sustained more than 35 percent casualties, and 25 percent of the infantry brigade commanders were killed or wounded.

Reckless assaults accounted for most of these Confederate casualties. At Stones River the 1st Louisiana charged across an open field. "Our loss was very severe at this place," wrote its commander. The regiment lost seven of its twenty-one officers and nearly 100 of its 231 men. Attacks made by other Confederate units were just as costly. Col. J.J. Scales, commander of the

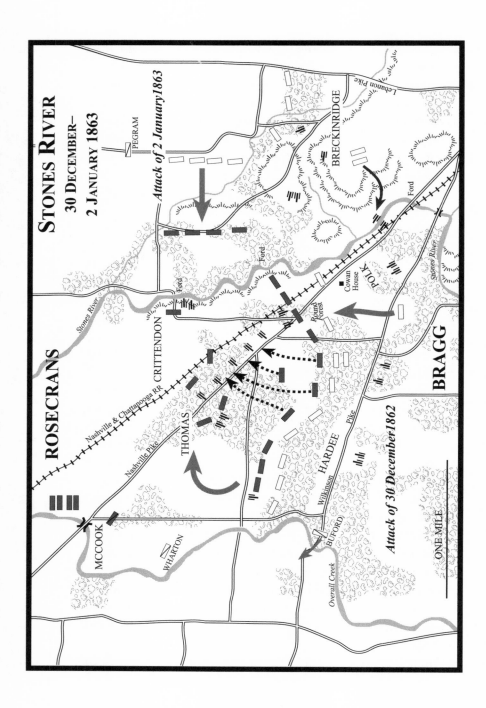

STONES RIVER
30 DECEMBER–
2 JANUARY 1863

PEGRAM

Attack of 2 January 1863

BRECKINRIDGE

Lebanon Pike

Ford

Ford

Ford

Ford

Stones River

Cowan
House

POLK

Round
Forest

Stones River

CRITTENDON

ROSECRANS

Nashville & Chattanooga RR

Nashville Pike

THOMAS

BRAGG

HARDEE

Wilkinson   Pike

MCCOOK

WHARTON

BUFORD

Attack of 30 December 1862

Overall Creek

ONE MILE

30th Mississippi, received orders to charge and capture several Federal batteries. Five hundred yards of open ground "lay between us and those . . . batteries," wrote Scales. "As we entered [this field,] a large body of [Union] infantry in addition to the Batteries on my flanks and front rained their leaden hail upon us. Men fell around on every side like autumn leaves and every foot of soil over which we passed seemed dyed with the life blood of some one or more of [my] gallant [men]. . . . Still no one faltered, but the whole line advanced boldly and swiftly to within seventy-five yds. of the battery when the storm of death increased to such fury that the regt. as if by instinct fell to the ground." This single charge cost the 30th Mississippi half of its 400 men. A young soldier in the 24th Alabama recalled how his regiment made three desperate charges at Stones River and that each time thirty or forty of his comrades fell. The commander of the 26th Alabama reported the Federal fire so heavy that thirty-eight of his men defected during the first thrust.

It requires courage to charge at any time, but it is almost unbelievable what some units endured. Gen. James R. Chalmers's brigade of Mississippians hit the strongest part of the Union line at Stones River. This in itself was in no way remarkable, but half the men in the 44th Mississippi Regiment went into battle armed only with sticks and most of the 9th Mississippi's rifles were still too wet from the previous night's rain to fire. Nevertheless, the men charged.

As the Mississippians faltered, Gen. Daniel S. Donelson's brigade of Tennesseans came up. No unit on either side fought harder than this brigade; it dashed itself to bits against the Union center in the Round Forest. One of Donelson's regiments lost half its officers and 68 percent of its men; another lost 42 percent of its officers and over half of its men. The 8th and 16th Tennessee Regiments spent several hours and 513 of their combined total of 821 men in brave but unsuccessful efforts to break the Federal line.

Sometime in the early afternoon, two fresh Confederate

brigades tried where Chalmers's and Donelson's men had
failed. Generals John K. Jackson and Daniel W. Adams led their
men across a field thick with bodies. Both of Jackson's two furious assaults aborted. In an hour of combat, he lost more than a
third of his men, including all of his regimental commanders.
One of his regiments, the 8th Mississippi, lost 133 of its 282 men.
Adams had no more success than Jackson, though his men made
what one Federal called "the most daring, courageous, and best-
executed attack . . . on our line." Adams was wounded and his
brigade, caught in a crossfire, retreated. One of his units, the
13th and 20th Consolidated Louisiana Infantry, entering the
fight with 620 men, lost 187 on the afternoon of December 31
and another 129 in an attack two days later.

Confederate losses at Chickamauga were even more severe.
At least twenty-five of the thirty-three Confederate brigades present lost more than a third of their men, and incomplete returns
indicate that at least forty-two infantry regiments suffered over
40 percent casualties. Nearly half of all regimental commanders
and 25 percent of all brigade commanders were killed or
wounded.

Just as at Stones River, the heaviest losses at Chickamauga
occurred when units assaulted strong Union positions. Gen.
Lucius E. Polk's brigade of about 1,400 men attacked the Kelly's
Field salient twice on September 20. The first attack, checked by
heavy guns and musket fire, cost the Confederates 350 casualties
in about ninety minutes. In the second attack the brigade lost
200 men. An assault against the Federal position on Horseshoe
Ridge cost the 22d Alabama 55 percent of its men, and two bat-
talions of Hillard's Legion lost nearly 60 percent of their effec-
tives in an attack on Snodgrass Hill, where the Federals had
thrown up breastworks.

Bloody battles like Stones River and Chickamauga took the
lives of the bravest Southern officers and men. Relatively few
combat officers went though the conflict without a single
wound, and most of those who did could claim, as did Brig.

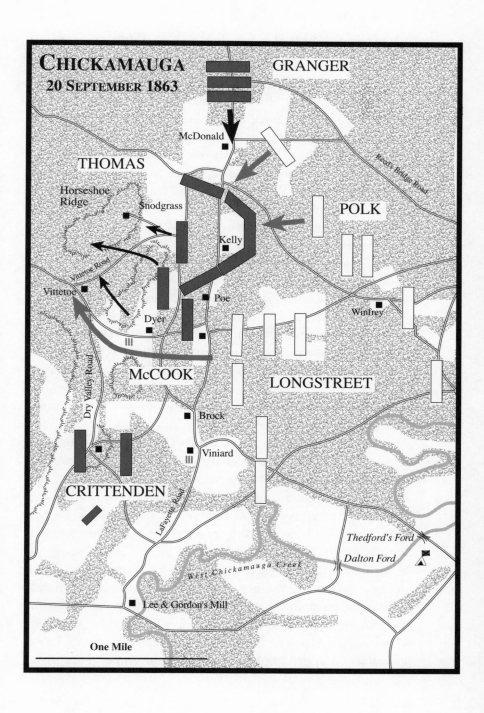

CHICKAMAUGA
20 SEPTEMBER 1863

GRANGER

McDonald

THOMAS

Horseshoe
Ridge

Snodgrass

POLK

Kelly

Vittetoe Road

Poe

Winfrey

Vittetoe

Dyer

McCOOK

LONGSTREET

Dry Valley Road

Brock

Viniard

CRITTENDEN

LaFayette Road

Thedford's Ford

Dalton Ford

West Chickamauga Creek

Lee & Gordon's Mill

Reed's Bridge Road

One Mile

Gen. Reuben I. Walker—who participated in no fewer than sixty-three battles—that "it was not my fault."

Only three of the eight men who commanded the famous Stonewall Brigade survived the war. What happened to the commanders of one regiment is told in a bare sketch penned by semiliterate Bartlett Yancey Malone, who "was attached to the 6th N.C. Regiment . . . which was commanded by Colonel Fisher who got kild in the first Manassas Battel. . . . And then was commanded by Colonel W. D. Pender untell [his promotion; he was subsequently killed in battle]. . . . And then Captain I. E. Av[e]ry . . . was promoted to Colonel and . . . in command untell . . . the day the fite was at Gettysburg whar he was kild. And then Lieut. Colonel Webb taken command."

Casualty lists prove that generals usually led their men into action. Of all Confederate generals, 55 percent were killed or wounded in battle. And more generals lost their lives leading attacks than in any other way; 70 percent of the seventy-seven Confederate generals killed or mortally wounded fell in offensives. In a single charge against Federal fortifications at Franklin in 1864, six Confederate generals were killed or mortally wounded—John Adams, John C. Carter, Patrick R. Cleburne, States Rights Gist, Hiram B. Granbury, and Otho F. Strahl.

Confederate leaders ignored the casualty lists and continually mutilated their armies. Throughout the war Jefferson Davis favored offensive operations, and five of the six men who at one time or another commanded the South's two largest armies were as devoted to aggressive warfare as was Davis. Albert Sidney Johnston, P. G. T. Beauregard, Braxton Bragg, John Bell Hood, and Robert E. Lee all preferred to be on the offensive; of the major field commanders, only Joseph E. Johnston really enjoyed defense. "What we have got to do must be done quickly," insisted Sidney Johnston. "The longer we leave them to fight the more difficult will they be to defeat." Beauregard, who helped Johnston plan the bloody assault at Shiloh, favored a Confederate invasion of Maryland in 1861, and in 1862 he wrote, "I desire to .

. . retake the offensive as soon as our forces . . . have been sufficiently reorganized." Bragg, who objected to trenches because he believed they destroyed an army's aggressiveness, attacked in three of the four major battles he directed.

Hood, who took command of the Army of Tennessee after Joe Johnston's removal, strongly favored assault tactics. Indeed, his major qualification for army command was his reputation as the hardest hitter in the Confederacy. Everyone knew Hood would attack Sherman's army; that was why he had been given command. The Confederacy needed a military miracle by that time. Joe Johnston did not believe in such things, but Davis and Hood did. So Davis, after many discussions about warfare with Hood, who was in Richmond recovering from the loss of his leg at Chickamauga, became convinced that Hood would fight just as Davis himself would have fought had he been able to take field command in Georgia. Hood—a gambler and a visionary, a man unaware of just how little he knew—wagered the lives of his men that he could beat the Federals by repeated attacks. Johnston's defense of Atlanta in May and June 1864 cost the Federals five thousand more men than the Confederates lost. Hood lost eleven thousand more men than Sherman in operations around Atlanta from late July to early September 1864.

Lee too liked to attack. He often suggested offensives to the president and urged other generals to be aggressive. In May 1862, a month after what Lee called the Confederate "victory of Shiloh," he advised Beauregard to invade Tennessee and approved Jackson's aggressive campaign in the Shenandoah Valley. When Lee assumed command of Confederate forces in Virginia in June, he promptly abandoned a defensive strategy and launched his own Seven Days campaign against McClellan on the Peninsula.

Though Lee was at his best on defense, he adopted a defensive strategy only after attrition had deprived him of the power to attack. His brilliant defensive campaign against Grant in 1864 made the Union pay in manpower as it had never paid before.

But the Confederates adopted defensive tactics too late; Lee started the campaign with too few men, and he could not replace his losses as could Grant.

Even after the Wilderness campaign, Lee wanted to launch another offensive. He continued to hope that he could maneuver Grant out into the open and attack him. In May 1864 Lee wrote Davis: "[Grant's] position is strongly entrenched, and we cannot attack it with any prospect of success without great loss of men which I wish to avoid if possible. . . . I shall continue to strike him whenever opportunity presents itself." Just two weeks before he surrendered, Lee lost 3,500 men in an assault on the Federal fortifications at Petersburg. "I was induced to assume the offensive," Lee explained to Davis, "from the belief that the point assailed could be carried without much loss." As it happened, Lee's push failed to break the Union line, and the Confederates lost three times as many men as the defenders.

Perhaps the best way to illustrate the advantage defenders enjoyed over attackers is by a comparison of casualties. In half of the twenty-two major battles of the Civil War, the Federals attacked. They lost 119,000 men when they assaulted and 88,000 when they defended—a difference of 31,000 men. The Confederates lost 117,000 men when they attacked, but only 61,000 when they defended—a difference of 56,000, or enough to have given the South another large army. Every time the Confederates attacked, they lost an average of at least ten men out of every one hundred engaged more than the Federal defenders, but when the Confederates defended, they lost seven fewer men out of every one hundred than the Union attackers.

Southerners may have attacked so regularly because of what Thomas Livermore called "the greater impetuosity of the Southern temperaments." He noted that "Southern leaders were, at least up to 1864, bolder in taking risks than their opponents, but also that they pushed their forces under fire very nearly to the limit of endurance." General Scott, himself a Southerner, insisted that Confederates were too undisciplined to fight a defensive war; they "will not take care of things, or husband [their] resources," he announced. "If it could all be done by one wild desperate dash [then Southerners] . . . would do it, but [they cannot] . . . stand the long . . . months between the acts, the waiting."

Their Celtic heritage influenced the way Southerners fought. Like their ancestors, Southerners who participated in the Civil War tended to be bold, reckless, and impatient. In *Attack and Die: Civil War Military Tactics and the Southern Heritage,* Perry Jamieson and I argue that the "Confederates bled themselves to death in the first three years of the war by making costly attacks more often than did the Federals." Offensive tactics, which had been used so successfully by Americans in the Mexican War, were much less effective in the 1860s due to the rifled musket, the repeating rifle, the use of entrenchments, the failure of bayonet charges, and the major change in the cavalry's role—all of these interacted with each other and created a revolution in tactics.

Southerners, imprisoned in a culture that rejected careful calculation and patience, often refused to learn from their mistakes. They continued to fight, despite mounting casualties, with the same courageous dash and reckless abandon that had characterized their Celtic ancestors for two thousand years. The Confederates favored offensive warfare because the Celtic charge was an integral part of their heritage.

Bismarck is reputed to have said that fools learn from their own mistakes; he preferred to learn from the mistakes of others. The Confederacy failed because its leaders made the same mistakes time and again. "The reb[e]ls," observed a Union private, "fight as though a mans life was not worth one sent [sic] or in other words with desperation; or like Gen. Lafayette [sic] said to [Gen.] Washington, there is more *dogs* where them came from." By 1865, Southern military leaders had exhausted their human resources. In attacking when they should have defended, they had, as Toombs's aptly stated, simply worn themselves out trying to whip the Yankees.

The First Shot

More than half a century ago, Charles W. Ramsdell charged
that Abraham Lincoln, "having decided that there was no other
way than war for the salvation of his administration, his party,
and the Union, maneuvered the Confederates into firing the first
shot in order that they, rather than he, should take the blame of
beginning bloodshed."

The ensuing uproar, especially among Lincoln scholars, was
predictable. Many distinguished historians joined the debate;
some supported the Ramsdell thesis, but most attacked it. In a
study published in the early 1940s, James G. Randall and David
M. Potter claimed that Lincoln sought peace rather than war. A
few years later Kenneth M. Stampp concluded: "one cannot
indict Lincoln for [sending relief to Fort Sumter] . . . unless one
challenges the universal standards of 'practical' statesmen and
the whole concept of 'national interest.' This was a thing worth
fighting for! If Lincoln was no pacifist, neither were his contemporaries, North and South. Southern leaders must share with

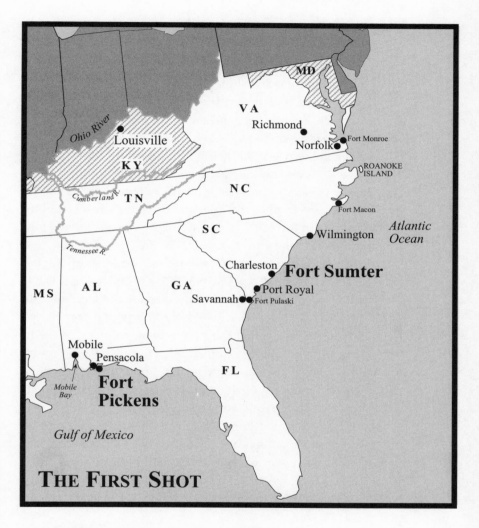

THE FIRST SHOT

him the responsibility for a resort to force."

More recent scholarship also contends that Jefferson Davis was as responsible as Lincoln, if not more so, for the outbreak of hostilities. "The firing on Sumter was an act of rash emotionalism," concluded Allan Nevins in 1959. "The astute Alexander H. Stephens, counseling delay, showed more statesmanship than Jefferson Davis." In 1963 Richard N. Current suggested that "the

Ramsdell thesis, turned inside out, could be applied to Davis with as much justice as it had been applied to Lincoln. One could argue that political and not military necessity led Davis to order the firing of the first shot. The very life of the Confederacy, the growth upon which that life depended, was at stake. So were the pride, the prestige, and the position of Davis." He then charged, "Biographers of Davis and historians of the Confederacy have evaded or obscured their hero's role in the Sumter affair. They have digressed to levy accusations or innuendoes at Lincoln. If they have any concern for historical objectivity, however, they should face frankly the question of Davis's responsibility for the coming of the war." "After all," Current concluded, "Lincoln did not order the guns to fire. Davis did."

Those who consider the Confederates aggressors have a strong case. As Current claimed, Southern historians and Davis biographers have evaded or obscured what the Confederate president and his associates actually did to bring on war. But so have Northern historians; they have been too engrossed in defending Lincoln against Ramsdell's charges to give much attention to Davis and the Confederates. Too few scholars have mined beyond the most obvious printed sources on the Confederate side or looked beyond Sumter.

The Lincoln-Sumter story, explained in elaborate detail by numerous historians, is too well known for recitation here. It probably has been overtold already. What has been neglected—what historians have missed—is how events at Fort Sumter were determined by what happened and by what failed to happen at Fort Pickens.

In March 1861 the only significant forts within the Confederacy still occupied by Federal forces were Sumter, in Charleston Harbor, and Pickens, near Pensacola, Florida. After a badly planned and bloodless attempt by Alabama and Florida militia to capture Fort Pickens in early January, Pres. James Buchanan and the Confederate government agreed to a truce. Stephen R. Mallory, a former U.S. senator from Florida, announced that

Southerners had no intention of attacking Fort Pickens, "but, on the contrary, we desire to keep the peace, and if the present status be preserved we will guarantee that no attack will be made upon it." Nine former senators—including Jefferson Davis and Judah P. Benjamin—joined Mallory in opposition to any Confederate attempt to take the fort. "We think no assault should be made," they wrote on January 18. "The possession of the fort is not worth one drop of blood to us."

President Buchanan also opposed any action that might appear aggressive. At his direction, the secretaries of war and the navy wrote the commander of the naval squadron off Pensacola on January 29, "In consequence of the assurances received from Mr. Mallory . . . that Fort Pickens would not be assaulted, you are instructed not to land the company on board the *Brooklyn* unless said fort be attacked." The day before this letter was written, the president asked Congress "to abstain from passing any law calculated to produce a collision of arms." Thereafter, through February, the Navy Department instructed the commanders of ships near Fort Pickens to "act strictly on the defensive."

Buchanan's successor was less cautious. In the preliminary draft of his first inaugural address, Lincoln wrote, "All the power at my disposal will be used to reclaim the public property and places which have fallen; to hold, occupy and possess these, and all other property and places belonging to the government, . . . but beyond what may be necessary for these, there will be no invasion of any State."

Secretary of State William H. Seward begged the president to substitute for this strong statement a promise to use his power "with discretion in every case and . . . with a view and a hope of a peaceful solution of the national troubles and the restoration of fraternal sympathies and affections." Lincoln's friend Orville H. Browning also suggested that the phrase "to reclaim the public property and places which have fallen" was too strong. "On principle the passage is right as it now stands," Browning agreed. "But cannot that be accomplished as well, or even better without announcing the purpose in your inaugural?" Lincoln did modify his address, but he left no doubt that he intended to hold Sumter and Pickens.

By early March, both Lincoln and Davis had decided to violate the truce, but neither knew what the other intended. On March 10 Brig. Gen. Braxton Bragg took command of Southern forces near Pensacola with instructions from the Confederate War Department to report his "wants in respect to artillery and the munitions of war, having in view the . . . reduction of Fort Pickens." Two days later a Union ship started south with an order to Capt. Israel Vogdes aboard the USS *Brooklyn*: "At the first favorable moment you will land with your company, reenforce Fort Pickens, and hold the same till further orders."

But the senior American naval officer off Pensacola, Capt. Henry A. Adams, refused to obey the order. "I have declined to land the men . . . as it would be in direct violation of the orders from the Navy Department under which I am acting," he wrote Secretary of the Navy Gideon Welles on April 1. To reinforce Pickens, argued Adams, "would most certainly be viewed as a hostile act, and would be resisted to the utmost. No one acquainted with the feelings of the military assembled under Genl Bragg can doubt that it would be considered not only a declaration, but an act of war. It would be a serious thing to bring on by any precipitation a collision which may be entirely against the wishes of the administration. At present both sides are faithfully observing the agreement entered into by the U.S. Government with Mr. Mallory." Adams reminded Welles: "This agreement binds us not to reinforce Fort Pickens unless it shall be attacked or threatened. It binds them not to attack it unless we should attempt to reinforce it. I saw General Bragg on the 30th ulto., who reassured me the conditions on their part should not be violated."

Bragg had been less than honest with Adams. Only insufficient means, not regard for the truce, prevented the Confederates from attacking Fort Pickens. By the end of March, Bragg commanded a force of 1,116 men, and 5,000 additional troops were on the way to Pensacola, but he was not yet ready to fight. He believed that the erection of a new battery at Pickens was "a virtual violation of the [truce] agreement; and the threat of President Lincoln in his inaugural is sufficient justification of the means we are adopting." But Bragg "deemed it prudent not to bring the agreement to an abrupt termination." The Union fleet off Pensacola was too strong, and the Confederates were still unprepared. "According to my notions," he admitted to his wife, "things here are in a most deplorable condition. . . . Our troops are raw volunteers, without officers, and without discipline, each man with an idea that he can whip the world, and believing that nothing is necessary but go . . . take Fort Pickens and all the Navy." It would not be that easy. The fort was on Santa Rosa Island, a mile and a half across Pensacola Bay from the mainland. Bragg had neither the firepower nor the ships necessary to isolate the Federal garrison. He believed that unless "U.S. troops attack us no fighting can occur here for a long time, as we are totally unprepared. . . . Fort Pickens cannot be taken without a regular siege, and we have no means to carry that on."

Yet the Confederate War Department insisted that Bragg submit a plan to take Pickens, and he suggested three possibilities— a regular siege, a flank assault on the fort from Santa Rosa Island, or a direct assault. If the operation was to be undertaken immediately, he favored an infantry assault on the fort after its walls had been broken by heavy guns and mortars.

The other alternatives would require many more guns and men than Bragg had or could reasonably expect to have for some time. He explained to Adjutant General Samuel Cooper on March 27: "I entertain little doubt of being able to batter [the fort's walls] . . . down with 10 inch guns . . . when an assaulting party from this side aided by a false attack on the island might carry the work with the Bayonet. It will be difficult at this distance to determine when the breach is fully effected, . . . and should the enemy resist us by landing heavy reenforcements it would be a desperate struggle. A knowledge, however, that success or entire destruction was inevitable would nerve our men to the work."

While Confederate authorities discussed what action, if any, Bragg should take, the Federals prepared to reinforce Pickens. On April 6, after Lincoln learned that his earlier reinforcement instructions had not been obeyed, Gideon Welles informed Capt. Henry A. Adams: "The [Navy] Department regrets that you did not comply with the . . . orders. . . . You will immediately, on the first favorable opportunity after receipt of this order, afford every facility to Capt. Vogdes . . . to enable him to land the troops under his command [at Fort Pickens]."

When Bragg received reports that additional troops might soon land at Pickens, he was uncertain what he should do. On April 5 he wired Secretary Walker, "Should the agreement not to re-enforce be violated, may I attack?" Walker replied that same day with three questions: "Can you prevent re-enforcements being landed at other points on Santa Rosa Island other than the docks? Do you mean by 'attack' the opening of your guns upon the fort or upon the ships? If the former, would your operations be confined to battering the fort?"

"I can control the dock," Bragg answered the next day, "but re-enforcements can be landed on the outside of Santa Rosa Island in spite of me. The ships, except the Wyandotte, are beyond my range. She can be driven off or destroyed. Any attack by us now must be secretly made by escalade. My batteries are not ready for breaching, and we are entirely deficient in ammunition. No landing should be made on Santa Rosa Island with our present means."

It was still unclear to him just what the War Department expected. In a letter to Adjutant General Cooper on April 5, Bragg asked how far he should "be governed by the articles of agreement now existing here?" He could not prevent the landing of reinforcements, but he might make it hazardous. Moreover, he might take Pickens by escalade before it could be reinforced. He would get ready for an escalade, "should it be deemed advisable at any time." Nevertheless, as "long as diplomatic intercourse is going on," he informed Cooper, "I shall not feel authorized to bring on a collision, as now advised." Yet the next day Bragg seemed less certain. To Secretary Walker he announced, "I do not hesitate to believe we are entirely absolved from all obligations under the [truce] agreement," but Bragg wanted to know if he was "free to act when a favourable occasion might offer?"

On April 6, the day he asked Walker for instructions, Bragg received from Jefferson Davis a remarkably candid letter, which historians of the first-shot controversy have overlooked. It was written, in the president's words, "freely and hurriedly" by "your old comrade in arms, who hopes much, and expects much for you, and from you."

> *Unofficial*
> Montgomery, ALA.
> April 3, 1861
>
> MY DEAR GENL,
> The Secty of War communicated to you last night by telegraph our latest information and the suppositions derived from it. It is, there is much reason to believe, with a view to exhibit forms and relieve the effect of the necessary abandonment of Sumter that is proposed to reinforce Pickens, but it is also possible that it may be intended to attempt the reinforcement of both. They will it is said avoid collision with you by landing their forces upon the Island and after the garrison is sufficient will bring in supplies defying your batteries.
> You will not have failed to notice that the tone of the Northern press indicates a desire to prove a *military* necessity for the abandonment of both Sumter & Pickens.
> It is already asserted that your batteries will not permit the landing of supplies, and soon this may be charged

among the short comings of Mr. Buchannan [*sic*]. Per contra there is manifested a desire to show what can be done at Pensacola as proof of what would have been done at Charleston. In the latter view they may seek to throw both men and supplies into Pickens by landing on Santa Rosa beyond the range of your guns. It is scarcely to be doubted that for political reasons the U.S. govt. will avoid making an attack so long as the hope of retaining the border states remains. There would be to us an advantage in so placing them that an attack by them would be a necessity, but when we are ready to relieve our territory and jurisdiction of the presence of a foreign garrison that advantage is overbalanced by other considerations. The case of Pensacola then is reduced [to] the more palpable elements of a military problem and your measures may without disturbing views be directed to the capture of Fort Pickens and the defense of the harbor. You will soon have I hope a force sufficient to occupy all the points necessary for that end. As many additional troops as may be required can be promptly furnished.

Instruction, organization and discipline must proceed with active operations; you will appreciate the circumstances which rendered such objectionable combination an unavoidable condition. Your batteries on the main shore are I am informed nearly complete and their converging fire may I hope compensate somewhat for their too distant location from the work to be battered.

To secure the time necessary for you to effect a breach will it not be necessary to embarrass the use of the guns of Pickens which bear upon your works? Can this be done by a mortar battery placed on the Island so as to take those guns in reverse? A mortar battery could I suppose be established in a night, secure from fire & from sortie when you have a sufficient force to justify a partition of your army. If that first step the establishment of a mortar battery was permitted you could establish gun batteries also, and then carry forward your approaches until you were attacked. Then all your batteries being opened, shells falling in the Fort from front and from rear must prove rapidly destructive to the garrison, and open to you several modes of success. Ist. By surrender. Second. By abandonment if you had not been able to command the shipping. Third. By breach of front wall or explosion of glacis mines exposing the work to capture by assault. Fourth. By evacuation on the plea that the means at the disposal of their government had not been sufficient to prevent the investment of the Fort and its reduction by famine.

I have written to you freely and hurriedly because I wished to exchange views with you and felt assured that you would understand that there was no purpose to dictate; and under an entire confidence that your judgment would control your conduct, and could only be influenced by a suggestion, in so far as it might excite a train of thought out of the channel which the constant contemplation of a particular view is apt to wear. Though you are addressed upon official matters yet I wish to regard this not as a letter of the President but of your old comrade in arms, who hopes much, and expects much for you, and from you.

Very respectfully & truly yrs,
JEFFN DAVIS

This letter indicates that Davis was willing to start the war. He would have liked to do precisely what Ramsdell claimed Lincoln did—maneuver the enemy into firing the first shot—but the Confederate president considered such a scheme, in his own words, "overbalanced by other considerations." Davis counseled action—"your measures may without disturbing views be directed to the capture of Fort Pickens"—and the tone of his letter implies that he expected Bragg to take the fort should he fire the first shot.

Bragg would make no such promise. In his reply to the president on April 7, he stated: "Subsequent information has strengthened the opinion against the attack by way of Santa Rosa Island. . . . Regular approaches by any but veteran troops are very difficult under the most favorable circumstances, but when attended, as in this case, by a combination of the most unfavorable circumstances, they become almost impossible. . . . The placing of a mortar battery on the Island as you suggest would have a good effect, but the same thing can be accomplished from this side without dividing our force." Bragg believed a Confederate landing on the island would result in the immediate reinforcement of Pickens. He could suggest only one possible and somewhat hazardous way to capture the fort before reinforcements landed. "The plan which just at this time might succeed," Bragg ventured, "is that of an escalade by ladders. My troops are eager, and will risk anything to avoid a long investment on this sand beach. Ignorant in a great degree of the danger they would go at it with a will, and with ordinary good luck would carry the point. Our greatest deficiency is the want of means to reach the Island properly and secretly."

Davis doubtless considered an escalade too risky. If it failed, the Confederates would be branded as aggressors and have nothing tangible to show for it. Though Bragg prepared for an escalade, permission to assault Pickens never came. On April 8 Walker ordered Bragg to prevent the reinforcement of the fort at "every hazard." The general might have considered this permission to attack had Walker written nothing else, but in a subsequent message the secretary of war warned: "The expression 'at every hazard' in my dispatch of this morning was not intended to require you to land upon the Island. The presumption is that reinforcement will be attempted at the Docks, and this I hope you can and will prevent, though it should lead to assault on your works. The belief here is that they will not only attempt to reinforce the Fort but also to retake the Navy Yard."

Bragg, who had been less than enthusiastic in his recommendation that the Confederates attack Pickens, began to doubt his ability to check a determined Union assault on the Pensacola defenses. "[We] will do our best," he promised Walker on April 9, "but supplies are short for a continued resistance. [We also] want transportation to move guns, shot and troops."

While Bragg strengthened his defenses, Confederate officials in Montgomery shifted their attention to Fort Sumter. Throughout March and early April, they had ordered the Confederate commander at Charleston, Brig. Gen. P.G.T. Beauregard, to prevent the reinforcement of Sumter but otherwise to remain on the defensive. But on April 10—after it became clear that Pickens was an unlikely place to start the conflict and Lincoln had informed the Confederates that supplies were on the way to Sumter—Walker ordered Beauregard to demand the fort's "evacuation, and if this is refused proceed, in such manner as you may determine, to reduce it."

The rest of the story is familiar enough. The Federal commander, of course, refused to evacuate Sumter, and at 4:30 A.M. on April 12, Beauregard's guns opened fire. The next day Walker wired Bragg, "Sumter is ours."

At that point Bragg was too busy with his own problems to rejoice. On the night of April 12, the first wave of Federal reinforcements reached Fort Pickens. A Confederate reconnaissance vessel discovered the landing on the seaward side of the island but was detained by the Federals until their troops were safely ashore. Bragg reported that when the reinforcements landed he "was making every effort for an escalade, had my party all detailed, and was waiting notice of the readiness of the Engineers. . . . Of course," he asserted, "such a movement now is impossible." Five days later four more companies of Union troops reached Pickens without opposition.

The first shot had been fired because neither Lincoln nor

Davis tried very hard to avoid a collision. Lincoln had no desire to shoot first, but he was determined to hold the forts, and he readily broke the informal truce Buchanan had established. Davis too had little regard for the truce agreement. He supported it only when it seemed advantageous. He encouraged Bragg to capture Fort Pickens, but when Bragg insisted that the only possible way to take Pickens was by a reckless assault that might become an embarrassing failure, Davis shifted his attention to Sumter and directed Beauregard to open fire. Thus, war came at Fort Sumter only because the Confederates were neither subtle enough nor strong enough to begin it at Fort Pickens.

CHAPTER NINE
Davis and His Generals

Jefferson Davis was, in the words of a contemporary, "the heart and brains" of the Confederate government. He spent fifteen or more hours a day at his duties, among them receiving visitors, writing letters, consulting his advisers, and revising or initiating projects to win the war. An informed contemporary claimed that Davis "managed the War Department, in all its various details, in addition to other manifold labors; finding time not only to give it a general supervision, but to go into all the minutiae of the working of its bureaux, the choice of all its officers, or agents, and the very disbursement of its appropriations." Davis appointed and removed generals, advised them on strategy and tactics, and often decided when and where they should fight. He was the man most responsible for the way the Confederacy fought the Civil War.

Davis seems to have had no doubts about his ability to direct a war. He had spent a dozen years in the army, including four years as a cadet at the U.S. Military Academy (1824–28), five years as a second lieutenant in the 1st Infantry (1828–33), two years as a first lieutenant in the 1st Dragoons (1833–35), and one year as colonel of the 1st Mississippi Volunteer Rifles during the Mexican War (1846–47). He had participated in the Black Hawk War (1832) and in two Mexican War battles. At Monterey and Buena Vista, where he had been wounded in the foot, Davis had fought courageously. In addition to his years in the army, he had served as Pres. Franklin Pierce's secretary of war (1853–57), and he had been chairman of the Senate's Military Affairs Committee. All of these activities had given him confidence in his mili-

Jefferson Davis and his generals

tary ability. "By early education, by years of service in the army, by other years spent in administering the U.S. War Dept.," Davis boasted, "I had learned the usages of war."

Before the Confederacy was formed, Davis had so much confidence in his ability as a soldier that he said he would rather be commander in chief of its army than its president. Of course, he knew that under the U.S. Constitution, the commander in chief of the army was the president; and he could have guessed that it would be so under the constitution the Confederates would adopt. Davis was not a devious man but neither was he overly modest. He told his wife during the war, "If I could take one wing [of the army] and Lee the other, I think we could wrest a victory from those people."

Contemporaries also had faith in Davis's military skills. In 1861 an enthusiastic newspaperman compared "Gen. Davis" favorably with Gen. George Washington, and Louis T. Wigfall, who later became one of the president's harshest critics, said: "Davis has the wisdom and sagacity of the statesman . . . , the courage and discretion of the soldier. . . . I know of no man so competent to inaugurate a Government at such a time." A few months later a clerk in the Confederate War Department noted the almost universal belief that Davis "possessed military genius of a high order." "When Jeff goes to the encampments [of soldiers]," Mrs. Davis noted in 1861, "they go on like wild Indians, scream, catch hold of him, call out 'I am from Tennessee, I'm from Kentucky, I'm from Mississippi, God bless your soul.' The other day a volunteer stepped up to the carriage and said 'God bless you, Madam, and keep you well,' with a deep bow. They seize little Jeff and kiss him. It seems as if Jeff's stock has . . . risen."

But Davis's popularity proved fragile, and his critics became more outspoken. An army physician believed that the president "placed too high an estimate upon his own individual military genius, and failed to grasp . . . the problem of the . . . young nation." An editor denounced Davis as "cold, haughty, peevish, narrow-minded, pigheaded, malignant"—"the cause of our undoing. While he lives, there is no hope for us." A major in the commissary department said that he "used to think of Jefferson Davis a *mule*, but a good *mule*. He has come to think him a jackass."

Such criticism of Davis would hardly have surprised Winfield Scott. The old general, with whom Davis had feuded when he was secretary of war, had declared at the war's outset: "I am amazed that any man of judgment should hope for the success of any cause in which Jefferson Davis is a leader. There is a contamination in his touch. . . . He is not a cheap Judas. I do not think he would have sold the Saviour for thirty shillings; but for the successorship of Pontius Pilate he would have betrayed Christ and the apostles and the whole Christian Church!"

If Scott's words seem unduly biased and exaggerated, it is worth noting that Davis's own chief of ordnance, Brig. Gen. Josiah Gorgas, stated: "The President seems to respect the opinions of no one; and has, I fear, little appreciation of services rendered, unless the party enjoys his good opinion. He seems to be an indifferent judge of men, and is guided more by prejudice than by sound, discriminating judgment." And Sen. C.C. Clay, a Davis supporter, admitted that the president "will not ask or receive counsel and indeed seems predisposed to go exactly the way his friends advised him not to go."

Nevertheless, a number of prominent men continued to support the president. The editor of *De Bow's Review* insisted that he was as "brave as Ajax and as wise as Ulysses," and Congressman Warren Akin wrote: "I had a long conversation with the President yesterday. He has been greatly wronged. . . . The President is not the stern, puffed up man he is represented to be. He was as polite, attentive and communicative to me as I could wish. He listened patiently to all I said and when he differed with me he would give his reasons for it. He was very cordial. . . . And many gentlemen tell me the same thing as to his manner with them. His enemies have done him great injustice. He is a patriot and a good man, I think."

Cabinet members understandably expressed appreciation of

Davis. The Confederacy's postmaster general considered him "the ablest man I have ever known"; his last attorney general claimed that Davis "was the most honest, truest, gentlest, tenderest, manliest man I ever knew"; and Judah P. Benjamin, who had served in several cabinet posts, insisted that neither in "private conversation nor in Cabinet council" had he ever heard Davis "utter one unworthy thought, one ungenerous sentiment." A soldier found him "one of the most approachable of men, as polite and affable to the humblest as to the most exalted," remembered Lt. Gen. Stephen D. Lee, who also praised Davis's physical and moral courage.

Different people simply saw different qualities in Davis. To those who admired him he appeared able, modest, polite, loyal, agreeable, and self-sacrificing—an accomplished and dedicated patriot. To his enemies he seemed ruthless, cold, stubborn, petty, and prejudiced—an incompetent executive with poor judgment.

On one point both friends and enemies of the president agreed: his health was poor. This sick man—who suffered constantly from insomnia, dyspepsia, and neuralgia—was often incapacitated by such diseases as malaria. "Jeff has been for nearly eight weeks confined to the house," admitted Mrs. Davis in 1858. The next year he wrote his friend Franklin Pierce, "I . . . have been seriously ill, though now free of disease, my strength has not been restored and there is therefore constant apprehension of a relapse."

Just before the war a reporter described Davis as having "the face of a corpse, the form of a skeleton." "You are surprised to see him walking," wrote Murat Halstead in 1860. "Look at the haggard, sunken, weary eye—the thin white wrinkled lips clasped close upon the teeth in anguish. That is the mouth of a brave but impatient sufferer. See the ghastly white, hollow, bitterly puckered cheek, the high, sharp cheek bone, the pale brow full of fine wrinkles, the grizzly hair, prematurely gray; and see the thin, bloodless, bony, nervous hands!"

Almost everyone who saw Davis during the Civil War commented upon his sickly appearance. He seemed, to English reporter William H. Russell, to have "a very haggard, care-worn, and pain drawn look." In 1861 a future congressman wrote, "The president looks thin and feeble." That same year a war clerk observed: "The President is sick. . . . I did not know until today that he is blind of an eye."

Two years later an English officer remarked that Davis looked "older than I expected. He is only fifty-six but his face is emaciated and much wrinkled. He is nearly six feet high, but is extremely thin and stoops. . . . I was . . . told he had lost the sight of his left eye from a recent illness."

Not only was the president sickly but so were many of his military advisers. Their gatherings sometimes resembled a hospital ward more than an assembly of war directors. An observer described Davis's first secretary of war, Leroy Pope Walker, as a "man . . . whose health is feeble." A war clerk noted in May 1861: "Mr. Walker . . . is fast working himself down. He has not yet learned how to avoid unnecessary labor. . . . He stands somewhat on ceremony with his brother officials, and accords and acts the etiquette natural to a sensitive gentleman who has never been broken on the wheel of office. I predict for him a short career." By June, Walker's health had failed; he remained secretary of war until September 1861, but most of the time he was too ill to come to his office. George W. Randolph, secretary of war for eight months in 1862, had pulmonary tuberculosis, and James A. Seddon, who had the longest tenure of any secretary of war, was often incapacitated by neuralgia and other illness. Albert T. Bledsoe, the assistant secretary of war, advised Davis that Seddon was too feeble to head the War Department. "The labor of the office would kill him in one month," insisted Bledsoe. "Mr. Seddon has no physique to sustain him," observed war clerk John B. Jones, who also stated that Seddon lacked both "energy and knowledge of war. . . . He is frail in health. . . . He will not remain long in office if he attempts to perform all the duties." Six months later Jones remarked: "Secretary Seddon is gaunt and emaciated. . . . He looks like a dead man galvanized into muscular animation. His eyes are sunken, and his features have the hue of a man who has been in his grave a full month." After two additional months of hard work, Seddon looked to Jones like a "corpse which had been buried two months. The circles round his eyes are absolutely black." Another contemporary remembered Seddon as "an old man broken with the storms of state."

Some of the soldiers Davis named to the War Department also looked and acted more dead than alive. Three of the most prominent were Col. Lucius B. Northrop, the Confederacy's often criticized commissary general; Adjutant and Inspector General Samuel Cooper; and Gen. Braxton Bragg. Colonel Northrop, whom Mrs. Mary Chesnut called an "eccentric creature" because he wore folded newspapers across his chest instead of underwear, had been on permanent sick leave from the U.S. Army for twenty-two years before Davis appointed him commissary general. "The reason for his appointment to . . . the most responsible Bureau of the War Department was a mystery," admitted a contemporary. Cooper, often described as too old and feeble for active duty, had not been in the field for nearly thirty years. During the war he was often ill and out of his office. "Genl. Cooper still sick & can't be seen," wrote an officer in 1862.

General Bragg, whom Davis brought to Richmond in 1864 to help him conduct military operations, was at the time the most discredited general in the Confederacy and one of the sickliest. Bragg had enough illnesses to keep a squad of doctors busy— dyspepsia, rheumatism, chronic boils, a liver ailment, extreme nervousness, and severe migraine headaches. Some of his illness—and perhaps his often erratic behavior—may even have been caused by the medicine he took.

A remarkable number of the South's highest ranking field officers had physical handicaps or health problems. Bragg was sick during much to the time he commanded various Confeder-

ate forces. Gen. John Bell Hood, who had lost a leg at Chickamauga and the use of an arm at Gettysburg, had to be strapped
into his saddle when he commanded the Army of Tennessee. In
1862 Gen. P.G.T. Beauregard had to take a leave of absence
because of illness. Gen. Joseph E. Johnston, who had been
wounded seven times in action against Indians and Mexicans
before the Civil War, was again hit twice at Fair Oaks—first by a
bullet in the shoulder and a few moments later by a shell frag-
ment that unhorsed him. For nearly six months during the critical summer and fall of 1862, he was incapacitated, and even
after he returned to duty, he often was, in his own words, "too
feeble to command an army." In April 1863, when President
Davis ordered him to take command of the South's second most
important army, Johnston was "seriously sick." He explained, "I
. . . am not now able to serve in the field." Later, when, he was
ordered to assume command of forces in Mississippi, Johnston
replied, "I shall go immediately, although unfit for field-ser-
vice."

Relations between the president and Joe Johnston were never
cordial; nevertheless, Davis respected Johnston's military skills.
In 1862, just before Seven Pines, the president assured the general, "my design is to suggest not to direct, recognizing . . . your
ability . . . it is my wish to leave you with the fullest powers to
exercise your judgment." Furthermore, three weeks after the
battle, Davis informed his wife, who was visiting in North Carolina: "Genl. J.E. Johnston is steadily and rapidly improving [in
health]. I wish he was able to take the field. Despite the critics
who know military affairs by instinct, he is a good Soldier,
knows the troops, never brags even of what he did do and could
at this time render most valuable service."

There is a tendency to think of Robert E. Lee as a superman
who was never ill, but he was bedridden for several days in the
spring of 1863 with "inflammation of the heart-sac" and a serious throat infection. This plus occasional attacks of rheumatism
"enfeebled" the general and forced him "to take more rest." In

August 1863, after the Gettysburg campaign, Lee asked Davis to relieve him from command of the Army of Northern Virginia:

> I do this with the most earnestness because no one is more aware than myself of my inability for the duties of my position. I cannot even accomplish what I myself desire. How can I fulfill the expectations of others? In addition I sensibly feel the growing failure of my bodily strength. I have not yet recovered from the attack I experienced the past spring. I am becoming more and more incapable of exertion, and am thus prevented from making the personal examinations and giving the personal supervision to the operations in the field which I feel to be necessary. I am so dull that in making use of the eyes of others I am frequently misled. Everything, therefore, points to the advantages to be derived from a new commander, and I most anxiously urge the matter upon Your Excellency from my belief that a younger and abler man than myself can readily be attained.

Though Davis refused to replace Lee, the general's health continued to decline. In October 1863 an attack of "sciatica," "rheumatism," or "lumbago" made it impossible for Lee to ride for about a week, and during the critical campaign against Grant in May and June 1864, Lee was debilitated for ten days by sickness.

Even Lee's trusted lieutenant, Thomas J. "Stonewall" Jackson, had or imagined he had a wide range of ailments—dyspepsia, liver disturbances, nervousness, eye strain, rheumatism, chilblains, cold feet, malaria, bilious attacks, neuralgia, fevers, "a slight distortion of the spine," and chronic inflammation of the throat, nose, and ears. By sitting "straight up, . . . without touching the back of the chair," Jackson believed that he "could keep his internal organs from being constricted." He also treated himself with buttermilk, freshly cooked cornbread, quantities of fruit—especially lemons—and cold water. "I have been quite unwell," he announced before the war, "and had it not have been for my judicious application of water, I can not say what would have been the consequences." Active campaigning seemed to improve his health.

The poor health of so many of Davis's subordinates does not necessarily suggest that the Confederate president had a psychological affinity for sick people, though one might speculate that this was the case. Sickness is after all an aspect of weakness, and there is abundant evidence that Davis liked to surround himself with weak subordinates. "He was not only President and secretary of five departments—which naturally caused some errors," stated a contemporary, "but the spice of the dictator in him made him quite willing to shoulder the responsibilities of all the positions." He had six different secretaries of war in four years.

If empathy bound Davis to some of his infirm subordinates, there is no evidence that these men received or retained their high offices solely because the president considered them fellow sufferers; indeed, he insisted that his military appointments were based on merit alone. "'Due care was taken to prevent the appointment of incompetent or unworthy persons to be officers of the army," Davis stated. And several historians have supported his claim. The president "gave just as few high commissions to politicians as possible," insisted one of his biographers. To a critic Davis wrote, "It would be easy to justify the appointments which have been made of Brig. Genls. by stating the reasons in each case, but suffice it to say that I have endeavored to avoid bad selections by relying on military rather than political recommendations."

Yet political considerations influenced Davis more than he admitted. Nearly 30 percent of the generals he named in 1861 were political appointees. For example, Humphrey Marshall of Kentucky, despite his military training and experience, was clearly a political general. Less than a year after his graduation from the U.S. Military Academy, Marshall had resigned from the army. He later served as a volunteer in the Mexican War, during which, according to one report, his "regiment did some fine running and no fighting." Elected to Congress seven times as a Whig, Marshall had tried to keep Kentucky neutral in 1861. After he failed, Davis appointed him a Confederate brigadier general. Marshall spent much of his time writing long letters of complaint to Davis. These finally goaded the president into a reply that revealed why he had appointed Marshall. "When you were offered a position of rank and responsibility in our army," he stated, "it was my hope that you would prove beneficial to our cause. . . . [I believed] in your assured conviction of your ability to recruit an army of Kentuckians, who would rally to your standard." But Marshall had proved to be neither an able recruiter nor an able general. In 1863 he resigned his army commission and entered the Confederate Congress.

Other political generals included John C. Breckinridge of Kentucky, who had been a member of Congress, vice president of the United States, and a candidate for president in 1860; Robert Toombs of Georgia, who resigned as Confederate secretary of state to enter the army; Louis T. Wigfall of Texas, who had been expelled from the U.S. Senate; James Chesnut Jr., a former senator from South Carolina and a member of the Provisional Confederate Congress, who became a member of Davis's military staff; Milledge L. Bonham, a South Carolina congressman; Lawrence O. Branch, a member of a politically prominent North Carolina family; Howell Cobb of Georgia, former speaker of the U.S. House of Representatives; John B. Floyd, at one time governor of Virginia and recently Pres. James Buchanan's secretary of war; Leroy Pope Walker of Alabama, who was for a short time Davis's secretary of war; and two former Virginia governors, William "Extra Billy" Smith and Henry A. Wise.

Pressure on the president to appoint political generals was strong. Davis had the thankless task of organizing an effective army while including in it officers of diverse political opinion from all states and regions of the South. In a letter of July 13, 1861, Gov. Isham G. Harris of Tennessee thanked the president for appointing three Tennesseans to the rank of brigadier general, "but," the governor noted, "they are all Democrats." He wanted Davis to name some "other generals" from Tennessee, including a few Whigs. "It is a political necessity," Harris explained, "that the Whig element be fully recognized." Davis agreed; in fact, he had appointed two additional generals from Tennessee just a few days before receiving Harris's letter. One of these men was Felix Zollicoffer, an influential Whig who had supported John Bell for the presidency in 1860 and had been a member of the aborted Washington Peace Conference.

A few of Davis's political generals were assets, but many proved to be worthless soldiers and sources of embarrassment. John B. Floyd, for example, was removed from command after he shirked his responsibility at Fort Donelson. Felix Zollicoffer rashly, and in violation of orders, attacked a Federal force at Mill Springs, Kentucky, in January 1862, where he was killed. After much criticism of his conduct at the battle of Elkhorn Tavern, Brig. Gen. Albert Pike, a prominent Arkansas Whig, resigned from the army. Brig. Gen. William H. Carroll, a Tennessean whose father had been governor of the state six times, was removed from command "for drunkenness, incompetency, and neglect of duty." Gen. Roger A. Pryor, a former Virginia congressman, left without a brigade in 1863, resigned and reenlisted as a private. Robert Toombs and Louis T. Wigfall soon resigned from the army and spent much of the war criticizing Davis. In the summer of 1863, Wigfall announced: "Davis's mind is becoming unsettled. No sane man would act as he is acting. I fear that his bad health and bad temper are undermining his reason, and that the foundation is already sapped." Henry A. Wise had been appointed a general because he was popular in the western counties of Virginia. After he had helped raise a number of regiments, Davis ignored him. "The war has produced no more emphatic a failure than Wise," remarked a member of the administration. Outraged by this ignominy, Wise denounced the president and his family as "little, low, vulgar people."

Davis liked to tell certain people that none of his appointees were political generals, but he told others—especially demanding politicians—that he also appointed a number of able politicians to high military positions. A general complained that professional soldiers "have seen themselves overlooked by their government, while their juniors in years of service and I think their inferiors . . . were put over them in rank." Civilians, however, often objected to what one man called the president's "irresponsible *West Pointism*."

Trying to defend himself against both charges, Davis wrote, "I know that among some of our people . . . an impression prevailed that I was unduly partial to those officers who had received an education at the Military Academy and was willing to concede something to that impression though I did not recognize its justice."

Davis knew that, whatever his personal desires, all of his generals could not be West Point graduates. First, there simply were not that many West Pointers available. A common misconception is that in 1861 most of America's experienced soldiers were Southerners who resigned their commissions in the U.S. Army to join the Confederacy. At the war's outbreak, Southerners did compose nearly 60 percent of regular-army officers, but of the army's 1,080 officers, only 286 entered Confederate service; 184 of these were graduates of the U.S. Military Academy. Over six hundred West Point graduates remained in the Federal army. Of the approximately nine hundred West Point graduates then in civil life, fewer than a fourth joined the Confederacy. Second, too many West Point graduates were young and inexperienced soldiers. Of the 286 men who resigned from the U.S. Army to enter Confederate service, only 24 held the rank of major or above in the "old army"; most of the others were junior officers, some quite recent graduates of West Point. Though the president welcomed those young men, he appointed few of them to high rank early in the war.

The eighty-eight men he appointed generals in 1861 fell into three categories: first, forty regular U.S. Army officers who resigned their commissions in 1861 to join the Confederacy (all but two of them—David E. Twiggs and William W. Loring— were West Point graduates); second, twenty-three West Pointers who had resigned from the regular army some years prior to 1861; and third, twenty-five men who had neither attended the U.S. Military Academy nor served in the regular army. All of these men had in common at least one thing—they were civil or military leaders. The forty regulars who became Confederate generals in 1861 had been captains or above in the U.S. Army at the war's outset.

But military training alone did not ensure high rank. Fewer than half of the West Point graduates who offered their services to the Confederacy ever became generals. Between 1861 and 1865, Jefferson Davis appointed 425 men to the rank of brigadier general or higher. Almost two-thirds of these had some military experience prior to the Civil War, but much of that experience consisted of militia service, attendance at military schools, or expeditions against Indians. No fewer than 153 Confederate generals were lawyers or politicians when the Civil War began; 55 were businessmen, and 42 were farmers or planters. Only 34 percent of Confederate generals were graduates of the U.S. Military Academy, and only 29 percent were professional soldiers when the war began.

Some men, it was charged, received or were denied high rank simply because the president liked or disliked them. William L. Yancey claimed that Davis's appointments "are often conferred as rewards to friends and are refused as punishments inflicted upon enemies." Sen. James L. Orr said that the "President's attachment for Genl. Bragg could be likened to nothing else than the blind and gloating love of a mother for a deformed and misshapen offspring."

Despite Davis's disclaimer to a critic—"nor will I consent to be influenced in the exercise of the appointing power which I hold as a trust for the public good, by personal favor or personal resentment"—there is evidence to support the charge that the president did reward his friends. Three of his general officers had been with him at West Point: Thomas F. Drayton, Hugh W. Mercer, and Leonidas Polk. All had left the U.S. Army while they were still lieutenants. Drayton became a planter and a railroad builder in South Carolina; Mercer became cashier of a bank in Savannah; and Polk became the Episcopal missionary bishop of the Southwest. At the time Davis appointed these men Confederate generals, they had been out of military service for twenty-five or more years. Polk, who had spent a grand total of five months as an officer after his graduation from West Point in 1827, was made a major general by Davis on June 25, 1861.

Richard Griffith, while a lieutenant in the 1st Mississippi Rifles during the Mexican War, had "formed a warm and lasting friendship with his commanding officer, Jefferson Davis." This brief military association must have been enough to convince Davis that Griffith had leadership ability. He was appointed a brigadier general in the Confederate service before he had been in a Civil War battle.

Richard Taylor, son of general and former U.S. president Zachary Taylor, was the brother of Davis's first wife. Taylor had no military experience prior to the Civil War except that gained from a childhood spent at various army posts, but Davis quickly promoted him to brigadier general. "This promotion," Taylor recalled, "seriously embarrassed me. Of the four colonels whose regiments constituted the brigade, I was the junior in commission, and the three others had been present and 'won their spurs' at the recent battle [of First Manassas], so far the only important one of the war. Besides, my known friendship for President Davis . . . would justify the opinion that my promotion was due to favouritism."

If Davis used his appointing power to reward friends, he also used it to punish his enemies. He apparently struck the name of Arthur M. Manigault off the list of colonels recommended for promotion to brigadier because of a published personal letter by Manigault that was critical of Davis. "I admit having written the letter and must abide the consequences," explained Manigault. "It is a matter of . . . great surprise to me . . . , its publication in any newspaper, . . . as to the best of my recollection, I placed it in the post office at Knoxville myself."

Contrary to the claims of Davis and certain historians, it is clear that qualities other than military ability and experience influenced the appointment of some generals, but what about the Confederacy's highest ranking officers? Did political considerations, friendship with the president, or other factors affect their selection and promotion?

Only six men—Samuel Cooper, Albert Sidney Johnston, Robert E. Lee, Joseph E. Johnston, Pierre Gustave Toutant Beauregard, and Braxton Bragg—ever became full generals in the regular Confederate army. The Confederacy's senior general both in age and rank was Cooper, who was sixty-four years old at the time of his appointment. No one could deny that he had years of military experience. At the time he joined the Confederacy, he could boast of forty-eight years of continuous service in the U.S. Army, but since 1838 Cooper had been in Washington, D.C., at a desk job. He became the adjutant and inspector general of the Confederacy, the position he had held in the "old army" since 1852.

In a time of peace, Cooper might have been a satisfactory figurehead for the Adjutant General's Office. But he was incapable of handling the complex and demanding task of organizing and administering the Confederacy's army. The chief of the Confederate Bureau of War, Robert H. Kean, claimed that Cooper was totally incompetent: "It is so manifest that nothing but the irrepressible *West Pointism* of the President, and that other peculiarity of preferring accommodating, civil-spoken persons of small capacity about him, can account for his retention."

Kean charged that Cooper had no idea of the condition of any army. "There has never been a time when the A[djutant and] I[nspector] General could give even a tolerably close *guess* of the whole force on the rolls of the army, still less of the *effective* force. He is most of the time *out* of his office. There is not one paper a week which bears evidence of his personal examination. He never decides anything, rarely ever *reports* upon a question, and when he does the report is very thin."

When Davis was President Pierce's secretary of war, he had worked closely and gotten along well with Cooper. "Having known him most favorably and intimately as Adjutant-General of the United States Army," recalled Davis, "the value of his services in the organization of a new army was considered so great that I invited him to take the position of Adjutant-General of the Confederate Army, which he accepted without a question either as to relative rank or anything else." Like most people, Davis generally favored individuals who agreed with him. If they did not, they usually left his administration.

Perhaps another reason why Davis appointed Cooper adjutant and inspector general was that there was simply nothing else to do with the man. Contemporaries agreed that he was unsuited for field service. What could the president do other than give Cooper the same job that he had held for the past nine years? To have done otherwise would have insulted Cooper—a native of New Jersey who had sacrificed a secure position to join the Confederacy—and created political problems for the Davis administration, for Cooper was married to the sister of Sen. James M. Mason of Virginia.

Had Davis been more astute and recognized Cooper's incompetence, he might have discouraged the Union's adjutant general in order to keep him at his post in the Federal capital and help Lincoln manage the Federal army.

If the appointment of Cooper appears to have been motivated by personal and political considerations, that of the second highest ranking Confederate general—Albert Sidney Johnston—

was based on personal friendship and admiration. Davis and Sidney Johnston had been friends for years. They may have met while students at Transylvania University; had attended West Point together, where Johnston treated Davis like a younger brother; had served together on the Illinois frontier as young lieutenants during the Black Hawk War; and had been under fire together at Monterey during the Mexican War.

Johnston was fifty-eight years old when the Civil War began; twenty-seven of those years had been spent in active military service or training. After four years at West Point (1822–26), he served eight years as a lieutenant in the 6th Infantry. He resigned from the army in 1834, but two years later he enlisted as a private in the Army of the Texas Republic. Johnston quickly rose to the rank of senior brigadier general in that organization, and then served two years (1838–40) as Texas's secretary of war. After Texas became part of the United States and the Mexican War began, Johnston assumed command of the 1st Texas Volunteer Infantry, holding the rank of colonel. A month later, when the unit's enlistment ended, most of the men went home and Johnston was left without a command. But he remained in Mexico, and Gen. Zachary Taylor appointed him inspector general on the staff of Brig. Gen. William O. Butler, commander of a division of volunteers. Johnston helped steady the volunteers when Butler was wounded at Monterey. After Taylor became president, he appointed Johnston a major in the army's paymaster department. Relief from this position, which Johnston disliked, came six years later when he was promoted to the rank of full colonel and given command of the newly formed 2d U.S. Cavalry. Political influence, including the support of Jefferson Davis, who was then secretary of war, helped Johnston get his new command. His next opportunity came in 1857, when he was selected to lead an army to Utah to prevent a Mormon uprising. His successful occupation of Utah won him promotion to brevet brigadier general.

When the Civil War began, Johnston was in California commanding the Department of the Pacific. He immediately resigned his commission and started overland with a small party. Arriving in Richmond in September 1861, he called at the Confederate White House only to be told that the president was too ill to see visitors. Davis, who from his sickbed heard sounds on the floor below, supposedly called out: "That is Sidney Johnston's step. Bring him up." Davis got out of bed, and "for several days at various intervals," he recalled, "we conversed with the freedom and confidence belonging to the close friendship which had existed between us for many years. Consequently upon a remark made by me, he [Johnston] asked to what duty I would assign him, and, when answered, to serve in the West, he expressed his pleasure at service in that section, but inquired how he was to raise his command, and for the first time learned that he had been nominated and confirmed as a [full] general in the Army of the Confederacy."

Robert E. Lee, a fifty-five-year-old professional soldier and the third highest ranking Confederate general, was also Jefferson Davis's friend. The president and Lee had been together at West Point, and while secretary of war, Davis had aided Lee's military career. Lee, in turn, had defended Davis against a newspaper critic. Davis later stated that in 1861 he had "unqualified confidence" in Lee, "both as a man and a patriot." Tactful, courteous, and modest, Lee proved repeatedly throughout the war that he knew how to get along with President Davis. Lee never demanded; he got what he wanted by subtle persuasion. He always referred to Davis as "Your Excellency."

The president even believed that Lee cared nothing about rank: "He had been appointed a full general," recalled Davis, "but so wholly had his heart and his mind been consecrated to the public service, that he had not remembered, if he ever knew, of his advancement."

The appointment of Lee was inextricably linked with that of Joseph E. Johnston, the fourth highest ranking Confederate general. Joe Johnston and Robert E. Lee were the same age, graduat-

ed from West Point in the same class (1829), were both professional soldiers, and had served together in the Mexican War,
where both had received the brevet rank of colonel for gallant
conduct under fire. After the war, and on the same date (March
3, 1855), both were promoted to lieutenant colonel and assigned
to cavalry regiments—Lee to the 2d Cavalry, Johnston to the 1st
Cavalry. On June 28, 1860, Johnston left the cavalry to become
the army's quartermaster general, with the rank of brigadier
general. Lee remained in the cavalry and was not promoted to
the rank of full colonel until March 16, 1861.

Thus, when the two men left the U.S. Army to join the Confederacy, Johnston, a brigadier general, outranked Lee, a colonel.
Consequently, when the list of Confederate full generals
appeared, Johnston was shocked and angered to discover that
his old friend and rival now outranked him. A proud man, Johnston believed that he had been treated unfairly by the president.
He recalled that he had not been Davis's choice for quartermaster general in 1860; Davis, then chairman of the Senate's Military
Affairs Committee, had favored Sidney Johnston for the position.

Now, it must have appeared to Joe Johnston, that Davis was
taking his revenge. Honor demanded a protest. In an angry letter to the president, Johnston argued that Confederate law guar-
anteed "that the relative rank of officers of each grade shall be
determined by their former commissions in the U.S. Army."
Since he was the highest ranking officer of the "old army" to join
the Confederacy, it was unfair and illegal to appoint others
above him. "I now and here declare my claim," he wrote, "that
notwithstanding these nominations by the President and their
confirmation by Congress, I . . . rightfully hold the rank of first
general in the Armies of the Southern Confederacy."

Davis considered the letter insubordinate; his reply was cold
and brief: "I have just received and read your letter. Its language
is, as you say, unusual; its arguments and statements utterly
one-sided, and its insinuations as unfounded as they are unbe-

coming." From that point on the men never trusted each other. In October 1863 a close observer noted: "the President detests Joe Johnston . . . and General Joe returns the compliment with compound interest. His hatred of Jeff Davis amounts to a religion. With him it colors all things." Curiously, in 1862 at least, Davis seems to have retained his confidence in Johnston's generalship. Just before Seven Pines, the president assured the general, "my design is to suggest not direct, recognizing . . . your ability . . . , it is my wish to leave you with the fullest powers to exercise your judgment." Furthermore, three weeks after the battle, Davis informed his wife, who was visiting in North Carolina: "Genl J.E. Johnston is steadily and rapidly improving [in health]. I wish he was able to take the field. Despite the critics who know military affairs by instinct, he is a good soldier, knows the troops, never brags even of what he did do, and could at this time render most valuable service."

The president also disliked and mistrusted the fifth highest ranking general, Pierre Gustave Toutant Beauregard—as much or more than Joe Johnston. Beauregard was one of the bright young professional soldiers who joined the Confederacy. Forty-three years old when the war started, he had graduated second in his class at West Point in 1838 and entered the elite engineering corps. During the Mexican War, while serving on Gen. Winfield Scott's staff, Beauregard had received brevet promotions to captain and major for gallant and meritorious conduct in battle. He became the Confederacy's first hero after Fort Sumter fell to his forces; he won additional fame at First Manassas. But his high opinion of his own military ability and his jealousy of those generals above him in rank, especially Joe Johnston, caused problems. After the war Beauregard explained why he considered himself better qualified in 1861 for high command than Johnston: "Having been attached . . . to the staff of . . . General Scott, in the Mexican War, General Beauregard had taken a leading part in the reconnaissances and conferences that had led and determined the marches and battles of that campaign; and as to what was really essential in those respects to the command of an army he had a practical military experience beyond any opportunities of General Johnston."

Beauregard, a vain man, could be haughty when he considered his prerogatives impinged. Soon after First Manassas he became engaged in a series of disputes with the administration over supplies, military law, and army command. For a time the president tried to be conciliatory, but gradually he grew impatient. In January 1862, after another argument between Beauregard and Davis, an observer in the War Department noted: "Beauregard has been ordered to the West. I knew the doom was upon him."

Following the death of Sidney Johnston at Shiloh, Beauregard became commander of the western forces, but in June 1862 he left his headquarters in northern Mississippi without the president's permission. Beauregard merely informed the government that his health was bad and that he was going to Alabama to recover. "I desire to be back . . . to retake the offensive as soon as our forces shall have been sufficiently reorganized," he explained. "I must have a short rest."

Davis jumped at this opportunity to appoint Braxton Bragg to the permanent command of the western department. Beauregard would never again command a major army in the field. The president no longer trusted him. Davis later told another general, "Beauregard was tried as Commander of the army of the West and left it without leave, when the troops were demoralized and the country he was sent to protect was threatened with conquest."

The sixth highest ranking general was Braxton Bragg, the man who replaced Beauregard as commander of the western department. Forty-four years old when the war began, Bragg too was a professional soldier, but he had left the "old army" in 1856 to become a Louisiana sugar cane planter. He had served for nineteen years in the 3d Artillery after graduating fifth in his class at West Point in 1837. He had received three brevet promotions during the Mexican War for gallant conduct. At Buena Vista he became a national hero when his battery stopped the final Mexican charge "with a little more grape."

It is easy enough, using hindsight, to blame Jefferson Davis for appointing at the war's outset too many generals who would later prove to be less than outstanding soldiers, but such a judgment is unfair—a misuse of history. Before censuring Davis for failing to pick the right men to lead the Confederate armies, historians should ask themselves what, given the circumstances, Davis could have done differently. He had to pick some political generals; he understandably picked some of his friends. What obvious leaders did he overlook? The six men he promoted to full general were all experienced and distinguished soldiers. They were reputed to be the elite of the "old army." Another man, less well acquainted with military affairs, might have selected different generals. But Davis simply could not. His own military experience and knowledge forced him to appoint the men he did to high rank. He had fought beside some of them, and—as secretary of war and as chairman of the Senate Military Affairs Committee—he had helped advance their careers. They were already, before the Civil War, his men. If, as has been charged, his judgment of military ability left something to be desired, if he relied too heavily upon his youthful impressions of men, and if he regarded criticism of his appointees as criticism of himself and stubbornly defended proved incompetents, it was because Davis was imprisoned by his own character and background. And so was the Confederacy.

If the fathers of the Confederacy failed, it was in their selection of Jefferson Davis to lead the "Lost Cause." Once he became president the pattern of leadership was established. The major appointments to high positions, especially to high military positions, were his. He picked, assigned, and replaced as he saw fit. When the Provisional Congress chose the Confederacy's president, it indirectly chose its generals.

CHAPTER TEN

Beauregard's "Complete Victory" at Shiloh

A telegram, sent from the Shiloh battlefield on the evening of April 6, 1862, to Confederate officials in Richmond, told what had happened, or at least what Gen. Pierre Gustave Toutant Beauregard thought and hoped had happened: "We this morning attacked the enemy in strong position . . . and after a severe battle of ten hours . . . gained a complete victory, driving the enemy from every position."

Pres. Jefferson Davis still had no reason to doubt the accuracy of this report when he informed the Confederate Congress two days later that "the enemy was driven in disorder from his position and pursued to the Tennessee River, where, under cover of his gun-boats, he was at the last accounts endeavoring to effect his retreat by aid of his transports." Davis admitted that "details of this great battle are as yet too few and incomplete to enable me to distinguish with merited praise all of those who may have conspicuously earned the right to such distinction," yet he announced, "with entire confidence, that it has pleased Almighty God to crown the Confederate arms with a glorious and decisive victory over our invaders."

The Confederate Senate, in response to the president's announcement, quickly passed a resolution thanking General Beauregard and his troops for the "exhibition of skill and gallantry [that they had] displayed" in gaining this "signal triumph."

During the next few days, it became distressingly apparent to everyone in Richmond and elsewhere in the South that the Confederates had not achieved a "signal triumph" at Shiloh. Beauregard had neither destroyed Maj. Gen. Ulysses S. Grant's army nor forced it to retreat across the river; indeed, the very day that Beauregard's telegram arrived in Richmond, the combined Union armies of Grant and Maj. Gen. Don Carlos Buell had dri-

P.G.T. Beauregard

ven the Confederates back to Corinth. "The news today from Ten[nessee] is not so favorable," a former member of the president's cabinet wrote on April 9. "Gen'l Beauregard telegraphs that he had fallen back from the river to his original position at Corinth."

There is no doubt what happened at Shiloh; the dispute that began almost immediately after the battle and continues today is over whether or not Beauregard should have called off the first day's action when he did. Jefferson Davis, who mistrusted Beauregard, became convinced "that, when General [Albert Sidney] Johnston fell, the Confederate army was so fully victorious that, had the attack been vigorously pressed, General Grant and his army would before the setting of the sun have been fugitives or prisoners."

Other writers agreed. Just after the war, Edward Alfred Pollard, editor of the *Richmond Examiner* and certainly no friend of Jefferson Davis, described Beauregard's decision as the "extraordinary abandonment of a great victory." Confederate units were ready to "sweep the enemy from the field," claimed Pollard. "The sun was about disappearing, so that little time was left to finish the glorious work of the day. The movement commenced with every prospect of success. But just at this time the astounding order was received from Gen. Beauregard to withdraw the forces beyond the enemy's fire!"

Similar complaints against Beauregard later appeared periodically in the pages of such journals as the *Southern Historical Society Papers.* "A great victory was just within the grasp of the Confederates" at Shiloh, insisted Col. William Allan in 1884, but Beauregard "allowed [it] to slip away from them." James Ryder Randall announced in 1896 that "Beauregard's unfortunate order of retreat [on the first day at Shiloh] saved the Federals from capture or destruction." John Witherspoon Du Bose stated in 1899 that "Beauregard, going on the field on a bed, wasted by protracted illness, . . . recalled the troops from the very arms of victory." Maj. Robert W. Hunter proclaimed in 1907 that, if Beau-

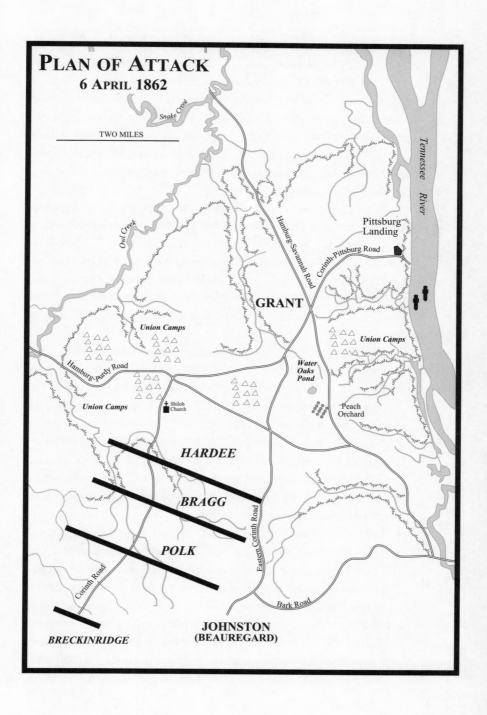

PLAN OF ATTACK
6 APRIL 1862

TWO MILES

Snake Creek

Owl Creek

Hamburg-Savannah Road

Pittsburg
Landing

Tennessee River

Corinth-Pittsburg Road

GRANT

Union Camps

Union Camps

Hamburg-Purdy Road

Water
Oaks
Pond

Union Camps

Shiloh
Church

Peach
Orchard

HARDEE

BRAGG

Eastern Corinth Road

POLK

Corinth Road

Bark Road

BRECKINRIDGE

JOHNSTON
(BEAUREGARD)

regard had allowed the attack to continue, "Grant would have been crushed before Buell's reinforcements could have saved him." In 1914 P. D. Stevenson summarized the views of Beauregard's critics. "Why," he asked rhetorically, when the Yankees were "disorganized and whipped, huddled together like sheep," did the Confederates fail to "go forward and complete their work? Alas!" he concluded, "they had changed commanders! And their new commander ordered them to halt and retire! And lo! the victory was lost!"

Beauregard, some of his friends and supporters, and a number of historians have insisted that his decision to stop the Confederate attack when he did "was the right one." They have accused Maj. Gen. Braxton Bragg, who commanded on the Confederate right at Shiloh, and Col. William Preston Johnston, son of Albert Sidney Johnston, of misstatements designed to diminish Beauregard's military reputation and to magnify Sidney Johnston's.

The pro-Beauregard accounts argue that their hero stopped the action because, first, the Confederates were "tired, hungry, and spiritless" after fighting all day; second, there was no real possibility that they might "break the Union line late in the evening" because the Federals enjoyed advantages in firepower and terrain that "a series of disjointed attacks [directed by Bragg] at that late hour upon a battery of over fifty pieces" could never overcome; and third, Beauregard "wanted to get his army in hand before darkness" so that he would be prepared for whatever might happen the next day.

Let us try to look at the military situation as Beauregard and others who were there saw it on that Sunday afternoon in April. The best of these eyewitness sources, of course, are the letters, diaries, and official reports that were written during or shortly after the battle. The memoirs and recollections, written later, generally are less reliable; after a time, people tend to forget or to distort the way things happened. But selective recollections and incorrect statements are not invariably or exclusively con-

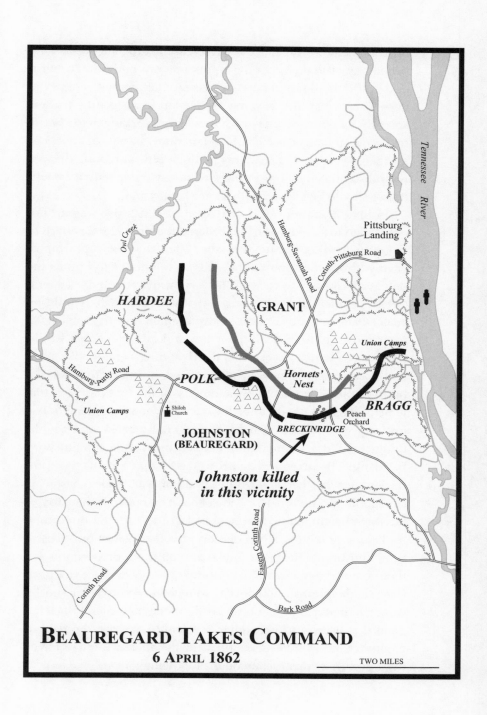

BEAUREGARD TAKES COMMAND
6 APRIL 1862

TWO MILES

fined to memoirs; documents written at the time the events happened may also be full of misrepresentations and lies. For writers of official military reports, whose reputations and careers can depend on what they say, the temptation to distort the truth is sometimes overpowering. That is why working with battle reports is so dangerous, commanders rarely admit to failures or mistakes. Therefore, statements made in official reports that are not substantiated by one or more relatively independent eyewitnesses should be viewed with some skepticism.

In his official report, dated April 11, 1862, Beauregard not only failed to state that he had ordered the Confederate attack to cease on April 6, but he even suggested that the capturing of enemy "stores and munitions" was as important to him as the defeat of Grant. "By a rapid and vigorous attack on General Grant," explained Beauregard, "it was expected he would be beaten back into . . . the river, or captured, in time to enable us to . . . remove to the rear all the stores and munitions that would fall into our hands . . . before the arrival of General Buell's army on the scene. It was never contemplated, however, to retain the position thus gained." In his summary of the first day of battle, which he says ended "after 6 P.M., . . . when the enemy's last position was carried, and his forces finally broke and sought refuge behind a commanding eminence covering the Pittsburg Landing," Beauregard again placed great emphasis upon retrieving what he called the "spoils of war." "Darkness was close at hand," he insisted, "officers and men were exhausted. . . . It was, therefore, impossible to collect the rich and opportune spoils of war scattered broadcast on the field left in our possession, and impracticable to make any effective dispositions for their removal to the rear. I accordingly . . . directed our troops to sleep on their arms . . . , hoping, from news received by a special dispatch, that delays had been encountered by General Buell . . . , and that his main force, therefore, could not reach the field of battle in time to save General Grant's shattered fugitive forces from capture or destruction on the following day."

Much later, after he had been accused of stopping the attack too soon on that critical April evening, Beauregard gave quite a different account of his actions. In an article published in *Battles and Leaders*, he claimed that he called off the Confederate attack because, first, units of Buell's army had already crossed the river and joined Grant; second, the Federals were protected by both gunboats and "some sixty guns [that] . . . commanded all the approaches" to the landing; and third, the Confederates were exhausted and out of ammunition, and "no serious effort was [being] made to press the victory by the [Confederate] corps commanders."

This summary of what Beauregard said caused him to end the assault, which might best be described as a postwar fantasy, is a mixture of hindsight, exaggeration, and misrepresentation designed to make the general appear sagacious. He was at Shiloh Church, two miles or more behind the front lines, when he ordered the action halted on the evening of April 6. From time to time during the afternoon, staff officers may have brought Beauregard information on various activities, but without visiting the front himself, which he failed to do, his knowledge of what was happening there was always fragmentary, dated, and imprecise; nor did he have any understanding of arrangements behind the Union lines. Yet he stated grandly, "Comprehending the situation as it was, at six P.M. I dispatched staff officers with orders to cease hostilities."

One should examine each of the general's claims. If, as he asserted in his article, Beauregard had known that units of Buell's army had already joined Grant's forces, it is most unlikely that he would have sent a telegram to the Confederate government on the evening of April 6 announcing a "complete victory."

In addition, there was no way for Beauregard to have known at that time how many guns protected the Federals near Pittsburg Landing. He says sixty guns threatened the Confederates, but this appears to be far in excess of the actual number. Grant in his official report mentioned only "four 20-pounder Parrott guns and a battery of rifled guns," later stating that about "twenty or more pieces of artillery" protected the Federals at nightfall. Historian Kenneth P. Williams, citing two unofficial accounts, claims that the total number of guns assembled was fifty, including some "moderately heavy siege weapons."

Actually, whether they numbered twenty or fifty, these guns may have been less formidable than their numbers suggest. Grant and other observers stated that most of the weapons on the Federal line were rifled guns and siege pieces, which were not as effective against infantry assaults as smoothbores firing canister; in fact, the Army of the Potomac's chief of artillery considered rifled guns generally less useful than smoothbores, and he regarded the rifled 20-pounder Parrotts as "unsafe," more dangerous to the users than to the enemy, because they often burst during firing. Regular-army artillerymen consistently favored smoothbore Napoleons over rifled guns.

Reports also indicated that elements of two units that formed part of the Union defensive line near Pittsburg Landing were battered and short of ammunition. The commander of Battery D, 1st Missouri Light Artillery, reported that during the day he had lost fourteen horses and expended over 200 rounds of ammunition; the commander of Battery H, 1st Missouri Light Artillery, reported losing twenty horses and being out of canister after having fired 275 rounds.

The Union gunboats, which Beauregard said "opened on our eager columns a fierce and annoying fire . . . of the heaviest description," did far less damage than he supposed. Few shells from the warships were hitting Confederates at the front because the guns, elevated to fire over the high riverbank, could hit only points some distance from the river's edge. "They were comparatively harmless to our troops nearest the bank," reported Confederate major general Leonidas Polk, "and became increasingly so as we drew near the enemy." A brigade commander called the shelling "more noisy than destructive," and General Bragg, who was at the front, stated that the fire from the gunboats, "though terrific in sound and producing some consternation at first, did us no damage, as the shells all passed over and exploded far beyond our positions."

Extant records also fail to support the other claims of Beauregard. His charge that his corps commanders at the front made "no serious effort . . . to press the victory" seems to be nothing more than a malicious attempt to discredit the official testimony of generals Polk, William J. Hardee, and Bragg about what happened in the late afternoon of April 6 after the fall of the Hornets' Nest and the capture of Union brigadier general Benjamin Prentiss and his men about 5:30 P.M.

One can understand why the reports of his corps commanders galled Beauregard. "The field was clear [following the surrender of Prentiss]," stated Polk, "the rest of the forces of the enemy were driven to the river and under its bank. We had one hour or more of daylight still left; were within from 150 to 400 yards of the enemy's position, and nothing seemed wanting to complete the most brilliant victory of the war but to press forward and make a vigorous assault on the demoralized remnant of his forces."

At this point, Polk insisted, the Union gunboats opened their noisy but relatively harmless fire, and Beauregard, unaware of the true situation at the front, made the mistake of stopping the action. Polk's exact words were: "Here the impression arose that our forces were waging an unequal contest; that they were exhausted and suffering from a murderous fire, and by an order from the commanding general they were withdrawn from the field." Beauregard was certainly displeased with Polk's report.

Nor was he any happier with Hardee's report, which declared that the Confederates "were within a few hundred yards of Pittsburg [Landing], where the enemy were huddled in confusion, when the order to withdraw was received." Even more upsetting to Beauregard was Hardee's statement that, after the death of Gen. Albert Sidney Johnston, there was "a lull in the attack on the right and precious hours were wasted. It is, in my opinion," declared Hardee, "the candid belief of intelligent men that, for this calamity, we would have achieved before sunset a triumph signal not only in the annals of this war, but memorable in future history."

Beauregard was equally displeased with the report of Bragg, whom he had recommended for promotion to the rank of full general on the night of April 6. Bragg's final report, which was not sent to the War Department until three months after the battle, also charged that Beauregard had stopped the action too soon. "The enemy had fallen back in much confusion [after the surrender of Prentiss]," he noted, "and was crowded in unorganized masses on the river bank, vainly striving to cross." At this point, said Bragg, he had ordered the Confederates nearest the river "to move forward at all points and sweep the enemy from the field." Brig. Gen. Patton Anderson remembered that one of Bragg's staff officers told him "to go wherever the fight was thickest." This forward "movement commenced with every prospect of success," claimed Bragg, but "Just at this time an order was received from the commanding general to withdraw the forces beyond the enemy's fire."

Eyewitness accounts, written both at the time and after, indicate that the Confederates were still pressing the Federals when Beauregard stopped the action. Bragg's chief engineer, Col. Samuel H. Lockett, recalled: "I was with General Bragg, and rode with him along the front of his corps. I heard him say over and over again, 'One more charge, my men, and we shall have captured them all.'" In a letter to his wife written a day after the battle ended, Bragg announced: "we literally swept . . . [the enemy] before us capturing his camps, artillery, men, horses, arms &c, &c. One whole battery was brought to me with the officers, men & horses all complete, and marched to the rear as if on parade. It was a sight rarely seen, and very impressive. It was now nearly sun set. We were close on the bank of the river just above Pittsburg, the landing place, driving . . . [the enemy] back, full well." Lockett remembered only a single enemy position still resisting at this point, and the Confederates could see confused Union masses huddled near the riverbank.

Men from Generals John K. Jackson's and James Ronald A. Chalmers's brigades actually had crossed Dill's Branch and charged up its banks in the face of heavy Union fire, but there were too few of them to break the Federal line without help. Jackson reported that his "men advanced under heavy fire from light batteries, siege pieces, and gunboats. Passing through the ravine, they arrived near the crest of the opposite hill upon which the enemy's batteries were, but could not be urged farther without support. Sheltering themselves against the precipitous sides of the ravine, they remained under this fire for some time."

Jackson, "believing any further forward movement should be made simultaneously along our whole line," sought support from his division commander, Brig. Gen. Jones Mitchell Withers, but before reinforcements arrived Jackson "was ordered by a staff officer to retire. This order was announced to me as coming from General Beauregard and was promptly communicated to my command."

Support for Jackson and Chalmers was on the way, according to several sources, when Beauregard's order to withdraw arrived. Brig. Gen. Patrick Ronayne Cleburne and Col. R.G. Shaver claimed that their brigades were moving forward toward Pittsburg Landing when they were "halted by . . . General Beauregard." Several regiments were assembled just behind the front ready to move forward when Beauregard's messengers arrived. Brig. Gen. Daniel Ruggles, commander of a Confederate division, reported that he was "advancing toward the river" with "a considerable force" when he received Beauregard's order to retreat. Withers reported that he was sending forward reinforcements "when, to my astonishment, a large portion of the command was observed to move rapidly by the left flank from under the fire of the enemy. Orders were immediately sent to arrest the commanding officers and for the troops to be promptly placed in position for charging the batteries. Information was soon brought, however, that it was by General Beauregard's orders, delivered thus directly to brigade commanders, that the troops were being rapidly [withdrawn]."

We can never be entirely certain why Beauregard stopped the battle when he did that April evening. Years after the event, one of his staff officers claimed that Bragg rode to Beauregard's headquarters shortly after the Hornets' Nest fell and said "in an excited manner: 'General, we have carried everything before us to the Tennessee River. I have ridden from Owl to Lick Creek, and there is none of the enemy to be seen.' Beauregard," according to this story, "quietly replied: 'Then, General, do not unnecessarily expose your command to the fire of the gun-boats.'" Other than this unsubstantiated recollection, there is absolutely no evidence that Bragg met Beauregard during the battle.

Col. Samuel H. Lockett of Bragg's staff recalled that Beauregard's order, brought to Bragg at the front by a messenger, read: "the victory is sufficiently complete; it is needless to expose our men to the fire of the gun-boats.'" Lockett said that upon hearing the order Bragg exclaimed: "'My, God, was a victory ever sufficiently complete? . . . Have you given the order to any one else?'" Told that the order had been delivered to other commanders as well, Bragg looked to his left, saw General Polk's forces withdrawing, and sobbed: "'My God, my God, it is too late!'"

There seems to be little doubt that Bragg objected to the withdrawal order, though his words may not have been exactly those Lockett remembered. "We drove the enemy from every position, captured nearly all his artillery, and were hotly pursuing him under my command when we were recalled," Bragg informed his wife soon after the battle. He admitted in his official report that his troops were "greatly exhausted by twelve hours' incessant fighting" when the withdrawal order arrived, yet he insisted that a final assault had "every prospect of success." Years later, Sidney Johnston's son wrote that Bragg believed Beauregard's order cost the South the battle.

It is unclear just how strong the Union position was when Beauregard called off the attack. Union reports can be cited to indicate either its strength or its weakness. Historians—many of them pro-Grant—have generally insisted that the Federal line would have held. But what if Beauregard had not stopped the advance?

The terrain over which the Confederates were advancing, though rough, was by no means as difficult to cross as some writers have suggested. "Anyone who thinks the Rebel attack in this area could have succeeded should spend some time tramping around in this ravine," asserted one historian.

I took his suggestion, spent much of a day in the summer of 1982 "tramping around in this ravine," and can report that even a fifty-four-year-old man accompanied by a much younger person had no problem crossing Dill's Branch or getting up and down its banks. Of course, we were not under enemy fire at the time. Test the terrain yourself; you will find nothing in the area, for example, comparable to what the Federals faced at Missionary Ridge.

Chalmers's and Jackson's men already had demonstrated that they could charge across Dill's Branch and up its northern bank despite Federal resistance; it does not appear impossible that Confederate reinforcements, which were advancing when Beauregard's order stopped them, could have done the same.

Of course, the claim by Beauregard that many Confederate units were disorganized and exhausted is true, but so were most Union units. General Buell reported that the river's edge "swarmed with a confused mass of men" and that "all efforts" to get this "throng of disorganized and demoralized troops" back into "the fight utterly failed." The commander of a Union regiment, who acknowledged that his retreat to the river without orders might subject him "to the criticism of military men," found it "difficult to rally and form the regiment" even behind the Federal guns. Another officer complained that his regiment was retreating "in good order until we were run into by the retreating artillery, cavalry, and rabble, which very much scattered my command." General Buell stated that by nightfall on April 6, some "7000 [of Grant's men] were killed or wounded, 3000 were prisoners, [and] at least 15,000 were absent from the ranks and hopelessly disorganized."

When Brig. Gen. William Nelson, who crossed the river at Pittsburg Landing about 5:00 P.M. with reinforcements from Buell's army, arrived, he "found a semicircle of artillery, totally unsupported by infantry, whose fire was the only check to the audacious approach of the enemy," and soon "the left artillery was completely turned by the enemy and the gunners fled from their pieces." Nelson's men "drove back the enemy and restored the line of battle. This was at 6:30 P.M.," he noted, "and soon after the enemy withdrew, owing, I suppose, to the darkness. I found cowering under the river bank when I crossed from 7,000 to 10,000 men, frantic with fright and utterly demoralized, who received my gallant division with cries, 'We are whipped; cut to pieces.' They were insensible to shame or sarcasm—for I tried both on them—and, indignant at such poltroonery, I asked permission to open fire upon the knaves."

"Darkness was close at hand" was another excuse that Beauregard and his defenders used to justify his stopping the battle when he did. But his argument, which seems plausible enough, is seriously flawed. Beauregard, by his own admission, issued the withdrawal order at 6:00 P.M., at least thirty minutes before sundown and considerably longer before real darkness. Capt. Clifton H. Smith, who delivered the withdrawal order to Bragg and returned with him to Beauregard's headquarters, testified that when they arrived back at Shiloh Church, it was just dark enough to prevent easy recognition. In other words, at least an hour, and probably longer, passed between the time Beauregard issued his order to end the attack and the onset of darkness.

Whether or not the Confederates could have broken the last Union defensive line during that time or later can never be determined and is, therefore, a counterfactual question. More appropriate considerations are why did Beauregard stop the battle when he did, and was his decision to do so the right one considering the existing military circumstances and the information that either he had at his disposal or he might readily have obtained.

As we have seen, the reasons given by Beauregard and his friends for stopping the attack—Union reinforcements, devastating artillery and gunboat fire, the poor effort by his own corps commanders to complete the victory, exhausted soldiers, and darkness—seem to be based on hindsight designed more to protect Beauregard's military reputation than to clarify his motives. Perhaps Col. William Preston Johnston, one of Beauregard's postwar enemies, was closer to the mark. "General Beauregard at Shiloh [Church], two miles in the rear, with the, *debris* of the army surging back upon him, the shells bursting around him, sick with his two months' previous malady, pictured in his imagination a wreck at the front," wrote Johnston. "Had this officer been with Bragg, and not greatly prostrated and suffering from severe sickness, I firmly believe his order would have been to advance, not to retire."

The illness of Beauregard may account not only for his failure to visit the front before halting the attack but also for his apparent willingness to accept the advice of captured Union general Prentiss. In explaining to his wife two days later why the attack on April 6 ended when it did, General Bragg wrote: "Gen'l Prentiss—a prisoner—had just told Gen'l Beauregard that they were defeated and in route across the river. The General tho[ugh]t it best no doubt to spare our men, and allow them to go. But unfortunately Buell came."

If Bragg's account is correct, Prentiss may have saved Grant's army from destruction twice on April 6—once when he bought precious time for the Federals by his stubborn defense at the Hornets' Nest and again when he influenced Beauregard to end the attack by telling him that Grant was beaten and retreating across the river.

Regardless of what or who influenced Beauregard to stop the attack, his decision to do so indicates unsound military judgment. Before ending the action he at least should have consulted the commanders at the front. Had his health been good, he might have done so. Stopping the attack without either consulting the generals directing the advance or going to the front himself to see the situation was a serious mistake.

Both the friends of Beauregard and the historians who attempt to justify his decision to halt the fighting when he did seem to overlook the basic reason why the Confederates were at Shiloh on April 6, 1862. They were there to capture or destroy Grant's army before it could be reinforced by Buell's. To accomplish anything less would be a failure.

If Beauregard believed that Grant was whipped and retreating, that should have been all the more reason to press on and destroy him rather than to stop and rest for the night. An aggressive commander would have refused to use the lateness of the hour or the tiredness of his troops as excuses to end a battle, especially when the enemy was in retreat and backed up against a deep and wide river. By continuing to attack the Federals, even in darkness, the Confederates had everything to gain and little more to lose than what they lost the next day. After all, their best hope of victory was to do as much damage to Grant as they possibly could before Buell's fresh forces arrived.

The "complete victory" that Beauregard failed to gain but so rashly claimed in his telegram to Richmond on the night of April 6 turned out to be a disaster for the Confederacy. And that disaster may well have been caused by the failure of Beauregard to follow the advice offered in the delayed official report of one of his corps commanders, Braxton Bragg. This report, written after Bragg had replaced Beauregard as army commander, was also self-serving and full of hindsight. Curiously, Bragg advocated tactics that he would never employ himself, yet his advice was sound. In part it read: "[Shiloh offers us] a valuable lesson, by which we should profit—never on a battle-field . . . lose a moment's time, but leaving the killed, [the] wounded, and [the] spoils [of war] . . . press on with every available man, giving a panic-stricken and retreating foe no time to rally, and reaping all the benefits of a success never complete until the enemy is killed, wounded, or captured."

Chapter Eleven
Davis and the Patronage

The almost universal consensus at the Civil War's outset that Jefferson Davis was the right man to lead the Confederacy soon changed. Early in 1862 Howell Cobb of Georgia told his wife that one "might almost use the term *odious*" in describing the attitude of Confederate congressmen toward Davis. "Only patriotism prevented them from rebelling against the president," wrote Cobb. "I . . . who have never received a kindness at his hands . . . have to interpose between him and his former pets to save him from bitter attacks on the floor of Congress." He concluded that "Davis is perverse and obstinate, and unless we can beat some liberal and just notions into his head, we shall have much trouble in the future."

Cobb was correct. Tennessee congressman Henry Stuart Foote

wasted no time in attacking the Davis administration, claiming the president only wanted "power for mischief" and would attempt to establish a dictatorship. According to Foote, Davis "was inclined to be too charitably disposed towards men. He excused acts too hastily." Indeed, he might best serve the Confederacy, Foote suggested, "by being placed in a mental institution."

As Federal military successes tested the stability of the Confederacy, criticism of Davis grew ever stronger. Nor were charges against him voiced only in Congress. Editors, military men, and ordinary citizens joined politicians in expressing their displeasure with the president.

Of all the various decisions Davis had to make, none was more important or more controversial than his appointments. He always insisted that his military appointments were based on merit alone. "Due care was taken to prevent the appointment of, incompetent or unworthy persons to be officers of the army," Davis claimed, and several scholars agree.

Davis, who had difficulty judging other men's motives, reacted sharply to criticism, especially to those allegations that may have contained an element of truth. When men questioned or challenged his judgment, he turned cold and rigid, stubbornly contesting every suggestion and every minor point.

Such obstinacy contributed to the deterioration of the once cordial relationship between Davis and William L. Yancey, the secessionist who had written the Alabama Ordinance of Secession. An "impassioned, eloquent and impressive" orator, Yancey "had no equal in the South before a popular audience," claimed an observer. "His voice was sweet and round, his articulation very clear and distinct—every word could be heard—and both his looks and manner were impressive and captivating. It was a treat to hear him." Quiet in his tastes, "very gentle and exquisitely refined," Yancey was a "considerate, courteous, well-bred . . . gentleman"—or, as another contemporary described him, "the embodiment of the highest type of southern chivalry." In other words, in manner and personality he was quite similar to Davis.

At the beginning of the war, Davis and Yancey were friendly. When Davis became president, Yancey had declared: "The man and the hour have met." He praised Davis as a "soldier, distinguished upon the field of battle, wise in council, terrible in the charge."

In 1861 Davis sent Yancey to Europe to represent the Confederacy. When he returned in 1862 to represent Alabama in the Confederate Senate, his relationship with Davis remained cordial. On April 6, 1862, Senator Yancey offered Davis some advice on obtaining weapons from abroad. "Pardon me for these suggestions," he concluded his letter. "They are dictated by a solemn sense of duty. I address them to you because I believe

William L. Yancey

that from the immense pressure upon you of every interest, you cannot comprehend all, unless with the aid of some plain spoken friends."

Davis said he appreciated this advice, thanked Yancey for it on April 16, and received another letter from him the next day saying he was "gratified" by the president's reply. "Finding the difficulty of obtaining your ear confidentially, which I would have preferred, I concluded to write," explained Yancey. "I did so from a sense of duty. I reply more explicitly from a sense of duty."

Up to this point, relations were still cordial between president and senator, but on April 22, 1862, Yancey and Sen. Clement C. Clay Jr. of Alabama sent a joint letter to Davis that angered him. The letter was written by Clay and only signed by Yancey, but Davis seemed more upset with Yancey than with Clay. The communication from the two senators infuriated Davis by informing him that only five Alabamians were generals, although some forty Alabama regiments were in the field. Clay and Yancey acknowledged that they "had heard that you objected to the promotion of some of the Colonels from Ala., that they had not shown themselves in action worthy of a Brigadier Genl's command; & that one must win his spurs before he could secure such an appointment. We concede the justice & sound policy of the rule when enforced in practice. Some of our friends from Ala. in command of Regts., to whom we have stated your rule, as a reason for their not having been promoted, think the rule departed from in your late nomination of Col. [Roger A.] Pryor [a former Virginia congressman] for a Brig. Genlship. Entertaining the same opinion, & thinking that there are Alabama Cols. whose commissions are of older date, & whose experience & previous course of life give them higher claims of confidence, we have felt it due to them & our State to call your attention to them."

Clay and Yancey concluded by "respectfully recommending" for promotion Colonels Sydenham Moore, Tennant Lomax, Thomas J. Judge, and Eli S. Shorter. As an afterthought, they added: "We think it proper to say further, that . . . we do not esteem Gen'l [Robert E.] Rodes and Gen'l [Danville] Leadbetter as Alabamians: the latter is a northern man who has been resident in Ala. for only a few years, & the former is a Virginian, who was only sojourning in [Alabama] . . . while superintending the construction of a Rail Road of which he was Engineer."

Davis responded with the following endorsement on the back of the letter: "It is the, province of the Executive to nominate and of the Senate to confirm or reject. Recommendations are willingly received and respectfully considered by me, but I will not argue as to their propriety and do not recognize the fairness of the within statement of my course, and assumption as to what it should be."

Obviously, the Alabama senators had made Davis quite angry. None of the men they recommended would ever be appointed a general. The president appointed Pryor and the Senate confirmed him, but apparently Pryor failed to please his commanders, Generals R.E. Lee and James Longstreet. Twice finding himself a brigadier without a brigade, he resigned in 1863, reenlisted as a private and a scout, and finished the war at that rank.

Yancey failed to realize at the time of his and Clay's letter just how deeply the president resented this intrusion into executive affairs. Some indication of this is the public praise Yancey gave Davis in June 1862. "My estimate of the character of Mr. Davis is on record," the senator told an editor; "in my opinion, he is conscientious in discharge of the high duties of his office."

But in the Senate, Yancey made no special effort to be either supportive or critical of the president; indeed, a casual observer might have wondered whether Yancey was for or against the Davis administration. On April 8, 1862, he proposed that the resolution honoring Gen. Albert Sidney Johnston for "the great victory [at Shiloh] be so amended as to tender the thanks of Congress to General Beauregard, and the surviving officers and soldiers, for their gallantry and skill on that memorable field."

Yancey must have known that Davis had no love for Beauregard. The next day, when the finance committee reported favorably on a bill to pay the state troops of Missouri a million dollars, Yancey objected. "We should avoid the reckless expenditure which characterized the government of the late United States," he insisted. When Missouri senator John B. Clark charged that Yancey's opposition "did not do credit to his liberality," Yancey replied "that the matter did not affect his liberality: he acted from a sense of duty." He professed the same reason for trying unsuccessfully to amend a routine postal bill to significantly increase the cost of mailing letters.

If duty compelled the Alabamian to take certain stands, his strong belief in individual liberty and states' rights influenced him in other actions. During a heated debate over the raising of partisan rangers, when a speaker received cheers from the galleries for denouncing those who believed that only regular armies should fight wars and most senators proposed clearing the galleries, Yancey objected. "I hope the galleries will not be cleared," he stated. "I approve of the sentiment that 'something should be pardoned to the spirit of liberty.'"

Several times in 1862 and 1863, Yancey spoke out against the administration. In September 1862 he announced in Senate debate that he "differed with the President, and he would not be true to himself if he did not express it." Yancey favored "increas[ing] our armies and carry[ing] the war into the heart of Yankeedom," but he opposed increasing Confederate authority and expressed strong states' rights views. "No General or officer of the Confederate States was the master of the humblest Justice of the Peace of Alabama," he contended. "He knew no citizen of the Confederate States but only citizens of States. The war-making power is not unlimited," he declared. "It could not touch the humblest State officer. If it could take a State constable it could take the Governor. This military power [required] . . . curbing. It was time that the civil law should arise. . . . These West Point men had been educated to believe war the great business of life," Yancey maintained, "but they must not be allowed to abuse the rights of citizens."

On September 22, 1862, five months after he had joined Clay in recommending to the president the promotion of some Alabama colonels, Yancey introduced a bill in the Senate "to regulate the nomination and appointment of brigadier-generals." His bill required the president to appoint brigadiers "with reference to the number . . . of troops that [the] . . . State [has] . . . in the [Confederate army] . . . , giving preference to [the] . . . State . . . [with] the least number of brigadier-generals in proportion to the troops it has in service." The bill also directed the president to assign any brigadiers he "appointed to the command of brigades . . . from the State from which they have been appointed."

When the Senate Judiciary Committee "decided that Yancey's bill was unconstitutional because the Confederate Constitution gave the president the exclusive right to appoint generals," Yancey disagreed. He argued that Congress had the right to appoint brigadiers either from certain brigades or from the states in which the brigades were raised. "The people of his state," asserted Yancey, "were dissatisfied with the present system and he believed that the people of other States were also. It was not right that all the honour that shall be gained in this war shall be divided among one or two States. If you put it upon the ground of favoritism, the people were not satisfied. If you put it upon the ground of superiority of talent among the favoured States, it was an insult to the other States. It was absurd to say that the States who furnished the soldiers who were fighting our battles could not furnish the military talent to command them. The old State of Virginia had an undue share of honours in this war," but Yancey did not begrudge it to her. "She had suffered much and made great sacrifices." But he mentioned the fact to show the working of the present system. "The President was surrounded by Virginians, and, as was natural, was influenced by them."

Alabama had some seventy-five thousand troops in Confederate service, but only four Alabamians were brigadier generals;

furthermore, at Seven Pines, Yancey claimed, "Alabama had . . . lost thirty percent more troops, in proportion to the number she had engaged, than any other State. Yancey also claimed that if he understood their manoeuverings, they had been led to unnecessary slaughter, which might have been averted had they been commanded by brigadiers from their own state. The same thing had occurred," he insisted, "at the battle of Shiloh, and the subsequent battles before Richmond."

Unable to convince his colleagues, Yancey tried to save the substance of his bill by introducing a substitute motion. His new proposal, even more strongly states' rights than his original bill, required that the troops raised in each state be organized into brigades with each brigade commanded by a brigadier who was "a citizen of the Confederate States, and of the State in which the troops of his brigade . . . [were] raised." The Senate rejected Yancey's substitute motion by a vote of fourteen to five; the vote against his original bill was fifteen to eight.

Yancey's proposals infuriated the president as well as a number of senators. Sen. Benjamin H. Hill denounced Yancey as erratic and antiadministration; Sen. William E. Simms said that when Yancey "denied the power of Congress to take the last man in the Confederacy . . . to repel the invader, [he] was, unwittingly, the best friend of the Lincoln government." The president was "deeply offended" by Yancey's attempt to regulate the nomination of generals.

Nevertheless, Yancey continued his defense of what he considered personal liberty, but which Davis viewed as attacks on his administration. "Look at the first step taken by your military commanders," Yancey charged, "the muzzling of a free press. Look at the next step, the suppression of civil law and the reported execution of a sovereign citizen by the order of a military commander." There was real danger, Yancey claimed, of Congress being abolished and "creating the President into an irresponsible military dictator." Yet Yancey told a reporter that "no man in the Confederacy . . . would give so little attention to any scheme to make him Dictator as [Davis] himself."

Outraged on another occasion by a rumor that an army commander had murdered "a citizen soldier," Yancey vowed that "the facts shall be reported to the President, and if he do[es] not remove the officer . . . , the President should be impeached."

Still later Yancey advocated "a liberal system of exemption" from the draft because he feared "that [no] more than one-third of the men to be raised under the conscription law would be used in the field, while the other two-thirds would be kept in camps of instruction," and as a consequence the "industrial interests of the country would be left to suffer."

In January 1863 Yancey introduced a bill to restrict the power of the secretary of the navy, who had forced an officer to stand trial twice for the same offense and then denounced the courts-martial for twice acquitting him. "Such a practice," insisted Yancey, "must be subversive of all justice." To criticism that he was trying to unduly restrict an administration official, Yancey replied that his "taste led him to condemn the order of the Secretary, and his Senatorial duty led him to offer the bill."

In the Senate debate over whether to establish a Confederate supreme court, Yancey argued against giving "this court . . . more honor and dignity than the State Courts" and proposed an amendment that he claimed would reduce by 40 percent "executive patronage, which did so much toward the destruction of the old Government."

Yancey claimed that he never realized that what he said in the Senate would be offensive to the president. Indeed, a little more than a year after Davis had returned the letter Yancey and Clay wrote regarding Alabama generals, Yancey seemed unaware that in Davis's mind their relationship had changed. Yancey's naiveté is confirmed by two letters he wrote the president: the first, dated April 26, 1863, asked Davis to appoint Yancey's son an officer; the second, dated May 6, 1863, withdrew that request. In his second letter Yancey confessed that he was "Entirely unaware that you entertained any personal enmity towards me," and since he had received no reply to the first of these letters, he was taking "the earliest moment after receiving information as to your personal feelings, to withdraw the application made to you in behalf of Dalton H. Yancey, a cadet in the University of Alabama."

Yancey should have ended his letter at this point, but his pride compelled him to devote several additional paragraphs to giving Davis a lecture on the responsibilities of public officials. "Holding that you are but the Trustee for the people in dispensing the offices of the government, and . . . that . . . even your enemy may consistently with his self-respect, lay before you an application of one of the places at your disposal," he stated, "I am also aware that places are often conferred as rewards to friends and refused as punishment inflicted upon enemies. Most assuredly I should never have placed myself in the position of asking a place for my son, if I had entertained the least idea that conscientious difference of opinion with the President upon some points of his administration had caused him to indulge towards me personal dislike."

Just before he wrote to Davis on May 6, Yancey had received a revealing communication from Senator Clay. "I am satisfied that Davis is not disposed to oblige you," Clay warned. "I left him in a bad humor with you. . . . I am sorry you have written to ask a favor of him. . . . He is a strange compound which I cannot analyze, although I thought I knew him well before he was President. He will not ask or receive counsel, and, indeed, seems predisposed to go exactly that way his friends advise him not to go. I have tried harder than I ever did with any other man to be his friend," confessed Clay, "and to prevent his alienating me or other friends. I have kept my temper and good will towards him longer than I could do with any other than an old and trusted friend. If he survives this war and does not alter his course, he will find himself in a small minority party."

When Davis replied to Yancey on May 26, the president denied that he "entertained personal enmity" toward the senator. "Will you have the goodness to inform me how you acquired that information," Davis requested, "not having made any declaration to that effect, I think I have a right to inquire." He admitted that "for sometime past the impression has been made upon me that you were in opposition to my administration, and that it was not of that measured kind which results from occasional difference of opinion, but does not disturb good wishes and desire to give support." Davis insisted that Yancey "had no right to feel personal hostility to me, and hoped you might not."

Davis also made what he must have considered a special effort at compromise by agreeing with Yancey that the presidential appointment power was a trust. Because Davis acted as a trustee, he informed Yancey, "your letter of recommendation will be referred and your note withdrawing the application will be retained by me as a private communication."

Yancey's response so upset Davis that he answered in five closely argued pages on June 20. First, the president charged that Yancey, without evidence, had made "the very grave charge that in my official action I have been 'influenced by feelings of personal hostility' to yourself." Davis denied "this charge as utterly untrue"; he also claimed "the right of inquiring on what information it is based. Notwithstanding your avowal that you have now 'allowed a natural resentment to gain an ascendancy in your breast' I can but expect that you will deem it due to yourself if not to me, to answer the inquiries of my former and present letter."

Davis had wanted to end his letter at this point, but he was prevented from doing so by "various statements in your letter which if unanswered might be supposed to be admitted, and to which I feel compelled to give a decided dissent."

Yancey had expected—indeed, he considered it a senator's prerogative—to have his candidate appointed postmaster of Montgomery, Alabama, but Davis ignored him and appointed another man. "I am not aware of the existence of any such usage in relation to the appointment of postmasters as you allege to have prevailed," stated Davis.

> In my whole official life both as an executive officer and as a Senator, no such usage was to my knowledge recognized or acted on. I will add, that if such a usage had actually existed in Washington, I should not for a moment have doubted as to the propriety of discontinuing it here, nor will I consent to be influenced in the appointing power which I hold as a trust for the public good, by personal favor or personal resentment. I must add that the Senate is no part of the *nominating* power, and that according, as I do, the highest respect to the opinion of Senators when they recommend applicants, I decline to yield to any dictation from them on the subject of nominations. Your statement that the Postmaster appointed for Montgomery was "recommended by an insignificant number of persons in Montgomery and hardly identified with the place" is so far from accurate as to satisfy me you have been misinformed in this as in almost every other particular connected with the nomination.

Davis said that he would have explained his appointment if Yancey had asked; "although," the President argued, "I must deny the *right* of any one to demand my motives for the nominations which I think proper to make, and which are subject to no other control than the approval or disapproval of the Senate."

Regarding the old question of the Alabama generals, which originally had set him and Yancey at odds, Davis insisted that Yancey's understanding of the situation was "entirely incorrect. If you will refer to my endorsement on [the letter]," lectured Davis, "you will find that it was not considered as a recommendation for the appointment of officers, but as the assumption of a right to question my motives in making nominations and to dictate the rules which should govern my action. Viewed in this light, I declined to retain it."

Despite the many harsh words he had used in this letter to Yancey, Davis tried to conclude graciously. He said that he was "gratified to learn" that Yancey's opposition to him and his administration was "uninfluenced by personal considerations. I likewise appreciate to the fullest extent your expressed purpose to preserve independence even at the expense of personal regard, while I regret that you should suppose the preservation of both to be impossible." Davis hoped that "unfriendly relations" would not "spring up between those to whom the people have committed their interest in this great struggle. For myself all of hostile feeling that I possess is reserved for the enemies of my country, not for those, who, like yourself, are devoted to our common cause. You promise a candid judgement and generous support to my administration so far as demanded by the interests of our country, whatever may be our personal relations. I accept your promise with pleasure as worthy of a patriot, and even were these relations of the most cordial character, could desire nothing more than the redemption of this pledge."

Yancey roughed out an eight-page reply to Davis on June 26 but never sent it. At the end of the letter, he wrote, "Not sent reconsidered." This endorsement suggests that after venting his anger and bitterness, Yancey waited to let his words cool and then decided that they were inappropriate. On the surface the evidence suggests as much, except that such a conclusion clashes with Yancey's personality. He was a "fire-eater," a secessionist—emotional, bold, and proud. He was never cool and calculating; he fought duels. His quick tongue was sharp and biting. He had called U.S. Senator Daniel Webster a man of "two characters, . . . as his interests or necessities demanded—the 'God-like' and the 'Hell-like'—the 'God-like Daniel,' and *'Black Dan.'*" Yancey also had provoked Confederate senator Benjamin H. Hill into attacking him with an ink well.

Waiting until his temper cooled and carefully planning his reply to Davis would have been uncharacteristic of Yancey. He may have delayed mailing his June 26 letter for a few days and then, after receiving a letter from Senator Clay written on June 30, decided to rewrite his letter before sending it to Davis.

In his letter—his second to Yancey on the subject—Clay revealed that he had recently visited the president, at his invitation, because Davis "wished to show me a . . . remarkable letter you had written him. After having yours and his letters placed before me," Clay remarked,

> I said that the only thing that surprised me was his denial of personal enmity to you; that I had not regarded him as your friend for more than twelve months past, and, in support of my opinion, recalled several expressions of his that one would not use toward another unless he disliked him; that I had refrained from repeating these expressions to you, or to anyone else, as my desire was to promote peace and prevent discord among all men, and especially my friends; but, that when you informed me you had asked the appointment of [your son] Dalton and requested my recommendation of him, I felt it due to you to say, in reply, that I would not ask anything . . . of the President and regretted you had done so, because I did not think his personal relations to you justified asking any favor at his hands; and that I thought it probable that you referred to me as the person who informed you that he was inimical to you.

According to Clay, Davis "did not show any surprise or make any reply, but commenced complaining of being misunderstood and maltreated—that he felt that there was a majority of the Senate opposed to him, etc., etc."

Clay confessed that during his visit he did not challenge the president's denial that "he was personally inimical to" Yancey, "as I might and perhaps should have done." Clay explained that the president's "official position, our past relations and the state of the country, all forbade my having any personal difficulty with him." But Clay claimed that he told Davis, "I did not think him your friend, had probably told you so, etc. I confess, however, surprise, not unmingled with indignation, at his positive and harsh denial of enmity to you—as I am sure all who have heard him speak freely of you, during the last twelve months, must feel. But it is perhaps possible for a man to abuse with offense and opprobrious epithets and innuendoes those whom he really likes as true friends; and this possibility may excuse his conduct. It is not my way of treating those for whom I profess friendship."

"I have thought it due to myself," continued Clay,

as well as to you, to tell you of the foregoing facts; and I think it proper to add that I think your entire correspondence puts you on the vantage ground, and evinces a frankness, manliness, patriotism and magnanimity which will do you honor. You did me only justice, as he knew, in saying that I would bear you out in your assertion that you had opposed the Administration with reluctance and regret, and had often expressed it to me. He has often been assured by me that he wronged you and misconstrued your opposition in terming it factious; that you were governed by principle in all your public conduct. I think it must have been a consciousness of the wrong he had done you that prompted his showing me the correspondence between you, in the hope that I would say something to justify him to himself. His official course grows daily more inscrutable, and the more I see of him the less I understand him. Some of my friends think he will show his friendship to me by trying to have me defeated next fall, if I run for the Senate. It would argue more friendship for me than he has expressed to me of you.

When he received Clay's letter, Yancey was dying. He had been in "bed 10 days with . . . pain & sickness," he informed his son on July 12. "I am utterly prostrate. I have no strength to stand these attacks," which he described as "bilious fever" with complications and which his biographer called "a disease of the bladder." Yancey wrote, "I have been afflicted for years with bleeding piles and they exhaust me." He would die on July 23, 1863.

But before he expired, Yancey wrote a final letter to Davis on July 11, which spelled out all his grievances but at the same time left the way open for reconciliation. "You state that you have not made any declarations to the effect that you were inimical to me," challenged Yancey, "but . . . in such matters, actions are more significant than words." He charged Davis with appointing to public office some of "the most inveterate personal foes I had in Alabama. Whatever doubts I may have entertained as to your feelings towards me . . . were dispelled by your [ignoring my recommendation] . . . for Post Master at Montgomery," a suggestion also supported by Senator Clay and Congressman William P. Chilton. Yancey, who had been "unwilling to believe that mere political differences of opinion would disturb our former good relations," was now much upset by Davis's actions. "Montgomery is the postal town of Mr. Chilton and myself," Yancey reminded the president. "I have understood that it has been a usage and a courtesy yielded to a Senator, as a part of the appointing power, to nominate as post master in his postal town one agreeable to him. Yet you overrode all these considerations, and appointed one unknown to you personally, [and] recommended by an insignificant number of persons in Montgomery, and hardly identified with the place." Moreover, said Yancey, "I have never been consulted by you as to a single appointment made by you, in Alabama."

In listing his complaints, Yancey returned to the old issue of Davis's ignoring his and Clay's letter and refusing to appoint additional generals from Alabama. "That letter of recommendation which, in my opinion, should have been filed," charged

Yancey, "was returned to us with your endorsement, to the effect that . . . it was your province to nominate, and that of the Senate to confirm or reject. The return to us of that paper and the endorsement, I considered then, and do now, an act of grave discourtesy."

"How, under these circumstances," he asked, could Davis claim that Yancey had no right to feel personal hostility toward him? "On the contrary," stated Yancey, "I think the circumstances evince a settled hostility on your part to me, and justify a return of such feelings on my part. But I had not allowed a natural resentment to gain ascendancy in my breast 'till I learned of your actions in the appointment of a post master at [Montgomery] . . . and the reasons which influenced you."

Yancey rejected Davis's claim that he had opposed the administration. "I have rarely differed with you on questions coming before the Senate when I did not find myself sustained by some of your truest friends in their opinions and votes," claimed Yancey. "When I have been compelled to differ with you—it has been done from a high sense of duty to the country. Upon administrative measures of a legislative character I have generally agreed with you. The chief questions upon which I have differed with you," he informed Davis, "have been questions of a purely executive character."

Yancey regretted that he and Davis were at odds.

> Your noble personal friend, Mr. Clay, a gentleman who would not flatter Caesar for his crown, can assure you that we have conversed together freely on these subjects of difference, and that they were invariably subjects of regret that we were compelled to take different views of them from those held by you. I had hoped that our personally kind relations might be maintained and made to harmonize with my independence as a public man. But if the two are inconsistent with your views, I shall adhere to my independence, and regret the loss of personal regards. I

regret that you did not accede to my request to return to me my application for a military appointment for my son. I am inclined to consider your course in the matter as conciliatory. My self-respect however calls for a return of the application, and I renew my request. I beg you to be assured that no matter what may be our personal relations, your administration will receive from me a candid judgement and generous support so far as it is demanded by the interests of the country; while the lively recollections of former personal friendship and good deeds, will always temper any opposition which I may feel called upon to make to any of your measures or acts.

His promise to support the president's administration "so far as it is demanded by the interests of the country" in no way ameliorated the deep division between Yancey and Davis. A year earlier, Yancey and Clay had asked the president, whom they had supported and considered a friend, to promote some additional Alabamians to the rank of brigadier general. Their request that the president share some of his patronage with them was neither outrageous nor unreasonable; they simply expected him to be considerate of their political needs. But Davis—by insisting that the appointing power was his to use as he pleased without making any concessions to interested politicians—had ignored them. Yancey wanted his constituents to consider him powerful enough to take care of their needs; otherwise, why keep him in office. Davis, by ignoring the Alabamians Yancey recommended and rejecting his preference for postmaster, not only embarrassed Yancey but also stripped him of powers that traditionally belonged to senators, especially those who claimed to be friends and supporters of the president. Consequently, Yancey felt humiliated and somehow betrayed.

Davis also felt betrayed, for a man he thought was his friend had asked him to compromise his right to make appointments. Such a request, Davis believed, was too great a burden on any friendship. It was, he had pointed out, the constitutional right of the president to nominate. Senators had no such power; they could only approve or disapprove the president's appointments. If Davis was too uncompromisingly rigid in his interpretation of the Confederate constitution, he was also unable to say and do the things that might have kept men like Yancey more friendly and supportive.

Not only were Davis and Yancey divided by their disagreement over what each man's political role should be, but also they were too proud to be successful compromisers. Both wrote in defense of their views and actions and grew ever more resentful and unbending when their arguments were rejected. At the end of their correspondence, Yancey promised to maintain his "self-respect" by rejecting even those presidential actions that he was "inclined to consider . . . conciliatory." The day after he wrote Davis for the last time, Yancey informed his son, "Vicksburg . . . has fallen—following the Presd's prejudices & littleness and this will be the verdict of history."

Yet Yancey, despite such bitter remarks, apparently hoped that somehow his friendship with Davis could be restored. As he lay dying, Yancey asked Clay "whether Davis appeared desirous of holding on to my regard or no." Clay's reply on July 25, written two days after Yancey died, was: "I answer, yes! I was surprised to find him unwilling to admit that he was unfriendly to you and much more to have you believe him unfriendly, and I can see no motive now, and saw none then, for his letters to you or his conversation with me, but to prevent making you an enemy. I think he begins to find himself in want of *friends* or *adherents*—and I do not know, really, which he wishes."

Chapter Twelve
A Bishop as General

One of President Davis's worst appointments was that of Episcopal bishop Leonidas Polk as a major general in the Confederate army. Polk, who graduated from West Point a year after his friend Jefferson Davis, had spent thirty years in church activities and agriculture before the Civil War. But he knew next to nothing about military affairs or the art of war. In just two months, while commanding the Confederacy's Western Department until Albert Sidney Johnston arrived from the West Coast to assume command, Polk had botched his first military assignment and managed to create problems that would plague the Army of Tennessee for the entire war.

General Polk feuded with his subordinates, exhibited what historian Thomas Connelly called a "sullen aloofness" that would hamper cooperation with his superiors, and planted "seeds of bitter personality and command conflict." He not only failed to establish an effective defense line across northwestern

Tennessee but also violated Kentucky's neutrality by seizing Columbus a week before Johnston took command. Polk's actions deprived the unguarded Tennessee border of the slim but important protection that neutrality had provided. Moreover, Polk violated orders by invading Kentucky and then dodged responsibility for the dishonesty of his actions by altering his correspondence with President Davis and Secretary of War Leroy P. Walker, forwarding to Richmond "recopied" correspondence for the War Department files.

All this was only a preview of the damage the apparently humble, sacrificing bishop would inflict on the Confederacy. To most observers, Polk seemed an asset to the Southern cause. "Wonderfully charming in conversation," over six feet tall, with

Leonidas Polk

broad shoulders, blue eyes, and a white lock overhanging his forehead, he possessed "all the manners and affability" of a nobleman. His troops, who never saw the darker side of his personality—his stubborn, childish, quarrelsome nature—adored him. As an aloof bishop he had learned to lead, but as a soldier he would never learn to follow. His treatment of all his commanding officers bordered on insubordination, but usually Polk got away with it.

Throughout his army career, he maintained the remarkable ability to evade the blame for situations he created—he accomplished this early in the war by imposing on his friendship with Sidney Johnston and Jefferson Davis. Polk knew how to flatter and manipulate Davis to protect himself from such army commanders as Braxton Bragg and Joseph E. Johnston. Three modern historians—Thomas Connelly, Steven E. Woodworth, and Judith L. Hallock—all have contributed to a revised view of Polk. Connelly insisted that the bishop, with his "amazing abilities to escape responsibility, was the most dangerous man in the Army of Tennessee."

Bragg, who never liked Polk, believed that just before the battle of Shiloh, the bishop contributed to General Beauregard's illness, distress, and worry. "Every interview with Genl Polk turns [Beauregard's recovery] . . . back a week," Bragg admitted to his wife. "But for my arrival here to aid him, I do not believe he would now be living."

Bragg also considered the troops that Polk commanded in northern Mississippi hopelessly undisciplined. "I thought my Mobile Army was a *Mob*," admitted Bragg, "but it is as far superior to Polk's . . . as the one at Pensacola was to it. . . . Such has been the outrageous conduct of our troops [here in northern Mississippi] that the people prefer seeing the enemy." Bragg claimed that Polk did "nothing to correct this. Indeed the good Bishop sets the example, by taking whatever he wishes."

Polk continued this policy. Later in 1862, during the Kentucky campaign, he ordered an officer "to dismount [three cap-

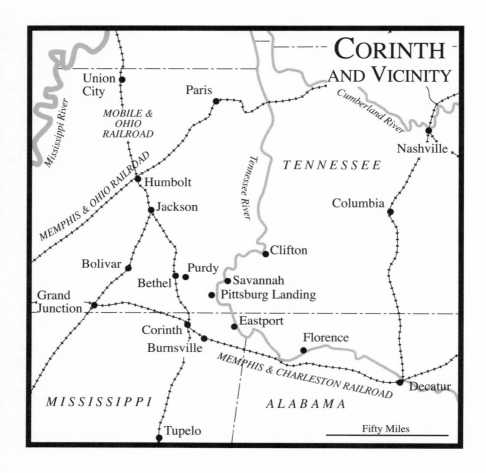

tured Federal cavalry officers], turn their horses over to the
quartermaster," and "make sure their excellent saddles were
specially reserved for [Polk] and his staff."

At Shiloh, in April 1862, Polk did nothing brilliant but neither did he do anything stupid. His command of one of the four
corps into which Gen. Albert Sidney Johnston divided his army
appeared to have been satisfactory, although a contemporary
called Polk's battle report the "Romance of Shiloh," implying
that much of what the bishop reported never happened.

Polk's troops and baggage train did delay the Confederate

march from Corinth, Mississippi, to Shiloh by jamming the streets. Maj. Gen. William J. Hardee, whose corps was scheduled to get underway by noon on April 3, found his route blocked by Polk's divisions and failed to get his men started until late that afternoon. Polk's inability to clear his men from Hardee's route may have been embarrassing, but it certainly was not the only mistake made by the Confederates during the Shiloh campaign.

If President Davis and Gen. Sidney Johnston tended to over-look Polk's little and big mistakes during 1861 and early 1862, the situation changed after Braxton Bragg became commander of the Army of Tennessee in June 1862. Bragg considered some of the army's highest ranking officers incompetent; he also believed that too many promising young officers had been killed at Shiloh or driven from the service by the rights granted Confederate soldiers to elect their own officers. To improve the quality of his officers, Bragg established promotion boards and stipulated that if elected officers were not accredited by those boards then the "elective franchise would be considered exhausted."

Bragg, who wanted to place some of his highest ranking sub-ordinates before such examining boards, reported in July 1862 that Hardee was the only "suitable" major general "now pre-sent." Such a remark by the army commander was a deliberate slap at Polk, whose military ability Bragg distrusted. "Among the junior brigadiers we have some excellent material," Bragg informed the government, "but it is comparatively useless, being overshadowed. Could the [War] Department by any wholesome exercise of power or policy relieve this army from a part of this dead-weight it would surely give confidence to the troops and add much to our efficiency."

Maj. Gen. Richard Taylor, son of Bragg's old Mexican War commander and who visited the Army of Tennessee while on his way from Virginia to Louisiana, heard Bragg call one of his senior generals "an old woman, utterly worthless." Taylor failed to name the "old woman," but apparently it was Polk.

During his Kentucky campaign in 1862, Bragg became even

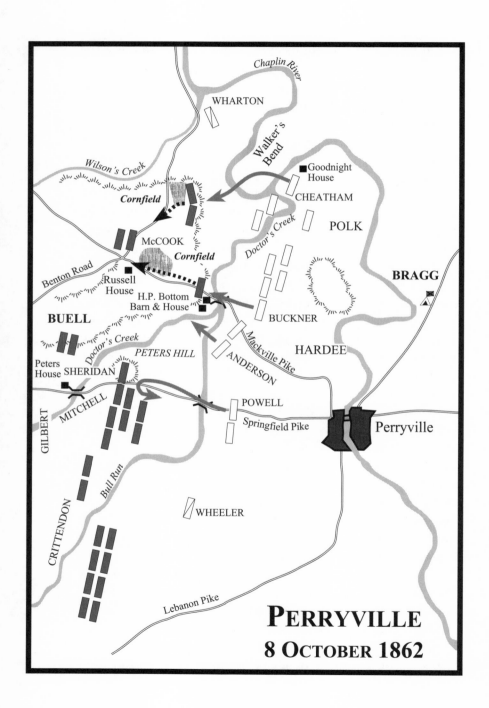

PERRYVILLE
8 OCTOBER 1862

more disgusted with Polk. On September 28 Bragg left his army temporarily under Polk's command at Bardstown, Kentucky, while he rushed to the state capital at Frankfort to inaugurate a pro-Confederate governor and to consult with Maj. Gen. Edmund Kirby Smith.

Bragg knew that leaving Polk in command of the army was a mistake, but he had no choice. The army commander had warned Richmond that Polk was incapable of holding the rank or exercising the responsibilities assigned to him. If the president refused to listen and insisted on retaining Polk, what could Bragg do? He must either use Polk in the position entitled by his rank and hope for the best or resign as commander of the Army of Tennessee, which Bragg was unwilling to do.

When reports indicated that the Federals were advancing from Louisville toward Frankfort, Bragg decided that "Polk [must] move on the enemy & assail the Federals in flank & rear, whilst [General] Smith [attacked] directly on his front." "The enemy is certainly advancing on Frankfort," Bragg informed Polk at 1:00 P.M. on October 2. "Put your whole available force in motion & strike him in flank, and rear. If we can combine our movements he is certainly lost."

Bragg's plan of a Napoleonic concentration of forces on the battlefield was bold but based upon inadequate information. He had only vague reports on the exact location of the Federals and misunderstood Union general Don Carlos Buell's strategy. Union troops actually had advanced from Louisville on four roads over a sixty-mile front. "The plan of my movement," Buell explained after the war, "was to force the enemy's left back and prevent him from moving upon my left flank and rear."

But on October 3 Bragg was confident that the Federals were where he thought they were and that Polk, as ordered, was on his way to Frankfort to cooperate with Smith. "The impression strongly prevails that the great Battle will be fought in this vicinity," wrote a staff officer. "With Smith in front and our gallant army on the flank," Bragg boasted, "I see no hope for Buell."

Actually, Buell was in no danger from Polk. The bishop, still at Bardstown, had no intention of marching to Frankfort or attacking Buell; indeed, Polk had sent neither aid nor orders to his subordinate Brig. Gen. Patrick Cleburne at Shelbyville, although Polk had known for two days that Federal forces threatened the Confederates there. Having done nothing to instruct or to reinforce Cleburne, Polk had the temerity to write Bragg, "It seems to me we are too much scattered."

He was correct, but Polk was about to scatter even further by retreating toward Danville in defiance of Bragg's orders. Believing the Federals were converging on Bardstown, Polk asked and received the support of his ranking generals for his extraordinary decision. Although Generals Hardee and Benjamin F. Cheatham later refused to reveal what they had advised, Brig. Gen. Sterling A. M. Wood readily admitted counseling Polk to disregard Bragg's order and to retreat. Apparently, only Patton Anderson, the junior general present at the meeting, favored obeying orders. Anderson pointed out that if Polk failed to march to Frankfort and cooperate with Smith, the results might be disastrous for the Confederates.

Polk explained his reasoning on October 3 in a dispatch to Bragg. "The last twenty-four hours have developed a condition on my front and left flank which makes compliance with [your] order not only eminently inexpedient, but impracticable," the bishop announced. "I have called a council of wing and division commanders, and find that they indorse my views. I shall therefore pursue a different course, assured that when the facts are submitted to you[,] you will justify my decision." Later, Polk would claim that he disobeyed no order; Bragg, he said, directed him to move with all his "available" force, but none of his troops were available for a march to Frankfort. This, of course, was the argument of a bishop, not a general; if his command was available for a retreat, it also was available for an advance to Frankfort.

Polk and some of his supporters insisted that Bragg's order was unclear, but Patton Anderson disagreed. "On the 3rd of

October, 1862, I was present at General Polk's quarters in Bardstown," he informed Bragg. "Your dispatch from Frankfort of
date 1 P.M. Oct 2nd was read after an interchange of views in
regard to our military condition, as junior officer present, I was
called upon by General Polk to give my views as to what was
best to be done. I hesitated to do so, whereupon General Polk
enquired as to the cause of my reluctance to advise. . . . And I
replied, that your order just read did not seem to admit of any
other course than that of compliance, and that if any other alternative then that of obedience to the order was adopted, it might
involve you and the forces with you near Frankfort in great
embarrassment if not defeat—that in your dispatch you distinct-
ly stated that Genl. Kirby Smith would attack the enemy then in
your front, and that *we* must move upon him and 'strike him in
flank and rear.'"

The decision of Polk to retreat demonstrated more than mere
cautiousness; it evidenced a distrust of his commander's judgment totally unsuitable for one considered second in command.
Older than Bragg and closer to the president, Polk had been a
bishop too long to be a successful subordinate. "With all his ability, energy and zeal, General Polk, by education and habit, is unfit-
ted for executing the orders of others," Bragg informed President
Davis. "He will convince himself his own views are better, and
will follow them without reflecting on the consequences."

During the Kentucky campaign, Polk made yet another mistake by misarranging troops at the battle of Perryville. Three roads
fanned westward from the town: one went northwest, another due
west, and the third southwest. Each crossed an almost dry stream
called Doctor's Creek, which trickled northeast into Chaplin River
about two miles above Perryville. Between the town and Doctor's
Creek, Polk had placed his fifteen thousand Confederates in a con-
cave line facing west. "This position was not so good," observed a
staff officer. "Genl Polk's line was weak, his right if outflanked by
the enemy would have cut us off from Genl Smith."

Bragg was furious when he rode over the field and saw what

Polk had done. At once he ordered Cheatham's division to move up and protect the exposed Confederate flank. "The distance to be marched [by Cheatham's men] was about two miles," recalled an officer, "and the interval which elapsed until their arrival, was a momentous one." Enemy skirmishers had already occupied high ground on the Confederate right, but before additional Federals advanced Cheatham's men arrived and secured the Confederate flank.

Late that afternoon, after a day of hard fighting, Polk believed that a Confederate unit was firing on St. John R. Liddell's brigade of Arkansans as they advanced in the twilight. "Dear me, this is very sad, and must be stopped," Polk muttered as he cantered over to ask the erring commander why he was shooting his friends. "I don't think there can be any mistake about it," replied the surprised officer. "I am sure they are the enemy." "Enemy," exclaimed the bishop, "why I have only just left them myself—cease firing, sir; what is your name, sir?"

After giving his name and *Union* regimental affiliation, the officer asked, "and pray, sir, who are you?" Polk, finally realizing his mistake but seeing nothing else to do, brazenly shook his fist in the Federal officer's face, saying: "I'll soon show you who I am. Cease firing at once."

Without waiting for an answer, Polk turned his horse and rode rapidly back to join Liddell. "They are enemies; fire upon them," the bishop shouted as he reached the Confederate line, "every mother's son of them are Yankees. I saw the colonel commanding the brigade." Liddell's men quickly fired deadly volleys into the startled Federals, but it was now dark and the battle was about over. Polk and Liddell rode forward to see the ground covered with dead and dying Yankees.

General Liddell considered the bishop "a good man, lofty in sentiment, gallant and enthusiastic in the cause," who "meant well and was a true patriot" but unfortunately saw things "with other eyes." Liddell even believed that Polk might have become a fair soldier if he had abandoned his "theatrical manner" and overcome his ignorance of strategy and tactics. A staff surgeon was less generous. "Genl Polk threatened wonders," wrote Dr. D.W. Yandell. "He was positively ferocious. But he can't be relied on. . . . He is great at talk, but is monstrous uncertain. I saw enough of the old grey beard at Shiloh & Perryville to cause me to place no great confidence in him. He will prevaricate. He did say he was going to do this and going to do that, but the old man forgets; [unless he is] transferred to [noncombat] house duties, we will all go to the Devil out here."

Following the Kentucky campaign, Polk rushed to Richmond to denounce Bragg to the president and to anyone else who would listen. The bishop-general not only criticized Bragg's leadership but also boasted that if he "had been in chief command, the strategy of the [Kentucky] campaign would have been very different—and the practical operations, as to tactics would have been very different [too]."

The strategy that Polk claimed he would have adopted revealed both his shortcomings as a general as well as how quickly he had forgotten what actually took place. The bishop said that he had favored "a more rapid and energetic campaign." Instead of the long detour of four hundred miles around by Chattanooga, he would have adopted a more direct and vigorous plan of falling first on one corps of the enemy and then on another, thus destroying the Federals in detail. Instead of marching on a line nearly parallel with that of Buell, Polk favored a cross march, falling on the Federal flank and crushing it before moving on to capture Louisville. And instead of fighting the battle of Perryville with divided forces, Polk said that he had favored concentrating the Confederate and "then falling on one corps of the enemy, and after crushing that, crushing the other corps—all of which," he insisted, "could have been easily done."

Polk's generalship got no better after the Kentucky campaign; indeed, his actions there may have been the highlight of his career. At Murfreesboro Polk made the mistake of sending his troops into action piecemeal and, at a critical point in the battle, announcing in a meeting with his commander that Bragg had only "three brigades that are at all reliable" and should immediately retreat. Weeks later the bishop admitted that he had meant to say that only three divisions, not just three brigades, were reliable. During the Confederate withdrawal from Tullahoma in the summer of 1863, Polk demonstrated how he could frustrate his commanding officer without actually disobeying orders. When Bragg ordered him to move his corps to Chattanooga "without delay," the bishop directed his division commanders not to move until they could make their "marches as expeditious as you can with convenience." At the battle of Chickamauga, Polk's actions and inactions were even more exasperating. At one point he failed to attack when ordered; at another, he failed to locate and notify Lt. Gen. D.H. Hill that Hill was expected to lead an attack. The person responsible for this poorly organized assault, which began nearly four hours later than Bragg had ordered, was the bishop, not Hill. Muddling and lack of concern by Polk had again disrupted Bragg's plans. As historian Judith Lee Hallock notes, Polk's generalship at Chickamauga was "his poorest in a long list of sorry performances."

The bishop's military ability failed to improve after Joseph E. Johnston took command of the Army of Tennessee. Polk apparently got along better with Johnston than he had with Bragg, but their relationship lacked cordiality. Friction between them never surfaced, but a certain lack of confidence in each other prevailed throughout their association. Polk discussed what he considered Johnston's deficiencies as a general with Hardee; in fact, Hardee wrote his friend Polk, "Johnston is wanting in all those particulars in which you feared he was deficient." Perhaps the bishop's major shortcoming was his failure to attempt to smooth the strained relationship, to ease some of the distrust and uncertainty that existed between his army commander and his close friend, the Confederacy's chief executive.

Polk made what some consider his greatest military contribution on June 14, 1864, when, while carelessly inspecting the enemy line from the summit of Pine Mountain, Georgia, the bishop moved a few feet nearer the crest for a final view. As he stood, arms folded, "a cannon-shot crashed through his chest."

His friends and some soldiers considered the death of Polk a great blow to the Confederacy. "He was every inch a gentleman, . . . simple and innocent, yet dignified and imposing," declared a staff officer. "Every private soldier loved him," remembered a Tennessean. "When I saw him here dead, I felt that I had lost a friend whom I had ever loved and respected, and that the South had lost one of her best and greatest generals."

These were pleasant and respectful words, to be sure, but not too helpful in evaluating bishop-general Leonidas Polk and his contribution to the Confederacy. Other contemporaries offered more realistic views. General Polk "is a slow coach—one who cannot be depended on," admitted Col. Taylor Beatty. Maj. Gen. Samuel G. French wrote kindly of the bishop as "a gentleman and a high Church dignitary" but remembered him as a soldier who was "more theoretical than practical." General Bragg described Polk as not just irresponsible and insubordinate but also "luxurious in his habits, rises late, moves slowly, and always conceives his own plans the best." Bragg concluded that he had been injured by Polk "on every field where I have been associated with him."

It may be time for historians of the Confederacy to admit that Bragg was not the Confederacy's worst general. Leonidas Polk may not be able to claim that title either, but he certainly was a bad general. Ignorant of military matters, quarrelsome, at times careless, lazy, insubordinate, and conspiratorial, he was dangerous not only because he knew so little about the art of warfare but also because he delighted in using his religious influence as well as his friendship with high government officials, especially the president, to promote himself and to undermine his enemies. Untrustworthy, he hurt every command and every commander with whom he served. The appointment of Polk to high military rank was one of Jefferson Davis's most serious mistakes.

CHAPTER THIRTEEN

Recklessness Destroys a General

Ambrose Powell Hill occupies a unique place in Confederate history. Both Lt. Gen. Thomas J. "Stonewall" Jackson and Gen. Robert E. Lee thought and spoke of Hill just before they died. In 1863, as Jackson took his last breaths, he cried out in his delirium, "Order A.P. Hill to prepare for action!" Seven years later Lee, on his deathbed, roused momentarily from half-consciousness and said so clearly that everyone in the room heard him, "Tell Hill he *must* come up."

The man called for so emphatically by Jackson and Lee as they lay dying was born in Culpeper County, Virginia, November 9, 1825. His parents—Maj. Thomas Hill, a merchant-politician respected for his courage and hospitality, and Fannie Russell Baptist Hill of Mecklenburg County, Virginia—named their third son Ambrose Powell in honor of his adventuresome,

Indian fighting great-grandfather, Capt. Ambrose Powell, who had settled the boundary line between Virginia and Kentucky.

Young Hill, whom his mother called Powell, spent his formative years in upcountry Virginia, where he would later lead men in combat. During his youth two strong forces shaped him. One was the traditional activities of rural Southerners. With his father, Powell fished, hunted, and rode; indeed, he became such an accomplished horseman that an admiring Confederate later claimed that Hill was "a perfect picture in the saddle and the most graceful rider I ever saw." The second forceful influence was a fondness for books, which Powell shared with his mother. His reading tastes included poetry, novels, the Bible, Shakespeare, and especially works on Napoleon. A boyhood friend remembered Powell as "self-reliant, forceful, and bright."

Influenced by the military exploits of his distinguished forbears as well as by his admiration of Napoleon, Powell decided upon a military career. He also may have been spurred to an

Ambrose Powell Hill

early decision by the conversion of his family to a religious orthodoxy that prohibited gambling, dancing, and attending the theater. Powell, already high spirited and independent, rebelled against such a straightlaced home environment. Over his mother's strong objections, he obtained an appointment to West Point through the influence of his father's political cronies. In 1842, some five months before his seventeenth birthday, Powell entered the U.S. Military Academy.

At West Point he was a better than the average student, who enjoyed frequent trips to Benny Havens's famous tavern and frolics with what his friend Henry Heth called "wild though not bad" girls. His schoolmates, besides Heth, included George B. McClellan, Fitz John Porter, Dabney Maury, George Pickett, Cadmus Wilcox, Ambrose Burnside, and Thomas J. Jackson. Because of an extended illness, Hill failed philosophy and chemistry and had to repeat a full year of studies. Thus held back from graduation until 1847, he finished fifteenth in a class of thirty-eight.

Adventures in Mexico awaited Hill. Appointed a second lieutenant in the 1st Artillery Regiment, he joined Gen. Winfield Scott's army and participated in several minor actions after Mexico City fell. From the conquered capital, Hill confessed to his father: "'Tis a fact that the ladies of Mexico are beautiful—and how beautiful—but very few of them have ever read Wayland's *Moral Science*. You know my failing. 'Tis an inheritance of this family, this partiality for . . . women." During one serious affair, he asked his parents, "How would you relish a Mexican daughter-in-law?" He left Mexico without a wife and sorely disappointed that he had experienced only limited combat.

For the next thirteen years, from 1848 to 1861, Hill suffered a typical antebellum military career. After becoming engaged and then disengaged to a beauty from Baltimore, he was sent to Florida to chase equally elusive Seminole Indians. After serving on the Texas frontier, he returned to Florida and spent months at such dreary garrisons as Key West and Barrancas Barracks, where he survived by fishing, hunting, and reading. Promoted to first lieutenant in September 1851, he was assigned to the coastal survey office in Washington, D.C., from November 1855 to October 1860, after which he secured a leave of absence.

During his stay in Washington, Hill fell in love again. First, he courted Ellen B. ("Miss Nelly") Marcy, the daughter of an army officer whose parents preferred that she marry someone with more "wealth and position in society." Hill also charged that Nelly's mother, in her determination to break up the romance, spread rumors "that from certain early imprudences, (youthful indiscretions I suppose), my health and constitution had become so impaired, so weakened, that no mother could yield her daughter to me, unless to certain unhappiness."

These rumors may have been true. In his excellent biography of Hill, James I. Robertson Jr. claims that his hero contracted gonorrhea in 1844 while a student at West Point and that the infection developed into prostatitis. This and related problems continued to trouble Hill and to shape his actions until his death; an invalid for the last six months of his life, he suffered from "swollen kidneys, flank pain, inability to urinate, drowsiness from taut nerves and lack of sleep," which "progressed into uremia." But historian Douglas Southall Freeman believed that Hill's problems were mainly psychosomatic, and another biographer suggested that Hill suffered from "chronic clinical malaria."

For whatever reason, Miss Nelly returned Hill's engagement ring and married instead Hill's old West Point roommate and friend, George B. McClellan. Years later, one of McClellan's veteran soldiers, tired of being hammered by Hill's Confederate Light Division, supposedly exclaimed, "My God Nelly, why didn't you marry [Hill]!"

Soon after Nelly broke their engagement, Hill boasted that a wealthy young widow, Kitty Morgan McClung, called "Dolly" by Hill, "has thrown her net around me." He praised her as "young, 24 years . . . gentle and amiable, . . . and sufficiently good looking for me." Her brother, John Hunt Morgan, would become a famous Confederate cavalryman and raider. Dolly married Hill at her mother's Kentucky home in 1859. Their marriage appears to have been a happy relationship that produced two daughters.

In 1860, as the sectional crisis loomed, Hill took an extended leave of absence from the army. He had never owned a slave and was not especially proslavery, but he believed in states' rights and was devoted to his native land. He was, in his own words, so determined to defend Virginia "to the death" that he resigned from the U.S. Army even before Virginia withdrew from the Union.

With the war came opportunities for combat and rapid promotions. First appointed colonel of the 13th Virginia Infantry in May 1861, Hill became a major general within a year. He favorably impressed both of the army commanders under whom he served, Joseph E. Johnston and Robert E. Lee. But not everyone believed that Hill deserved high rank. An old lady from his hometown, recalling that as a youth he was something of a mama's boy, exclaimed, "Heaven help us if Powell Hill is going to be a colonel in the Confederate Army!"

Hill was more impressive looking than the old lady's comments might suggest. Five feet, ten inches in height, he seemed taller because of his erect carriage. He weighed about 160 pounds, but his frame was so slight that Pres. Jefferson Davis always called him "little A.P. Hill." His long face—with high cheekbones, Roman nose, and intense eyes that blazed in anger—became gaunter as the war continued and his health deteriorated. His curling hair and luxuriant red beard matched the bright red hunting shirt he often wore in battle. Colorful and proud yet surprisingly gentle, he spoke in a soft, low Virginia drawl.

Hill missed action at First Manassas, where his regiment remained in reserve, but he got his chance to fight in 1862 during McClellan's attempt to take Richmond. Hill's first important action came on May 5 at Williamsburg, Virginia. There Gen. Joe

Johnston decided to punish the pursuing Federals before moving further up the Peninsula, and for seven hours Hill hurled his brigade of four Virginia regiments against the enemy. In these spirited assaults, Virginians pushed back the Federals and captured some guns, prisoners, and battle flags, including one bearing the inscription "To Hell or Richmond."

As the Confederates resumed their withdrawal, Hill and his men received high praise for their fighting. Maj. Gen. James Longstreet reported that Hill's brigade was so "ably led" at Williamsburg that its organization remained "perfect throughout the battle, and it was marched off the field in as good order as it entered it." Nothing was said about Hill's losses—326 men—the heaviest casualties of any brigade engaged on the Confederate right.

His actions at Williamsburg left little doubt that Hill was what the Confederate high command revered—an officer who would lead his men courageously against the enemy regardless of casualties. Given command of a division in May 1862, Hill took no part in the battle of Seven Pines, but he saw plenty of action after Robert E. Lee replaced the wounded Joe Johnston as army commander.

In preparation for action against McClellan, Lee expanded Hill's division to six brigades, numbering some fourteen thousand men. Hill immediately christened his command the "Light Division," perhaps in honor of British general Crawford's "Light Division" in the Duke of Wellington's army that once marched sixty-two miles in sixteen hours. A Confederate veteran admitted that he never knew why Hill's command was called the Light Division, "but I know that the name was applicable, for we often marched without coats, blankets, knapsacks, or any other burdens except our arms and haversacks, which were never heavy and sometimes empty."

Hill assumed a pivotal role in the Seven Days campaign. On June 26 he was ordered to wait until Stonewall Jackson and Maj. Gen. D.H. Hill had turned Union general Fitz John Porter's

JACKSON

Mechanicsville, 26 June

LEE

PORTER
V CORPS

Gaines' Mill, 27 June

FRANKLIN
VI CORPS

Richmond   *Oak Grove, 25 June*   SUMNER
                                       II CORPS

                              KEYES
                              IV CORPS   *Savage's Station,*
                                                29 June

                              HEINTZELMAN   McCLELLAN
                              III CORPS

                                          White Oak Swamp
                                          30 June

Glendale, 30 June

CHAFFIN'S
BLUFF

DREWRY'S
BLUFF   *Malvern Hill, 1 July*

Pamunkey River

Richmond & York River R.R.

Chickahominy River

Harrison's Landing

James River

SEVEN DAYS' BATTLES
25 JUNE–1 JULY 1862

Ten Miles

exposed right flank and then attack Porter's center at Mechanicsville. After waiting hours for Jackson to initiate the action,
Powell Hill lost his patience. "Three o'clock having arrived, and
no intelligence from Jackson," Hill later reported, "I determined
to . . . [attack] at once rather than hazard the failure of the whole
plan." Without consulting Lee, who was only a short distance
away, Hill assaulted the Federals and drove them back several
miles but suffered heavy losses himself.

Lee did not censure Hill for rashly and injudiciously initiating a costly encounter that Lee had hoped a skillful flanking
movement might avoid. But another Confederate called Hill's
attack "courageous, . . . impetuous, [and] . . . exceedingly impru-
dent."

Unabashed, Hill continued to fight as furiously as ever. On
June 27 he assailed the Federal center at Gaines's Mill with what
General Lee called "the impetuous courage for which that officer and his troops are distinguished." Three days later Hill's and
Longstreet's men led the assault at Frazier's Farm, where Hill
urged some of his exhausted soldiers to shriek their bloodcur-
dling rebel yell as they charged. At one point during the action,
Hill became concerned that President Davis and General Lee
had ventured too near the front. Davis recalled that Hill dashed
up and, "in the high pitched tone his voice assumed when excited," ordered them both to leave the battlefield.

Hill and his Light Division played only a minor part at
Malvern Hill, where the Seven Days campaign ended. In earlier
battles Confederate attacks usually had forced the enemy to give
ground, but at Malvern Hill numerous bloody assaults failed
because the Federals, protected by massed artillery and securely
entrenched around their new base along the James River, were
too strong. Lee reluctantly decided to disengage rather than
bleed his army to death.

Hill's men, along with other Confederate survivors of the
Seven Days, could boast that they had fought gallantly and
"withstood many hardships." They had indeed, although their

accomplishments fell far short of what they and their leaders had hoped to achieve. The Confederates had checked McClellan's advance on Richmond, but Lee had failed in his major goal—to destroy or capture McClellan's army. Moreover, his rash assaults had cost Lee more than twice as many casualties as he inflicted on the Federals. Hill's division alone suffered in excess of five thousand casualties—more than a third of its men.

Understandably, the Richmond press, both during and after the campaign, focused more on Confederate success than failure. Glowing accounts of the army and the achievements of its leaders filled every newspaper. Articles in the *Richmond Examiner,* written by a former member of Hill's staff, extolled the exploits of the Light Division and its commander, often at the expense of General Longstreet. An exchange of letters over the matter only fueled the quarrel, and ultimately, Hill and Longstreet agreed to fight a duel. Lee managed to avert this encounter by transferring Hill and his entire division to Jackson's command just in time for the Second Manassas campaign.

Soon after the fighting ended on the Peninsula, Lee detached Jackson to meet a growing Union threat in northern Virginia from a newly created Federal army commanded by Maj. Gen. John Pope. Hill and the Light Division reinforced Jackson's command along the Rapidan River in late July.

Joining Jackson gave Hill new concerns as well as new opportunities. He found Stonewall, as always, cold and secretive—still quite like the humorless cadet he had known at West Point. Jackson's reticence to take subordinates into his confidence infuriated and further alienated Hill, who developed what at best might be called a strained relationship with Jackson.

As Jackson moved against the Federals, he encountered Union general Nathaniel P. Banks's corps at Cedar Mountain on August 9. Jackson hurled two of his three divisions—commanded by Richard S. Ewell and Charles S. Winder—against Banks, who not only withstood the attack but also launched a massive counter assault that broke Winder's division and threatened the entire Confederate line. Only the prompt arrival of Hill's Light Division checked the Federal advance and saved Jackson from a disaster.

Ironically, Hill's men were in the right place at the right time because Jackson had modified his marching orders without notifying Hill, thus creating confusion and delays but perhaps also saving Hill's life and reputation. Had not Jackson's modification of the march forced Hill's men to follow Winder's rather than precede them—as originally planned—Hill might have been killed at Cedar Mountain, as was Winder, and the Light Division might have been driven from the battlefield.

Less than a month later, at Second Manassas, Hill's men demonstrated that when necessary they could be just as steadfast defenders as they were spirited attackers. Five times on August 29 General Pope dashed his divisions piecemeal against the Light Division's strong defensive position. Before the day ended more than four thousand dead or wounded Federals lay heaped in Hill's front, but such a dogged defense nearly exhausted both the Confederates and their ammunition. As Pope prepared for yet another attack, Hill discovered that his troops, even after stripping cartridges from the dead and wounded, were down to one round per man. Uncertain that the Light Division could withstand another assault, Hill reported his critical situation to Jackson, who at first merely sent a message informing Hill that somehow he "must beat them"; then Stonewall decided to ride over to Hill's headquarters and personally reiterate his message. When Hill again expressed doubt about the outcome, Jackson replied, "General, your men have done nobly; if you are attacked again you will beat the enemy back." Sounds of musketry from the Confederate left ended the conference. "Here it comes!" exclaimed Hill, and he rode off in the direction of the firing. Jackson called after him, "I'll expect you to beat them."

Hill did just that. Overwhelming numbers of Federals forced the Confederates back, but the Light Division refused to break.

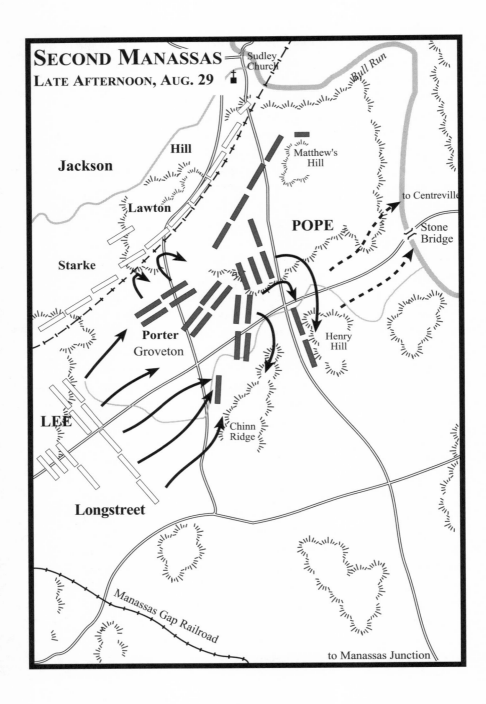

SECOND MANASSAS
LATE AFTERNOON, AUG. 29

Sudley
Church

Bull Run

Jackson

Hill

Lawton

Matthew's
Hill

POPE

Starke

to Centreville

Stone
Bridge

Porter
Groveton

Henry
Hill

LEE

Chinn
Ridge

Longstreet

Manassas Gap Railroad

to Manassas Junction

Some units, such as Gen. Maxcy Gregg's South Carolina brigade, met the final Union assault with only their bayonets. "Let us die here, my men," exhorted Gregg. Many did, but the South Carolinians held and with help from reinforcements ultimately drove back the enemy. At sundown Hill reported that the Federal attack had failed. Jackson, with a hint of a smile on his face, said to the messenger, "Tell him I knew he would do it."

The Confederates achieved overwhelming success the next day. Unaware that Lee and Longstreet had arrived and taken a position on Jackson's right, Pope moved to occupy terrain he mistakenly believed Jackson had abandoned. Several Federal assaults failed as Jackson's men stood firm and Longstreet's guns raked the exposed Union left flank. Then Lee counterattacked. Along a five-mile front, Confederates surged forward in double lines and routed Pope's army.

Following this success, Lee invaded Maryland and Hill renewed his feud with Jackson. Stonewall, convinced that Hill had neglected his marching orders, gave instructions directly to one of Hill's brigadiers. Hill was furious. In a face-to-face confrontation, he said to Jackson, "You have assumed command of my division, here is my sword; I have no use for it!" Jackson replied: "Keep your sword General Hill, but consider yourself under arrest for neglect of duty." Without a command and "as mad as a bull," Hill marched along on foot with the rear guard of the army for several days.

But when action seemed likely, Hill bridled his pride and asked to be reinstated. Jackson relented, and Hill resumed "command of his division to the delight of all his men." Their assignment, along with other units of Jackson Corps, was to capture the Union garrison at Harpers Ferry, which blocked Confederate communications through the Shenandoah Valley, while the remainder of the Army of Northern Virginia moved northward.

The Federals at Harpers Ferry surrendered without much of a fight. Since the Light Division, which lost only sixty-nine men in capturing the post, had "borne the heaviest part of the engagement," Jackson left Hill and his men behind to parole prisoners and to collect captured supplies. Stonewall and the rest of his corps rushed to reinforce Lee at Sharpsburg, Maryland.

For two days Hill let his men enjoy themselves. Of course, some helped get the captured military stores, arms, and prisoners moving, but most members of the Light Division delighted in this break from marching and fighting. They gorged on Yankee food and appropriated needed apparel.

Meanwhile, Lee was in trouble. With fewer than twenty-five thousand Confederates, he faced some eighty-seven thousand Federals at Sharpsburg. During the night of September 16, he sent a note to Hill requesting him to join the main army at once. Hill received the message at 6:30 A.M. the next day. Leaving one brigade behind to complete the removal of captured supplies, Hill got his other five brigades underway within an hour.

The march to Sharpsburg was not only one of the great military movements of Confederate history; it was an example of Hill at his best. By acting decisively and moving rapidly, he saved Lee from what probably would have been a disastrous defeat. When Hill's men arrived at Sharpsburg, Lee's lines were ready to break. All day the Confederates had fought gallantly against overwhelming odds, but now they were exhausted and the final Federal push by Maj. Gen. Ambrose Burnside's corps was about to crush Lee's thinned right flank and cut the Confederate line of retreat to the Potomac.

Hill could not have reached the battlefield at a better time. About 3:40 P.M., just as a Federal victory seemed certain, he arrived and unleashed his brigades. Hill's men had marched some seventeen miles in seven hours. They were weary and footsore, but they attacked without resting. Yelling wildly, they smashed into Burnside's flank, and within an hour the battle was over. The surprised Federals, unable to withstand Hill's assault, retreated to the high ground around Antietam Creek. "At the critical moment," observed an admiring Confederate,

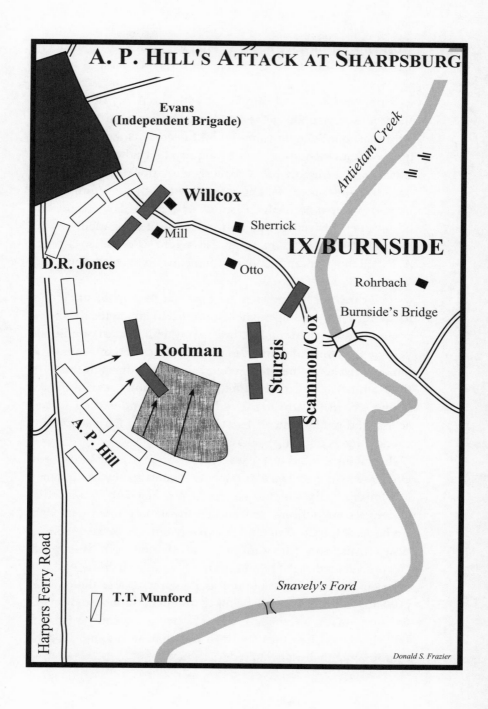

A. P. HILL'S ATTACK AT SHARPSBURG

Evans
(Independent Brigade)

Willcox

Mill

Sherrick

IX/BURNSIDE

D.R. Jones

Otto

Rohrbach

Burnside's Bridge

Rodman

Sturgis

Scammon/Cox

A. P. Hill

Antietam Creek

Harpers Ferry Road

T.T. Munford

Snavely's Ford

Donald S. Frazier

"A.P. Hill was always at his strongest." Thanks to the timely arrival of the Light Division, Lee's army had survived to fight again.

After the Maryland campaign, with the Army of Northern Virginia safely south of the Potomac, Hill renewed his dispute with Jackson. Believing that he had been "treated with injustice," Hill insisted on a court of inquiry to vindicate his honor. When Jackson ignored this request, Hill appealed to Lee—not once but several times. Lee, concerned with more important matters, wanted no further dispute between his lieutenants, but he revealed his regard for Hill in a letter to President Davis. Next to Jackson and Longstreet, Lee wrote: "I consider General A. P. Hill the best commander with me. He fights his troops, and takes good care of them."

Hill cared for his men less well in their next action at Fredericksburg, Virginia, on December 13, 1862. In taking his defensive position on the right flank of Lee's army, Hill left a six-hundred-yard gap between the brigades of Gen. James H. Lane and Gen. James J. Archer. When the Federals attacked through the gap, they almost broke Hill's line. Only stubborn resistance by Gregg's South Carolinians, whose commander died in the action, and reinforcements from Maj. Gen. Jubal Early's division checked the Federals.

Lee won a relatively easy victory at Fredericksburg, but Hill's men suffered twice as many casualties as any of the other Confederate divisions engaged. Lee refused to blame Hill, although some officers insisted that the gap between Lane and Archer cost the Confederates needlessly and could have led to a disaster. Jackson, for example, candidly stated in his report, "before General A.P. Hill closed the interval which he had left between Archer and Lane, it was penetrated, and the enemy, pressing forward in overwhelming numbers through that interval, turned Lane's right and Archer's left." For whatever reason, Hill displayed ineptness both in positioning his men and in coordinating their rally at Fredericksburg.

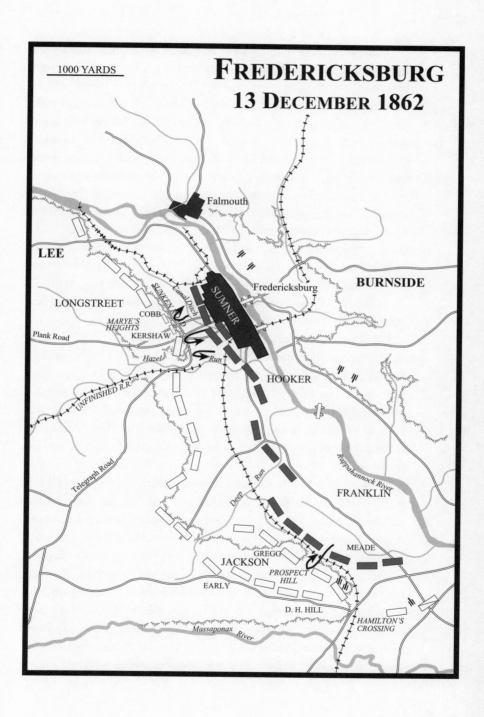

1000 YARDS

FREDERICKSBURG
13 DECEMBER 1862

Falmouth

LEE

BURNSIDE

LONGSTREET

Fredericksburg

COBB

MARYE'S HEIGHTS

Plank Road

KERSHAW

Hazel

Run

SUMNER

Canal Ditch

SUNKEN RD

UNFINISHED R.R.

HOOKER

Telegraph Road

Deep Run

FRANKLIN

Rappahannock River

GREGG

MEADE

JACKSON

PROSPECT HILL

EARLY

D. H. HILL

HAMILTON'S CROSSING

Massaponax River

Hill performed better the following spring during Jackson's famous flanking movement at Chancellorsville. While Lee with less than half the army confronted Union general Joseph Hooker, Jackson's corps marched to attack the exposed Federal right flank. The Confederate assault, which began in the late afternoon, continued after dark. As the advance slowed, Jackson rode forward to reconnoiter. Hill followed some distance away but within sight of his corps commander. Having been stopped by the sound of axes preparing Union barricades, Jackson and Hill, still within sight of each other, were riding back toward the Confederate lines when some North Carolina troops from Hill's own division, mistaking their returning commanders for Federal cavalry, opened fire. Hill escaped unhurt, but several members of his staff were killed or wounded. When he learned that Jackson also had been shot, Hill rushed to his fallen commander, removed his sword belt and gloves, and held him in his arms until Stonewall could be moved from the field.

As senior division commander, Hill assumed command of Jackson's corps, but shortly thereafter he came under fire again, this time from the Federals, and was wounded in the calves of both his legs. Unable to walk or ride without considerable pain, he was forced to relinquish corps command to Maj. Gen. J.E.B. Stuart, chief of the army's cavalry, who decided to halt action for the night.

Hill, still unable to walk or ride the following day, impatiently followed the battle from behind the lines by ear and by dispatch. He lamented that the Federals managed to escape being crushed and that he and the Light Division had not played a more conspicuous part in the battle, but he generously praised Stuart, whose "indomitable energy," in Hill's words, allowed him to overcome "all difficulties and achieve a glorious result."

When Lee reorganized the Army of Northern Virginia into three corps after Jackson's death, he entrusted the Third Corps to Hill. Lee informed President Davis that Hill was "the best soldier of his grade" in the army and recommended his promotion.

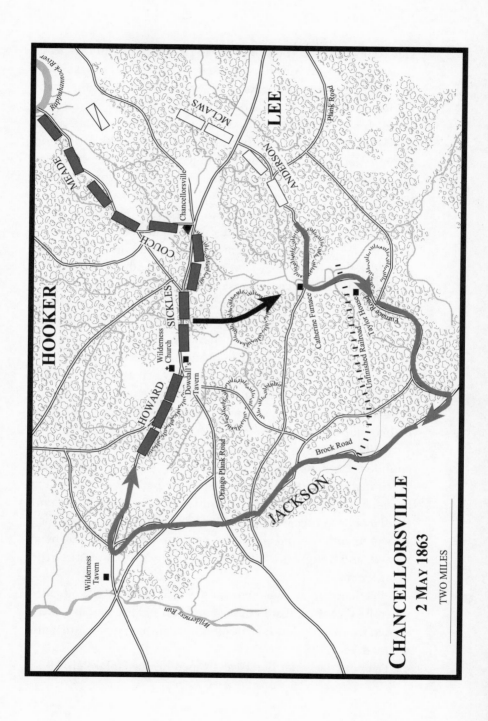

CHANCELLORSVILLE
2 MAY 1863

TWO MILES

Davis concurred, and on May 24, 1863, Lee called Hill to head-quarters and told him he was now a lieutenant general. Maj. Gen. William Dorsey Pender, the new commander of the Light Division, believed that as a corps commander Hill "would give as much satisfaction as he had in divisional command." Other Confederates had equally high hopes for Hill. "As a division commander he had few equals," noted a staff officer. "He was quick, bold, skillful, and tenacious . . . ; he did his work dashing-ly and well."

But something had gone out of Hill. He would never be as successful as a corps commander as he had been as a division commander. During Lee's Pennsylvania campaign, Hill's men located the Federals near Gettysburg and, without waiting for orders from Lee, moved against them. Hill, feeling miserably ill, nevertheless directed the action that followed on July 1. It was the only large engagement of the war in which the initiative and whole responsibility rested with him. At first his units sustained heavy losses and gained little ground, especially against the Union's famous Iron Brigade. But later in the day, having received reinforcements, the Confederates drove the Federals back though the town to Cemetery Hill. At that point, Hill halt-ed his troops for the day.

Hill's actions on the first day at Gettysburg have received abundant condemnation. Critics have accused him of recklessly precipitating a battle that Lee wished to avoid and then failing to press a beaten enemy. Hill admitted in his after-action report that he believed the enemy had been "entirely routed," but then wrote, "prudence led me to be content with what had been gained, and not push forward troops exhausted and necessarily disordered."

"Prudence" may indeed explain why Hill halted the advance when he did; if so, it was quite untypical of Hill. He had never shown much "prudence" before—either in his personal or mili-tary actions.

The next day, after Longstreet's men hit the Union left, Hill's corps again took up the offensive. But the charges made by his various brigades lacked coordination. Moreover, Hill failed to throw in his reserve division at the critical moment. The Federals held their ground, and soon after dark Hill's depleted and disheartened men fell back to where their assault began.

July 3 was yet another day of frustration for Hill. He enthusiastically supported Lee's plan to attack the Federal center on Cemetery Ridge. Indeed, Hill wanted to lead the assault himself and begged Lee to let him take in his entire corps. Instead, Lee detached ten of Hill's brigades to Longstreet's command for that grandest of Confederate failures—Pickett's Charge. "What remains of your corps will be my only reserve," Lee told Hill, "and it will be needed if General Longstreet's attack should fail."

Perhaps Lee should have granted Hill's request. Hill had complete confidence in Lee's plan, the action took place on Hill's front, and two-thirds of the troops engaged on July 3 were from Hill's corps. Furthermore, Hill had the deserved reputation of being one of the hardest hitters in the Confederacy. Later, his supporters would suggest that if he had led the attack the Confederates might have been victorious. Lee anticipated such hindsight when shortly after Gettysburg he told General Heth: "my mistakes are never told me until it is too late."

But, in fact, Hill's generalship after Gettysburg was no better than adequate. In October 1863, without reconnoitering, Hill launched a headlong attack at Bristoe Station that was both humiliating and costly to the Confederates. Fighting in the Wilderness in May 1864, Hill more than held his own, but he was outflanked and faced a disaster that only the timely arrival of Longstreet's corps prevented. Hill and his men were not heavily engaged in the fighting from the North Anna to Cold Harbor, but they shared in most of the action on the Confederate right throughout the eight-and-a-half-month siege of Petersburg.

Late in March 1865, Hill left the front lines to recuperate but

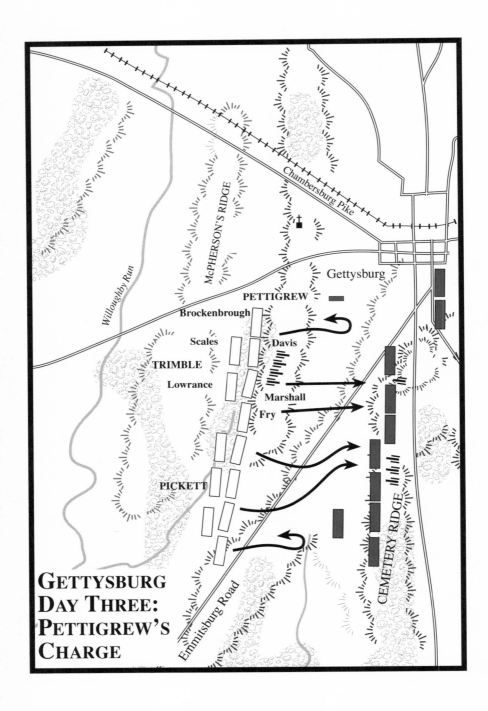

Chambersburg Pike

McPHERSON'S RIDGE

Willoughby Run

Gettysburg

PETTIGREW

Brockenbrough

Scales   **Davis**

TRIMBLE

Lowrance

                              Marshall

                              Fry

PICKETT

CEMETERY RIDGE

**GETTYSBURG
DAY THREE:
PETTIGREW'S
CHARGE**

Emmitsburg Road

cut short his furlough when he learned that the Federals were threatening his right flank. On April 2, while inspecting his line and accompanied only by a courier, Hill encountered two enemy infantrymen, whom he recklessly attempted to capture. "Surrender," demanded Hill. Instead, both Federals fired. One bullet missed, but the other killed the general.

A.P. Hill the soldier possessed both solid strengths and serious weaknesses. Dashing, gallant, and forthright, he participated in all the great battles fought by the Army of Northern Virginia except for the operations around Spotsylvania Court House. Restless for action, he could be as aggressive as Lee or any of Lee's lieutenants. Hill moved his troops promptly and enjoyed the good opinion of his subordinates and the unquestioning confidence of his soldiers. "Affable and readily approached by the humblest private," cordial and courteous in manner, Hill nevertheless demanded strict attention to duty. "No commander was ever more considerate of the rights and feelings of others under him," recalled a contemporary, "or sustained the authority of his subordinate officers with more firmness and tact."

Along with all his admirable qualities, Hill had some serious faults. Especially touchy about his honor, he quarreled with all of his superiors except Lee. At times Hill could be willful—as in July 1862 when he violated Lee's order to cut transportation to a minimum—but perhaps impetuosity accounted for most of his mistakes, military and personal. He often acted without knowing the enemy's strength or location and just as often paid a heavy price in casualties for his negligence. He was almost never cautious or reluctant to fight; indeed, he seemed willing to risk heavy losses—frequently terrible losses—for what he hoped to gain. His men usually suffered more casualties than comparable Confederate units.

Nor can any evaluation of Hill escape the conclusion that he lacked certain higher administrative abilities. He simply could not coordinate and direct a corps as well as he could a division.

As a corps commander, he never rose above being ordinary. His great achievements occurred while he was leading the Light Division at such places as Cedar Mountain, Second Manassas, and Sharpsburg. On those battlefields he attained magnificence. How appropriate that when Jackson and Lee lay dying they each called for A.P. Hill. He had saved them before, but ultimately his own recklessness destroyed him.

CHAPTER FOURTEEN

Needed but Misused

As the Confederacy collapsed, a Georgia girl wrote in her diary: "Generals Bragg and Breckinridge are in the village, with a host of minor celebrities. General Breckinridge is called the handsomest man in the Confederate army, and Bragg might be called the ugliest . . . ; he looks like an old porcupine."

Braxton Bragg, the sixth ranking Confederate general, was no beauty; perhaps the kindest remark ever made about his appearance came from a young lieutenant who thought Bragg looked "just like a General you see in pictures," but most comments were less favorable. A captain described Bragg as "a tall, slim, rough looking man with a little round head, covered with gray frizzly hair. . . . he has a wild abstracted look, and pays but little attention to what is passing around him; his mind seems to be in a constant strain. His apparel consists of long gray hunting shirt, pants stuffed in his boots, . . . his hard looking head is ornamented with a military cap [to which] some white cloth [is attached to cover] his neck." An English visitor called Bragg "the least prepossessing of the Confederate generals."

Civil War writers in general have been hard on Bragg. He "was as baffling a mixture of high ability and sheer incompetence as the Confederacy could produce," wrote Bruce Catton. David H. Donald called Bragg "tense, punctilious, arrogant, a martinet and a dawdler." He was, to Clifford Dowdey, a "psychotic warrior" who "at the ultimate test of committing an army to battle . . . shrank from the decision." Bragg "lacked the determination to carry through his purpose," charged T. Harry Williams; "he did not have the will to overcome the inertia of war."

Most scholars have censured Bragg for his failure to win the loyalty of his officers and men. Douglas Southall Freemen praised Robert E. Lee for "realizing that the volunteer leaders of

Braxton Bragg

a revolutionary force could not be given the stern, impersonal treatment that can be meted out to the professional soldier of an established government. How different," concluded Freeman, "might have been the fate of Bragg and perhaps of the Confederacy if that officer had learned this lesson from Lee!"

The judgment of Bragg's contemporaries was no less severe. "Bragg is not fit for a general," a soldier confided to his diary in 1863. "If Jeff Davis will just let Bragg alone, I think he will do us more damage than the enemy." A Georgian complained, "Napoleon says the art of war consists in knowing how to separate to subsist, and how to unite to fight. The art of Bragg has been to unite to starve, and to separate to be whipped." In one canard an old lady said: "I wish General Bragg were dead and in heaven. I think it would be a God send to the Confederacy." "Why, my dear," replied her friend, "if the General were near the gates of heaven, and invited in, at the critical moment he would 'fall back.'" An army surgeon's diagnosis in 1862 concluded: "General Bragg is either stark mad or utterly incompetent. He is ignorant of both the fundamental principles and details of his noble profession. He has lost the confidence of both his men and officers."

Many of Bragg's subordinates were certain something was wrong with their commander. One general swore he would never fight again under Bragg's command; another threatened to resign from the army and challenge Bragg to a duel. Maj. Gen. Henry Heth simply explained that Bragg "lost his head" in the enemy's presence. "General Bragg did not know what had happened," Lt. Gen. Leonidas Polk reported to Pres. Jefferson Davis after the battle of Chickamauga. "He let down as usual and allowed the fruits of . . . victory to pass from him by the most criminal incapacity." About the same time Lt. Gen. James Longstreet wrote the secretary of war: "our chief [Bragg] has done but one thing that he ought to have done since I joined his army. That was to order the attack [at Chickamauga] upon the 20th. All other things that he had done he ought not to have done. I am convinced that nothing but the hand of God can save us or help us as long as we have our present commander." Generals D.H. Hill and Simon B. Buckner joined Longstreet in ridiculing Bragg; they also signed a petition requesting his dismissal from army command. Buckner later recalled that he told President Davis in 1863: "Mr. President, . . . frankly, General Bragg as a military man, as a commander is wanting in imagination. He cannot foresee what probably may occur. When he has formed his own opinion of what he proposes to do, no advice of all his officers put together can shake him; but when he meets the unexpected, it overwhelms him because he has not been able to foresee, and then he will lean upon the advice of a drummer boy."

Curiously, hardly anyone doubted Bragg's ability when the Civil War began. Mexican War hero, retired army lieutenant colonel, he was one of the most distinguished soldiers to join the Confederacy, and for a time one of the most impressive. He rose quickly from brigadier to full general, and in 1862 a congressman wrote him: "no General in the army has more of public confidence and admiration. Your praise is on the lips of every man. Mr. [Secretary of War Judah P.] Benjamin told me that you were 'the greatest General we had.'"

Yet less than two years later, Bragg was the South's most discredited commander. He had done as much, or appeared to have done as much, as any Confederate general to lose the war. Longer than anyone else—from June 27, 1862, to November 30, 1863—Bragg commanded the principal western army. Under his direction the Army of Tennessee fought four major campaigns and retreated from Kentucky to Georgia. Its failures were justly considered his failures. But only after his rout at Chattanooga in November 1863 was Bragg relieved of field command.

The man who drove him from Missionary Ridge, Ulysses S. Grant, boasted: "An Army never was whipped so badly as Bragg was. So far as any opposition the enemy could make, I could have marched to Atlanta or any other place in the Confederacy." This view exaggerated Confederate demoralization, but even Bragg admitted, "The disaster . . . is justly disparaging to me as a commander."

Instead of retirement to the obscurity most people believed he so richly deserved, Bragg received a remarkable promotion. He went to Richmond as President Davis's military adviser soon after relinquishing command of the Army of Tennessee. Called the Confederacy's general in chief, Bragg supervised all army operations. Few were surprised that his failures in this position were less apparent than they had been as a field commander.

Much of the criticism of Bragg is justified, but too often he has been blamed for the mistakes of others; his faults have been exaggerated. A failure is always an easy target. Unfortunately for Bragg, his enemies published more than his defenders, and many writers have accepted uncritically the opinions of Bragg's critics. That officious chronicler of Confederate life, Mary B. Chesnut, frequently denounced Bragg as "a worthless general." Her popular diary has become a standard source for Civil War writers, and her estimate of Bragg is often cited as the opinion of all Southern civilians.

But Bettie R. Blackmore, a native of Tennessee, also kept a diary. Her journal is not as famous as Chesnut's, nor is it as easy to find in libraries. Yet Blackmore, who claimed Bragg did "more with his men and means than any other general," is just as reliable an authority on Bragg as Chesnut: neither lady served in Bragg's army, neither knew much about generalship, and neither is a major source for anyone trying to evaluate Bragg.

It is important to note that too many Civil War historians have based their evaluations of Bragg upon inadequate sources. If scholars cite Chesnut's diary against Bragg, it is only fair that they cite Blackmore's diary for him. It is unjust to use only the opinions of the general's enemies.

Bragg, it is often charged, received promotion to full general only because he and President Davis had long been friends. Such was not the case. One reason why Bragg had resigned from

the U.S. Army was because he disliked Davis, who was then secretary of war. In 1855 Bragg informed his friend William T. Sherman: "To judge from high sounding words in reports and bills
before Congress, Mr. Jeff. Davis intends to have an Army after
his own heart (not a very good one by the way). We are all to be
placed at his mercy, and to be rearranged to suit his pleasure
and convenience." Bragg considered Davis "a good deal of the
pettifogger and special pleader." Years later, Sherman recalled
that "Bragg hated Davis bitterly" for sending him to the frontier,
"as Bragg expressed it 'to chase Indians with six-pounders [can-
nons].'"

Davis certainly never knew that for years Bragg had disliked
and distrusted him. When the Civil War began, Bragg feared
that he would be ignored by the Confederate president. Nor was
Bragg reassured when Davis gave him command of forces near
Pensacola, Florida, in 1861.

Only after receiving extensive reports from people he trusted
did Bragg become convinced that the president was not his
enemy. In the spring of 1862, Congressman James L. Pugh, formerly a soldier at Pensacola, wrote that he "was delighted to
find" in the Confederate capital "the highest confidence in my
old Genl. Bragg. . . . President Davis said that 'you had shown a
most self sacrificing devotion to the cause, and was about the
only General who had accomplished all you undertook.'" And
Bragg's brother, who was a member of Davis's cabinet, noted
that the president "spoke [favorably] of Gen'l Bragg—said he
had put down drinking and that his had been the only well disciplined and managed army in the field. That he set a proper
example to his men. In speaking of other Generals, their qualities &c, he [Davis] ranked him [Bragg] with Sidney Johns[t]on."

Bragg owed his promotion to full general after Shiloh not to a
close friendship with the president but to the reputation he had
gained as an organizer and administrator. When Bragg moved
north to reinforce Sidney Johnston before Shiloh, Davis wrote his
old friend, "General Bragg brings you disciplined troops, and

you will find in him the highest administrative capacity."

James Longstreet's memoirs, D.H. Hill's biased articles in *Battles and Leaders*, P.G.T. Beauregard's autobiography (ghost-written by Alfred Roman), Simon B. Buckner's recollections, Basil Duke's reminiscences, and the biography of Leonidas Polk {written by his son) all present unfavorable views of Bragg. These are important sources to be sure, but they paint only part of the picture. Scholars should recognize them as biased accounts and use them cautiously.

Throughout the war Bragg had numerous supporters inside and outside the army. Perhaps the clearest proof of his popularity was the deluge of letters he received after he retired from command of the Army of Tennessee. These expressions of regret were written by generals as well as by privates, by high government officials as well as by common citizens.

"I express to you my sense of the loss which the Army of Tennessee has sustained in your retirement," Gen. Joseph E. Johnston wrote Bragg. "Let me assure you, too, of a fellow soldier's appreciation of your high military ability—and a fellow citizen's admiration of the disinterested patriotism which you have exhibited from the commencement of the war."

Generals Richard Taylor and St. John R. Liddell asked Bragg to take command of the Trans-Mississippi West. "It is the general desire of the Army and people of Louisiana that you come to this side of the Mississippi," wrote Taylor. "No one indulges this hope more than myself." In Louisiana, promised Liddell, Bragg would be "free from all unjust public clamor. You will know . . . your friends; [everyone] . . . will . . . follow you."

Brig. Gen. James R. Chalmers told Bragg, "I have seen no man in this war who looked, talked & acted on all occasions so much like my beau ideal of a General; you have shown yourself a great military chieftain & history will give you an everlasting page in the records of the Southern struggle for independence."

On December 10, 1863, the inspector general of the Army of Tennessee informed Bragg: "I have just inspected the Army . . .

and I find a general regret at your leaving. It is . . . evident now to all that the rank and file of the Army and the more efficient and honest officers prefer you to any other leader that could be sent here and would hail your return with earnest satisfaction."

"The news had just reached us that you have been relieved of the command of the Army of Tennessee," wrote Brig. Gen. Philip D. Roddey. "You will please pardon this intrusion but I am so mortified that I cannot in justice to my own feelings resist the temptation to say that we can never be as well satisfied with a commander as we have been with you. Nor do we believe that any officer on the continent could have done more or better with the Army of Tennessee than you have done. I have heard a general expression from the officers and men of my brigade and without exception they prefer you as a commander to any officer in the Confederate Army."

Several months later Brig. Gen. Alpheus Baker told Bragg that his "real friends were among the rank and file and the regimental and company officers in this army. I find everywhere the most devoted attachment and respect for you among them all," stated Baker, "and I have yet to meet the first man who has not spoken as your friend."

A civilian reported similar sentiments among the soldiers with whom he had talked. "I cannot but believe that you will soon be restored to the command of the Army you have so long and so gallantly led," H.W. Walters of Atlanta wrote Bragg. "I have no doubt but that such a restoration would be hailed by almost every man of the army with pleasure. Such is the uniform declaration of all who come from the Army of Tennessee. I meet daily with persons from the Army and I find but one sentiment, that of deep respect, amounting to affection for you, and but one wish, that you will again be placed in command."

Maj. Gen. Joseph Wheeler expressed the same view. "I hear from many sources that the soldiers and many subaltern officers express indignation that it should have been said they did not like you as a commander. I have been serenaded twice in the last few days by troops who said they had come to hunt up General Bragg's friends, for whom they expressed the greatest devotion," explained Wheeler. "They said the only enemies you had were a few bad Generals and some newspaper editors. They might have included a few soldiers who had been misinformed and influenced by designing men."

One of the editors to whom Wheeler referred was L.J. Dupree, of the *Atlanta Register*. On February 25, 1864, he wrote Bragg: "I was influenced, I must confess, in all that I have written of you, to a greater extent than I should have been, by the whispered slanders of your enemies. I could not escape this influence General. It filled the very atmosphere of all newspaperdom. All sorts of influence were brought to bear upon the Press I controlled. My opinions of your generalship were fixed by these influences, but I was misled. I have since learned that I did you injustice. I shall find an occasion to make amends worth more than this tendered apology."

Of the many letters Bragg received from common soldiers, perhaps the most charming was a note from J. H. Fraser, Company H, 50th Alabama Volunteers, dated December 2, 1863. Fraser wrote:

> my heart is full of sorrow; in fact, our camp is full of sorrow and sadness, for we had learned to love you as a child loves his father, and the thought of being separated from you, and losing perhaps forever your paternal-like care sends pangs most bitter through our insides. Many of us have followed you with gladness from Mobile up to the present, and the longer we remained with you the more we loved you, and the more confidence we had in your skill and ability as a military chieftain; we always felt sure that while General Bragg commanded no evil could ever befall us. Your old army was never dissatisfied with you and we love you today better, and can yield a more willing service at your command, than we can to any untried leader. But for fear I weary you with the

length of my letter I bid you good bye for the Regiment—
we all love you alike. Should you retire from the Army
entirely—which God forbid—[we hope] you may find the
peace and joy and rest which you so much need, and
praying that you may live to see us a free, happy and independent nation; and that when at last your career on Earth
shall have ended you may be received into that heavenly
abode where no vile slanderers are allowed to enter.

The assumption that once a soldier hated Bragg he continued
to do so is disproved by the letters of Capt. E. John Ellis. His
early dislike of Bragg changed slowly to admiration. In November 1862 Ellis wrote his father, "We do nothing in this department nor will the matter be mended as long as our poor partisan
President keeps this miserable tyrant Bragg at the head of
affairs." In December of the same year, he wrote his sister: "I
wish, I long to come home, but I can't for old Bragg would
rather see a man hung than have a leave of absence and Bragg is
right, for we need every man at his post now." In July 1863 Ellis
happily informed his brother that Beauregard might replace
Bragg. "Yet I do not want Bragg . . . taken away from the Army,"
admitted Ellis. "Let Beauregard supervise and Bragg . . . discipline. Bragg is one of the greatest of our leaders and though the
present generation will not do him justice, Time the great rectifi-
er, and History will." Ellis wrote in October 1863: "Bragg is truly
a great man; he metes out justice to the high as well as [to] the
low." Ellis concluded in his last letter home, written in November 1863, just before he was captured, that it was the "firm and
unbending justice [Bragg] . . . meted out . . . to his Generals, his
Colonels, his captains and privates alike that brings the ire of
officers high in rank down upon General Bragg." The troops
loved Bragg, insisted Ellis:

His army has been held together and has been so disciplined and organized by him as to nearly compensate in

efficiency what it has sadly lacked in numbers. All this is attributable to General Bragg. The papers say he is incompetent! His career and history gives this the lie! They say the army has no confidence in him, but as I know the men of this army (and my acquaintance extends to many Brigades including men from every state) I am prepared to pronounce this like the former, a lie. No army ever had more confidence in its leaders and Napoleon's guard never followed his eagles more enthusiastically than this ragged army has and will follow the lead of its gaunt grim chieftain.

Unpublished letters and diaries suggest that Bragg was neither as unpopular nor as tyrannical as most historians claim. A soldier said most men knew Bragg only as a "chieftain of rough and somewhat forbidding exterior," but this was only because he "avoided giving public evidence of the tender feeling" he had "for the suffering and unfortunate." One staff colonel noted, "I was too frequently cognizant of [Bragg's] . . . good deeds of mercy to delinquents . . . to let him rest under the imputation of a heartless man, or one who wielded his great power cruelly."

Throughout the war Bragg took a sincere interest in the welfare of his soldiers. He was constantly about their camps, checking, inspecting, questioning, setting things right. Were they getting enough to eat? Did their clothing fit? Did their tents leak? Often he visited the hospitals and cheered the wounded with his sometimes less than humorous jokes. On one visit he told some ladies who were comforting the patients that if one of their sweethearts died, "they must hug the harder with the one that was left." The following day Bragg wrote his wife: "The ladies seemed to enjoy my little jest as much as the men, and all were better for a little diversion."

Bragg was a diligent commander. He rose early, retired late, ate little, and drank less. A soldier called Bragg "industry personified." Recalled a staff officer, "He was untiring in his labors, methodical and systematic in the discharge of business." A chaplain wrote, "whenever or wherever I have seen Bragg, I have found him at work;—night and day, always laboring for the cause;—thinking not of self indulgence or enjoyment;—living hard!" Lt. Gen. Richard Taylor said that he had never "known a more conscientious . . . man" than Bragg. "Whatever may have been General Bragg's defects," wrote a colonel, "he was conspicuous for one trait . . . , a profound sense of public duty."

Moreover, Bragg was a talented organizer and disciplinarian. After taking command of Gen. P.G.T. Beauregard's disorganized forces at Tupelo, Mississippi, in June 1862, he developed the second finest army in the Confederacy. "Bragg is beyond doubt the best disciplinarian in the South," a soldier wrote in September 1862. "When he took command . . . the army was little better than a Mob. . . . Firearms could be heard at all hours of the day. Now a gun is never fired without orders from the Brigade Commanders. Bragg had one man shot for discharging his gun without orders. . . . Since that time the discipline of the troops [has] improved very much. Men are not apt to disobey orders when they know death is the punishment."

As a disciplinarian, Bragg "far surpassed any of the [other] senior Confederate generals," stated General Taylor. And according to Union general L.H. Rousseau, "all the officers who knew Bragg [before the Civil War] thought he was perhaps the best disciplinarian in the United States Army. . . . That is the universal opinion as far as I have heard, and I have conversed with a great many of the old Regular Army officers." Discipline occupied a special place in Bragg's thinking. He once wrote his friend William T. Sherman: "Where do we find the fewest mutinies, revolts and rebellions? In the best disciplined commands. Human nature is the same throughout the world. Give us all disciplined masters, managers, and assistants, and we shall never hear of insurrection." The entire Confederacy could have used more of Bragg's discipline.

It is sometimes forgotten that Bragg was the Army of Tennessee's most successful commander; after eighteen months and five major campaigns under his leadership, that army was still one of the best fighting forces ever organized in North America. In March 1863 Gen. Joseph E. Johnston informed his friend Sen. Louis T. Wigfall: "I think you under rate [Bragg]. . . . he has exhibited great energy & discretion in his operations. . . . Thinking that great injustice has been done to him by the country— that is to say by the press & congress—I should regret very much to see him removed. Since the battle at Murfreesboro he has brought up his army to its former strength—indeed to a greater [strength]. This could have been done by nobody else."

Though by no means the Confederacy's worst general, Bragg was not as able as Johnston's letter suggested. After the war Beauregard called Bragg "a good subordinate" but an "inferior" commander. Another officer, Col. John H. Savage, was more blunt: "Bragg had none of the instincts and elements of a great soldier."

Notoriously inept at getting along with people he disliked, Bragg failed to win the loyalty of his chief lieutenants. His disputes with subordinates eventually undermined his army's morale and efficiency. Bragg was not solely responsible for these quarrels; yet he contributed to each.

He had been contentious throughout his career. A man who knew Bragg well told him: "Your best friends admit that your temper is irritable—that under excitement you are sometimes harsh when there is no necessity for it & sometimes even wound an innocent man." Ulysses S. Grant, who had served with Bragg in the U.S. Army before the Civil War, remembered him as "a remarkably intelligent and well-informed man, professionally and otherwise," who had an "irascible temper, and was naturally disputatious." Despite a high moral character and correct habits, Bragg "was in frequent trouble. As a subordinate he was always on the lookout to catch his commanding officer infringing his prerogatives; as a post commander he was equally vigilant to detect the slightest neglect, even of the most trivial order." Grant recalled a popular story about Bragg, who at the time was both company commander and company quartermaster. "As commander of the company he made a requisition upon the quartermaster—himself—for something he wanted. As quartermaster he declined to fill the requisition, and endorsed on the back of it his reasons for so doing. As company commander he responded to this, urging that his requisition called for nothing but what he was entitled to, and that it was the duty of the quartermaster to fill it. As quartermaster he still persisted that he was right." Unable to resolve the dilemma, Bragg referred the whole matter to the post commander, who exclaimed: "My God, Mr. Bragg, you have quarreled with every officer in the army, and now you are quarreling with yourself."

Poor health doubtless was one reason for Bragg's cantankerousness. Throughout the Civil War Bragg suffered from a number of complaints and illnesses. His persistent sickness helped make his "temper sour and petulant." Often he was too sick to command. In the spring of 1863, a siege of boils resulted in what Bragg called "a general break-down." He continued working and insisted he was still fit, but Lt. Gen. William J. Hardee considered Bragg too feeble "either to examine and determine his line of battle or to take command on the field." English colonel James Fremantle, who saw Bragg about this time, also noticed how weak he looked. "He is very thin," reported Fremantle. "He stoops, and has a sickly, cadaverous, haggard appearance." Bragg "was mentally and physically an old, wornout man, unfit to actively manage an army in the field," charged one of his regimental commanders.

Some of his illness—and perhaps his often erratic and irascible behavior—may have been caused by the medicine Bragg took. Before the war he admitted that he was suffering from his "old Florida complaint of the liver. . . . Every summer I have these attacks," he explained to a friend, "and I can now only keep about by almost living on Mercury (Blue Mass & Calomel).

No constitution can stand it."

Whatever the cause, Bragg lacked that imperturbability and resolution so necessary in field commanders. He did not have that "will to win" that made such commanders as Grant and R. E. Lee great generals. Bragg was courageous and at times imaginative, resourceful, and bold. But he was never patient, either with his own men or with the enemy; he was unable to wait out his opponents. During battle he became unduly excited, at times confused and almost panicky. Often he "is as blind as a bat to the circumstances surrounding him," admitted his chief of staff. At Perryville and Murfreesboro, Bragg lost his nerve; under the strain of combat, he changed from a bold aggressor to a cautious retreater.

Two additional characteristics hampered Bragg as a field general. He was temperamentally unsuited to lead an army composed overwhelmingly of individualistic citizen-soldiers. By training and preference, Bragg was a regular-army man, contemptuous of volunteers and a democratic military establishment. He strongly objected to the Confederate policy of letting troops elect their own officers. "I have . . . neither the capacity nor the desire to command troops, where the officers are made subservient to the men by this disorganizing and ever recurring universal suffrage," Bragg informed the government in 1862.

Even more significant, Bragg was a mediocre tactician. He was unimpressed by the tactical revolution that during the Civil War gradually shifted the advantages that attackers had long enjoyed to entrenched defenders armed with rifled muskets and supported by artillery. In nearly all of his battles, Bragg was the attacker. Such tactics cost him more casualties than he inflicted; he never entrenched his army and let the enemy attack him. "General Bragg says heavy intrenchments demoralize our troops," reported President Davis's aide. Had Bragg been receptive to the lessons of the tactical revolution, he would not have ordered repeated infantry charges against strongly posted Federals at Shiloh, Perryville, Murfreesboro, and Chickamauga; nor would he have rejected the opportunity to entrench as he did at Murfreesboro and elsewhere.

Despite all these shortcomings, Bragg might have been successful if he had learned from his own mistakes. Some of his contemporaries grew as soldiers as the war progressed, but Bragg was little better as a combat leader at the end than he had been at the beginning. He had not developed that flexibility, the ability to modify his tactics to meet a new situation, which all students of the art of war consider indispensable to a great soldier. Bragg had perfected neither an efficient intelligence system nor a capable staff to assess information and to make plans. At times he had moved his forces rapidly and deceived the enemy, but he had demonstrated little understanding of the economy of war. Repeatedly, he had wasted men in rash attacks when he could have accomplished much more by skillful defenses at a fraction of the cost to the Confederacy. As for security, he obviously had not heeded Frederick the Great's advice: "Never deceive yourself, but picture skillfully all the measures that the enemy will take to oppose your plans, in order never to be caught by surprise. Then, having foreseen everything in advance, you will already have remedies prepared for any eventuality."

Though Bragg had little talent for field command, he had characteristics that the Confederacy needed desperately but used inadequately. Intelligent, diligent, and patriotic, Bragg by all accounts was an excellent organizer and disciplinarian. He "possessed qualifications such as, rightly directed, would have made him as great in the Confederate army as Moltke in the Prussian," asserted Col. J. Stoddard Johnston, a staff officer. Higher-ranking officers also thought that the president should have appointed Bragg inspector general or chief of staff of the Confederate armies. In February 1863 Beauregard wrote Confederate congressman William Porcher Miles, chairman of the House Military Committee, "with Bragg in [Adjutant and Inspector General Samuel] Cooper's place . . . all would go right." And in March 1863 Lt. Gen. Leonidas Polk asked President Davis to transfer Bragg "to another field, where his peculiar talent—that of organization and discipline—could find a more ample scope. For that kind of service he has, undoubtedly, peculiar talent. . . . His tastes and natural inclination fit him for it. . . . The application of that talent is not always easy or agreeable where it exists, yet there are few armies which would not be benefited by it. . . . My opinion is that the general could be of service to all the armies of the Confederacy, if placed in the proper position. Such a position would be that of . . . Inspector-General. . . . The whole family of idlers, drones, and shirks, of high or low degree, far and near, would feel his searching hand and be made to take their places and do their duty."

That a bad general could make such a good suggestion enhances slightly the bishop's standing. But it is surprising that the president ignored his friend's excellent proposal. One of the great ironies of Confederate military history is that Jefferson Davis, who prided himself so on his knowledge of the capabilities of those former regular-army officers who fought for the South, failed early in the war to assign Bragg to a position where his talents could be best used. Instead, the president placed and retained Bragg in a post—as commander of the South's second most important army—where he made a major contribution not to Confederate victory but to Confederate defeat.

CHAPTER FIFTEEN
An "Unsuccessful" Davis Biographer

A scholar defined Francis Butler Simkins as "one of the most interesting intellectual forces of his generation." As an academic who questioned conventional thinking, he "helped lay the foundation for the Civil Rights Movement." Yet when these momentous events of the 1950s and 1960s challenged the traditional order in the American South, Simkins "discovered much . . . that he believed should be conserved and [thus] became a spokesman for tradition."

I knew him only from 1950 until his death in 1966. He was a complex individual who enjoyed nothing more than questioning and offering a fresh look at the past. He delighted in ideas and unusual individuals; only dullness bored him. As a scholar, he stood ahead of most of his contemporaries, not just because of his perceptive views and insights but also because he wrote the kind of history that upset people—Northerners as well as Southerners.

Born in Edgefield, South Carolina, December 14, 1897, Simkins took his undergraduate degree in 1918 from the University of South Carolina, where he studied history with Prof. Yates Snowden. In 1920 he received his M.A. and in 1926 a Ph.D., both from Columbia University.

During the next forty years, Simkins became a distinguished historian, teaching briefly as a regular or a visiting professor at a number of institutions: Randolph Macon College, the University of North Carolina, Emory University, Louisiana State University, the University of Mississippi, Mississippi State University, the University of Texas, and the University of Massachusetts. But he spent most of his long academic career at Longwood College in Farmville, Virginia.

A great teacher whose students called him "Doc," his tech-

Francis Butler Simkins

nique was simple; he made friends with his students and treated them as a patient father would his children. I recall how Doc dealt with my first graduate paper, written in the summer of 1950 at Louisiana State University. After reading what I had written, he invited me to discuss it with him at a campus cafe. He paid for our iced tea with the most crumpled dollar bill I had ever seen, which he finally found, after a lengthy search, deep in one of his pockets. He told me that he liked my paper (its thesis probably appealed to his iconoclastic nature), but he explained—tactfully, to avoid hurting my feelings—that my "effort" needed revision before an editor would consider it for publication. When I expressed fear that I lacked the skill to make a significant improvement on what I had done, Doc offered to become my coauthor. I accepted, and one hot day our collaboration began. Under the shade of a great live oak (neither faculty offices nor the library were air conditioned then), he rewrote our piece; Doc scratched out my awkward and amateurish words, moved sentences about, and added colorful phrases. What he did both amazed and pleased me. He turned a rough draft into an article. More important to me, he explained why he thought certain words or phrases belonged or did not belong; graciously he asked me—and always got—my approval of each change. It seems to me, looking back, that I learned a good bit about writing that day.

During his career, Doc received many honors: the Dunning Prize, the Guggenheim Fellowship, the Fleming Foundation Lectureship, a number of other awards, and election in 1954 as president of the Southern Historical Association, which much later honored him by establishing the Francis Butler Simkins Prize awarded for the best first book in Southern history.

An appropriate honor, this book award, because Doc wrote so ably and sympathetically about the South. His most important works were *The Tillman Movement in South Carolina*, published in 1928; *South Carolina during Reconstruction*, published in 1932 and written with Robert H. Woody; *Pitchfork Ben Tillman*, published in 1944; *A History of the South*, published in 1947, with many subsequent revised editions; and finally *The Everlasting South*, published in 1963.

In his early works, when most historians still accepted the traditional view of Reconstruction, Doc become one of the first revisionists. During the 1930s and 1940s, because his work placed blacks at the center of Reconstruction history, progressive liberals claimed him as a hero. But after World War II, when nearly all historians boasted of their liberalism, Doc became one of the few vocal conservatives in the profession. "His study of Reconstruction in South Carolina . . . seemed to put him among the enlightened revisionists of the dark period," wrote his friend and coauthor Robert H. Woody. "But more and more he came to stress the distinctive characteristics of the 'everlasting South,' and to question the validity of such that passed for progress in the modern South. His forte was the propounding of ideas rather than the systematic marshalling of facts. He was a stimulating conversationalist, a ready lecturer, and always boldly free to give a reason for the faith that was in him."

Another academic who knew Simkins considered him "the most informal man" he ever met. Gregarious and overflowing with challenging questions, Doc enjoyed interesting people, but if the conversation lagged, he often dozed. As a friend admitted, Doc could not "endure being bored by an empty mind." When the new president of the Southern Historical Association came on stage during the annual banquet, he snoozed through the presidential address. He did the same at the home of his department chairman at Louisiana State, who inflicted a violin solo upon his guests after dinner. The story of Doc's sleeping through the chairman's solo spread across campus, delighting faculty and students, who had nicknamed the outraged administrator "the pope" to emphasize his pompous and overbearing ways. But the sleeping incident doubtless speeded Doc's leaving LSU and returning to Longwood, where he happily reported, "They don't understand me but they tolerate me."

Another example of how his informality often upset people

occurred just before Doc left LSU. Taking advantage of an open invitation to drop by and discuss books, a graduate student called at Doc's home one afternoon. Doc and his young son, Chip, had been taking a nap in the summer heat and humidity that made pre–air conditioned Baton Rouge so uncomfortable. Both came to greet their visitor. Because they had been napping naked, they answered the door without either attire or embarrassment. The startled visitor, suddenly aware that neither Chip nor his father intended to burden themselves with clothing, admonished, "For Heaven's sake, Doc, go put some clothes on."

Doc's dress, as well as his undress, attracted attention. He usually dressed correctly, though often in a somewhat careless, quaint style. On trips he frequently wore an old homburg hat. As you may know, homburgs used to be stylish, but Doc never gave his hat a fraction of the care and attention it needed. So instead of adding to his appearance, his hat gave him an outdated and slightly scruffy look.

Nearly daily a dressing difficulty surfaced. Doc had trouble keeping his shirttail in his trousers; usually by midmorning half or more of it had escaped. After years of patient effort, his wife finally taught him to tuck it into his shorts. Yet even that failed. By afternoon Doc's shirttail might still be inside his shorts, but by then his trousers had slipped down several inches below the tops of his shorts.

Toenails were another problem—Doc never cut them. But because his shoes hurt his feet, he always removed his shoes during seminars and propped his feet up on a chair, displaying quite unselfconsciously the huge holes his long toenails had cut through his socks.

I doubt that Doc's wife Margaret ever accused him of being too informal, but I know she did call him a number of things. One of her milder charges was that he could wreck a house with only a New York Times and an orange. His habit was to peel and discard pieces of both as he walked through the house. He had a curious habit of playing with a newspaper—that is, tearing off pieces, rolling them, sticking them in his ear, and then tossing them aside.

One of his former students, after visiting the Simkins family, claimed that Doc rejected the germ theory of disease. It seems that he decided to invite his guests out in the yard and treat them to some homemade ice cream, which he somehow managed to prepare without accident in a primitive freezer. The trouble began when Doc opened the container and began dispensing ice cream to his guests. At that point several neighboring dogs joined the party. As the dogs attempted to get into the ice cream container, Doc continued to serve his guests with a wooden spoon that he also used to beat off the dogs. Soon he got ice cream on the dogs and dog hair on the spoon and in the ice cream. Undaunted, Doc discarded the spoon and, in the words of his horrified guest, "stuck his grubby little hand down in the container and began scooping out and serving ice cream mixed with dog hair."

At cocktail parties Doc remained courteous and mannerly while eating everything on his plate with his fingers, whether it was finger food or not. As one observer noted, Doc's tastes were catholic. His friends certainly never doubted his appreciation of good food and drink. Eating with Doc could be a memorable experience. On our first visit to New Orleans, he informed me that any good restaurant had checkered tablecloths and male waiters. He also introduced me to lobster, telling me, a country boy from north Louisiana, that it was just a big Yankee crawfish.

He was generous and so was his wife. During the first week of my graduate career, I was alone in a room used by graduate assistants when Doc opened the door and asked, "Have you eaten?" I had not, and he invited me to his home for lunch. At the university parking lot, he handed me his car keys, saying, "You drive." Before doing so, I had to repair a badly bent windshield wiper that had been scraping the windshield rather than wiping it.

Doc was no mechanic; nor had he called ahead to prepare his wife for our coming. When we arrived at his house, he said,

"you wait here." I had no idea why I should remain in the car
while he went inside to eat. I was already beginning to realize
that Doc was not just informal; he was downright eccentric. But
soon he emerged from his house, waved to me and announced,
"Come on in, Margaret says it's okay." The lunch, featuring a
delicious homemade soup, was excellent.

Doc loved tasty food as well as visiting in the grand old
Southern style. While single, "Old Fetch" Simkins, as he was
affectionately called, frequently spent months at a time with various prosperous families, enjoying their comfortable homes. A
number of South Carolinians boasted that "Old Fetch" not only
spent the winter with their family but also claimed he wrote a
specific book while visiting them. The trouble was that different
families claimed him for the same book! He readily availed himself of their openhanded hospitality so frequently and for such
long periods of time that some wit claimed Doc's initials stood
not for Francis Butler Simkins but for "Free Board" Simkins.

Once when he was visiting a professor at Princeton University, Doc stayed overnight with my wife and me in New York City,
where our accommodations failed to match the plantation hospitality he had enjoyed as a young man. We lived in a cramped
apartment befitting graduate students. Unfortunately, while
using our small bathroom, Doc dropped and broke his false
teeth. This upset him tremendously, because he feared his wife
would badger him if he returned to Princeton with broken teeth.
"Margaret thinks I'm a damn fool anyway," he admitted.

To ease his dread, I called a place that promised to repair his
teeth within a few hours and off we went on the subway to find
it. Assured that he would not have to go back to New Jersey
with broken teeth, Doc thoroughly enjoyed our wait to have
them fixed. He quickly decided we would lunch at a place that
served German food and beer. Without his teeth, Doc had a few
problems with the food, but he compensated by indulging himself with beer.

Doc may have been a sensualist, but he was too innocent to

be a lady's man. I recall a story told by his wife, who informed Doc when he came home one afternoon that she had been to visit the doctor. Preoccupied with something else, Doc asked vaguely about Dr. Smith's health. Margaret informed him that she had not been to see Dr. Smith about his health but her own. Sitting Doc down, she told him she had some important news— she was pregnant. This shocked him so much that Doc stammered a bit before apologetically admitting, "My God, Margaret, I feel partly responsible."

Because Doc was so kind and unassuming, so hospitable and courteous, everyone who loved him forgave his faults. Knowing that his wife never gave him more than a dollar at a time, for he invariably lost whatever money he had with him, we joked about his carelessness and forgetfulness. Graduate students put their theses and dissertations in Doc's hands with mixed emotions. They appreciated his careful editing and helpful suggestions for improving their work, but they lamented his habit of misplacing and sometimes actually losing some of their pages. They all admitted that Doc took as much care with their manuscripts as he did with his own, but it came to be expected that he would lose several pages of any paper he read. I recall him complaining to me at a history conference that he had misplaced some of the essay he had intended to present and had been compelled to scratch out a replacement in longhand from memory.

Ordinarily, Doc wrote at odd hours on an antique typewriter. An early riser, he liked to set up under a shady tree at first light, but when his noisy typing in his yard annoyed his neighbors, he removed his table and typewriter to the local graveyard, where apparently his hunt-and-peck typing disturbed not a soul.

What distinguished him from so many of his contemporaries was that he refused to truckle to current historical fads; indeed, to use his phrase, he believed that historians ought to "tolerate the past." Unlike many historians of the South, Doc was unashamed of being a Southerner; he was proud of his origins and ancestry. This alone, he knew, was reason enough for most

Yankees and "Yankeefied" Southerners to object to his views.

Doc wrote about a wide range of Southerners but concentrated on understanding and justifying historically the plain white people of the South, especially postbellum Southerners and such of their heroes as Benjamin R. (Pitchfork Ben) Tillman of South Carolina.

"I do not attempt to emphasize here the contributions of the South to the history of the United States," Doc explained in his Southern history textbook. "I propose instead to stress those political and social traits that make the region between the Potomac and the Rio Grande a cultural province conscious of its identity." To him the changes that occurred over time in the South were not nearly as significant as the persistence of cultural continuity in the region. "The militant nationalism of the Southern people supplemented rather than diminished their provincialism; devotion to state and region went along with devotion to the United States," Doc observed. "Gloating pride in growing cities and imported industries went along with retention of country habits. The interest of the youth of the region in rifles, dogs, and wildlife, like that of the Virginia gentlemen of the eighteenth century, was often greater than their interest in classroom studies."

Doc often provoked conventional historians by saying or writing things that they did not want to hear. Invited to become a visiting professor at the University of British Columbia, he willingly admitted to the administrators that he was something probably no Canadian university had ever had on its faculty— the grandson of a Confederate field officer. Doc even delighted in revealing the full name and regiment of his ancestor—Lt. Col. John Calhoun Simkins of the 3d South Carolina Artillery.

At times Doc seemed to do and say things just to shock people. A few months before his death, I saw him at a party in Richmond, Virginia, arm-in-arm with Prof. Eugene D. Genovese. Doc was taking this famous radical historian about and, to their mutual delight, introducing him to the most sheltered of Southern ladies with these words, "I'll bet you never met a real live communist before!"

He sometimes acted the bumpkin, but seriousness prevailed when he spoke or wrote in opposition to the nationalizing of Southern history. In his Southern Historical Association presidential address, "Tolerating the South's Past," he denounced the tendency of modern historians to judge the South and its people by the modern standards of today rather than by those of the past. "Chroniclers of Southern history," he charged, "often do not grasp the most elementary concept of sound historiography: the ability to appraise the past by standards other than those of the present. They accept a fanatical nationalism which leaves little room for sectional variations, a faith in Darwinian progress which leaves no room for static contentment, and a faith in the American dream of human equality which leaves little room for one person to get ahead of another except in making money."

In his later years, Doc knew that most historians disagreed with his views. He also understood that his outspoken opinions, together with his personal eccentricities, kept him from receiving either the academic position or the professional recognition that his ability merited. He once said, regarding a paper he was about to deliver at a history conference, "I fear it will be hooted by patriotic Southerners who are ashamed of the South."

He confessed to me in 1961, "I have submitted about 10 of my essays to LSU Press, but I fear they will be adjudged too reactionary." When, to his surprise, they agreed to publish his essays, he discovered that he still had a problem. He feared that it would be impossible to get a Southern historian to endorse his book. "If I was young enough to be ambitious I would shut my mouth," Doc wrote. "The New York Times magazine editor called me up, asking me to write an article, and then changed his mind in another phone call."

Doc wisely turned for an endorsement of his final book, The Everlasting South, to his former student, coauthor, and friend Charles P. Roland, then a distinguished historian at the University of Kentucky. "Probably a great majority of historians today disagree with Professor Simkins' logic," Roland admitted in his foreword. "But probably a great majority of the common folk of the South, wittingly or unwittingly, agree with the gist of it."

Just as Doc expected, nationalistic historians generally ignored or dismissed *The Everlasting South* as the work of an aberrant. "Conservatism gets no attention in the U.S.," Doc complained. "Everyone, even multimillionaires, imagine themselves radicals."

In the late 1950s and early 1960s, powerful people in publishing either rejected Doc's work or forced him to modify it to suit liberal values. "While [in New York City] . . . I delivered the ms of 'The Seaboard South' . . . to A.A. Knopf in a short interview along with a letter of commendation of my effort from Prof. Walter Johnson, editor of the series," wrote Simkins in 1959. "Knopf then went into a gassy tirade saying Walter and the other contributors to the regional history series were no good. I left feeling rather gloomy thinking that despite my contract, the autocratic old publisher will throw my ms out of the window."

A few weeks later Doc received a letter that confirmed what he had feared. "Knopf sent me a devastating report on my book which may indicate that I shall not be able to revise it to his satisfaction," Doc admitted. "A very able critic of the neo-abolitionist variety . . . is adverse to the idea of trying to treat the Seaboard South as a separate segment of the nation and he seems to think the only wise way to treat the Radicals, Bourbons, Negroes, and the Agrarians is in the [C. Vann] Woodward manner. But at least the objections to my book are concrete, and it may be possible to meet many of them. Knopf accepts what this critic says as gospel and the only way I could have of evading the criticism would be to throw the ms in the garbage. Naturally I am discouraged. . . . I hate like hell to abandon 'The Seaboard.' I foolishly abandoned [writing a biography of Jefferson] Davis in favor of it. It is not supposed to be original scholarship, and I may not have the flair to write semi-popular stuff."

Despite various attempts to revise that manuscript, including seeking a coauthor who was closer to what Doc called "the Knopf-Woodward-University of NC Press . . . position than I am," "The Seaboard South" never found a publisher. But this was not because Doc insisted that his work be published without alterations; he accepted criticism, even when he disagreed with it, and he believed ardently that revision improved his writing.

On another occasion, he confessed: "At the suggestion of [Prof. Howard] Quint I rewrote the article on 'Reconstruction,' eliminating most of the Confederate 'bias.' He said my 1st version was too 'conventional,' so I have gone all out for revision."

Doc could be amazingly forbearing of those who refused to tolerate either his work or the South's past. "As I grow older I try to be free of prejudice and at the same time tolerate the prejudices of others," he wrote just before his death. He liked thoughtful people regardless of what they believed. For example, he strongly supported the appointment of an Italian-Irish Catholic, a New Yorker, to the history faculty at Longwood. "I believe L[ongwood] will be satisfied with T., but will T. be satisfied with this place?" Doc asked. "I want you to write him a note in the light of your acquaintance with the Farmville community. Tell him we have a teachers' college, [but that] we are tolerant enough to keep . . . diverse persons. He seems civilized and animated enough not to make the girls sleep. [Tell him that] this is a Protestant community, but it has a thriving Catholic [church]. One can get away with being an integrationist. The town is provincial, but tolerant of mannerly Yankees and other foreigners."

In his attempt to "tell the stark truth" as he saw it, Doc never pulled his punches, not even on "big name" historians. "Allan Nevins spent the day here [at Longwood] lecturing on the glories of Big Business," Doc once observed. "The Old Abolitionist spoke in private bitterly of the persecution of the Negro [but kept quiet on this subject in his public speech]. Of course all liked his glorification of Rockefeller and Ford."

Doc was always modest. For a time there were two doctors named Simkins in Farmville—one was a black M.D. When Doc received phone calls asking if he was Doctor Simkins, he always answered: "Yes, but I'm not the one that can do you any good." To a critic who complained about a paper that Doc proposed to read at an historical meeting, he replied: "I am distressed that . . . you are upset by the tone of the paper I plan to read. Seemingly I have given you too severe a dose of Southern prejudice. I am taking [out] some of the phrases . . . as tactless and in bad taste . . . I like to be frank but I do not wish to offend unduly."

In his letter to this outraged Northerner, Doc explained what he believed was his responsibility, as an historian of the South, to the Southern plain folk. "You may not understand that I am attempting to give what actually the ordinary white Southerner thinks," he wrote.

> Our press—liberal and reactionary—and our politicians will not give publicity to what is actually happening; they want to be overtactful so as to attract Northern industry. . . . As a historian I believe that all significant historical events—even Nazi Germany and Communist Russia— have explanations—perhaps even justifications. This even applies to the South. The historians, even the Southern ones . . . , have of late abandoned the Southern heritage.
>
> The common white people—except as they try to lure Northern investors—have not. Don't you think they have the right—at least in an historical session—to be justified?

Doc once told me that there were many disappointments in scholarship. He certainly had his share, especially toward the end of his career. Dismissed from LSU in 1951, Doc returned to Longwood, where he had taught happily for twenty years before going to Louisiana and where he would spend his remaining years. "The work [here at Longwood] is quite elementary," he explained. "I like that. It is conducive to . . . research. . . . Getting hired in a teachers' college may be terminal," he admitted, "but it may lead to greater scholarship. You have freedom here to be a good or a bad teacher, to be lazy or industrious." Later he stated: "I like this place. I don't give all my time to the students' frolics. They tolerate me and I have more time for my work than I did at L.S.U." Yet in giving students advice, he warned that they might be making a mistake to follow his example. Those who hoped to become successful historians should "not stay in the South"; anyone who did remain "would [soon] be talking about autos, how wonderful the little college is, and grinning at the girls."

Though he never expected liberals to admire his work, Doc was disappointed that Southerners so often misunderstood and rejected his views. During his last years, as his health failed, a touch of despair seemed mixed with his characteristic energy and enthusiasm. "I have about completed for Van Nostrand . . . a paperback, 'The Reconstruction of the South, 1865–1965,'" which he wrote just before his death. "It may be too pessimistic to please."

His greatest disappointment was that he had not spent the last years of his life on a biography of Jefferson Davis. "God, I wish I were working on J. Davis," Doc wrote in May 1958; "I am—perhaps 6 or 7 hours a day—grinding out something on the Seaboard South. It may be worth little; just a pot-boiler." A year later, he complained: "I regret much having not continued with my Davis. It was a great error to turn aside for the Seaboard South. . . . If Knopf reacts favorably to my [Seaboard South] b[oo]k, I shall go again after J. Davis. . . . I have written about 1/3 of it in long hand. I'll copy that off on triple-space typewriter. That will perhaps give me enthusiasm to write the rest. I should never allowed myself to be diverted to the Seaboard book." Four years later he lamented: "I regret getting diverted from Jeff Davis. If I am not too old I'll return to that thesis." Doc was then sixty-six; he never got back to his biography of the Confederate president.

Believing just as Davis did in tolerating and justifying the South's past, Doc doubtless would have given his hero a sympathetic yet critical understanding that he deserved but had not received at that time. "The historian of the South should join the social novelist who accepts the values of the age and the section about which he writes," Doc declared. "He should learn to identify truth with facts. By mixing sympathy, understanding, and a bit of kindness with his history, he might attract the people about whom he writes to read his books. And this could be done without sacrificing scholarly integrity."

Doc's most lasting contribution to his native land may not have been his fine study of Reconstruction in South Carolina, or his excellent biography of Ben Tillman, or even his popular History of The South, but rather his understanding that it is just as possible and just as scholarly for historians to be Southerners as it is for them to be Americans. Historians of the South should not be "ashamed of the peculiar standards of their section," Doc declared. "Some of them write 'the literature of accommodation.' The Southern historian [Douglas Southall Freeman], who has won the greatest applause, writes of the heroes of the Confederacy without arguing whether or not they were quixotic. The best recognized historian of the Old South [Ulrich B. Phillips] pictures plantation life without assuming that it was a grand mistake. Another historian examines the literature of the poor whites without moralizing against them because they were not as thrifty as their social betters. A recent historian of the New South joins William Faulkner in exposing the true tragedy of the South; it was not the defeat at Appomattox, but the truckling of both scalawag and Bourbon, both materialist and idealist, to alien values."

As Doc lay dying, he made two requests: first, "I hope you can help me defend the toleration of the past, which I think is the chief duty of the historian"; second, "Don't forget me." How could a Southern historian fail to tolerate the South's past, and **who could forget Doc?**

CHAPTER SIXTEEN
The Unforgiven President

During and after the Civil War, Jefferson Davis was accused of a wide range of villainies. Not all of his accusers were Yankees— a former member of his cabinet denounced Davis as a "scoundrel," and a popular Southern writer called the Confederate president senile and foolish.

But the most extensive and lasting attacks on Davis were made by Northerners. In a letter embossed with an American eagle crushing "Secession" and "cotton" in its talons but holding proudly in its beak a U.S. flag and a banner announcing "Death to Traitors," a man from Rochester, New York, wrote: "Now Jeff Davis you rebel traitor here is the beauty of America one of the greatest treasures that ever waved over your sinful head. Now I want you to look at this motto and think of me for I say death to cession [sic] and death to all traitors to their country and these cession [sic] and death to all traitors to their country and these are my sentiments exactly. Yours not with respect for I can never respect a traitor to his Country a cursed traitor." The same view of Davis as being "among the archtraitors in our annals" was expressed just as emphatically in 1887 by Theodore Roosevelt and Harvard University professor Albert T. Perkins.

Davis quickly became, and would remain to most Northerners, the quintessential wrongdoer. Immediately after the war Federal authorities put Davis in jail, and left him there for two years without trial, while they tried to implicate him in the assassination of Abraham Lincoln, the alleged cruelty to Andersonville prisoners, and treason itself. Though never brought to trial or convicted of any crime, Davis was much abused by Yan-

An older Jefferson Davis

kees in the press and on the podium. Between 1863 and 1866 in *The New York Times* alone, he was depicted as a murderer, a cruel slaveowner whose servants all ran away, a liar, a boaster, a fanatic, a confessed failure, a hater, a political adventurer, a supporter of outcasts and outlaws, a drunkard, an atrocious misrepresenter, an assassin, an incendiary, a criminal who was gratified by the assassination of Lincoln, a henpecked husband, a man so shameless that he would try to escape capture by disguising himself as a woman, a supporter of murder plots, an insubordinate soldier, an unwholesome sleeper, and a malingerer.

Several incidents suggest that anti-Davis sentiment was more than mere newspaper talk. Just after the war the citizens of Sacramento, California, true to their vigilante tradition, hanged Davis in effigy. A few months later the Kansas Senate passed a resolution to hang him in person. More than ten years after the war ended, there was still widespread opposition to his being allowed to speak anywhere in the North. In 1876 an editor answered the question "ought Davis to be given amnesty" with a resounding "no," and in 1880 a man was shot in Madison, Indiana, because he cheered for Jefferson Davis.

"Malice and slander have exhausted their power against you," a Southerner assured Davis in 1884, but that speaker was wrong. Davis continued to be criticized and sneered at in such repeated stories as his supposed attempt to escape capture by dressing in "petticoats." An observer wrote in 1898, "I believe there never was a time when a whole people were more willing to punish one man than were the people of the North . . . to punish Mr. Davis for his alleged crimes." As late as 1907, eighteen years after his death, handbills accusing Davis of complicity in Lincoln's assassination were still being displayed. And in 1909 an editorial was published in *The New York Times* denouncing the plans of a Southerner to present for use on the new battleship USS *Mississippi* a silver service with the likeness of Jefferson Davis etched on each piece.

More than a hundred years passed before the Congress of the

United States officially forgave Jefferson Davis for being president of the Confederacy. No other Confederate leader had to wait so long for either official or unofficial exoneration. By the early 1900s, Robert E. Lee, the greatest Yankee killer of all time, had become a national hero, absolved of his sins. Soon he was considered so harmless that the government would allow his picture to be hung on the walls of Southern public schools alongside those of Washington and Lincoln.

The failure of Davis to receive a reprieve, even after his death, bothered many Southerners. "Mr. Davis was never a particular friend to me or mine," wrote John S. Wise in 1905. "I never believed he was a very great man, or even the best President the Confederate States might have had. But he was our President. Whatever shortcomings he may have had, he was a brave, conscientious and loyal son of the South. He did his best, to the utmost of his ability, for the Southern cause. He, without being a whit worse than the rest of us, was made to suffer for us as was no other man in the Confederacy. And through it all he never, to the day of his death, failed to maintain the honor and the dignity of the trust confided to his keeping. Yet the North seems not to have forgiven him." Wise could not understand why. It all seemed so unfair. "It distresses me to this day," he admitted, "whenever I hear anybody speak disparagingly of this man, who was unquestionably devoted to the cause for which he lived and died, and who was infinitely greater than his traducers."

Davis was well aware that he was a special target for criticism. He rejected an invitation to visit the North in 1875, he explained, because "the tide of unreasoning prejudice against me, in your section, was too strong to be resisted." Davis also thought he knew why he was so despised. "The portion of the people of the North who are the least informed as to the events immediately preceding the war between the states have naturally fallen into the erroneous belief that I instigated and precipitated it," claimed Davis. "Demagogues, who know better, have found it easier to inflame and keep alive the passions of the war by personifying the idea, and thus . . . I have been the object against who revilings have been mainly directed."

Such an analysis was true as far as it went, but there were other reasons why Northerners singled out Davis for attack. He was, after all, a wholehearted supporter of those symbols of Southern wickedness that Union military might had discredited—slavery, states' rights, and secession. Davis had not only defended slavery but also insisted that it restrained blacks "from the vicious indulgences to which their inferior nature inclines them." His views on the sovereignty of the states had been stated just as forcefully. "To all which has been said of the inherent powers of this [Federal] Government," Davis declared in 1846, "I answer, it is the creature of the States; as such it could have no inherent power, all it possesses was delegated by the States." And on the legitimacy and the necessity of secession, he was equally emphatic. "The temper of the Black Republicans is not to give us our rights in the Union, or allow us to go peaceably out of it," he declared in January 1861. "If we had no other cause, this would be enough to justify secession, at whatever hazard." A few days later he reported to his old friend Franklin Pierce: "Mississippi, not as a matter of choice but of necessity, has resolved to enter on the trial of secession. Those who have driven her to this alternative threaten to deprive her of the right to require that her government shall rest on the consent of the governed."

There were still other reasons why Northerners considered Davis especially villainous. He was denounced in the Yankee press for "hopelessly prolonging the war." It certainly was true that Davis wanted to continue the struggle. No one could accuse him of being a traitor to the Confederacy, as William Faulkner's fictional Mr. Nightingale did Robert E. Lee, because he quit when his army could still fight. The determination of Davis to carry on the war after Lee and Gen. Joseph E. Johnston had surrendered inspired a Confederate officer to write in his diary in

April 1865, "The armies of Dick Taylor and Kirby Smith are still left, and no one should give up the cause so long as there is an armed man in the field, and I feel that I would be disgraced if I should consent to such a course while we have an army ready to do battle, and our President is still firm and resolute, and even now perhaps with the army of his brother-in-law General Taylor."

The invidious comparisons made between Davis and Lincoln during and after the war by certain foreigners further embittered Northerners. For example, William Howard Russell's published diary contained this unflattering contrast: "[Davis] is certainly a very different looking man from Mr. Lincoln. He is like a gentleman." Or consider the remarks made by Percy Greg, whose article "Tribute to Confederate Heroes" appeared in print in 1882. He praised Davis as having more "moral and intellectual powers" than any twenty Federal statesmen and a man vastly superior in every way to "the 'rail-splitter' . . . whose term, had he died in his bed four or five years later, would have been remembered only as marking the nadir of American political decline; the culmination of . . . vulgarity. . . . Lincoln's uncleanness of language and thought," insisted Greg, "would hardly have been tolerated in a Southern 'bar.'"

Perhaps Yankees also were stung by the contrast between the "gentlemanly" warfare advocated by Davis and the comprehensive destruction practiced by such terrorizers of civilians as Generals William T. Sherman and Philip H. Sheridan. To Davis, war should consist solely of combat between organized armies. He abhorred the killing of civilians or the destruction of private property during hostilities. Years after the war, when Gen. U. S. Grant was dying of cancer, Davis wrote, "I . . . have felt a human sympathy with him in his suffering." Judah P. Benjamin recalled that "when it was urged upon Jefferson Davis, not only by friends in private letters, but by members of his Cabinet in council, that it was his duty to the people and to the army to endeavor to repress . . . outrages by retaliation, he was immovable in his resistance to such counsels, insisting that it was repugnant to every sentiment of justice and humanity that the innocent should be made victims for the crimes of such monsters." Davis proudly proclaimed after the war, "I am happy to remember that when our army invaded the enemy's country, their property was safe."

What made Davis utterly intolerable to most Yankees was his refusal to admit any guilt or to apologize for his actions and the cause he had led. He told veterans of the Army of Tennessee who came to Mississippi to 'honor him' in 1878, "Your organization was appropriate . . . to preserve the memories and cherished brotherhoods of your soldier life, and cannot be objectionable to any, unless it be to one who holds your services to have been in an unworthy cause and your conduct such as called for repentance and forgiveness." Davis reminded these old soldiers that they must maintain pride in their cause as well as in their soldierly conduct. "The veteran who shoulders his crutch to show how fields were won must not be ashamed of the battle in which he was wounded," Davis affirmed. "To higher natures success is not the only test of merit; and you, my friends, though you were finally unsuccessful, have the least possible cause to regret the flag under which you marched or the manner in which you upheld it."

Given this opportunity to explain his views to an understanding audience, Davis unburdened himself. "Every evil which has befallen our institutions is directly traceable to the perversion of the compact of union and the usurpation by the Federal Government of undelegated powers," he contended. "The events are too recent to require recapitulation, and the ruin they have wrought, the depravity they have developed, require no other memorial than the material and moral wreck which the country presents." Davis still believed in secession. "My faith in that right as an inherent attribute of State sovereignty, was adopted early in life, was confirmed by study and observation of later years, and has passed unchanged and unshaken, through the severe ordeal to which it has been subjected." He could express such views, he told his listeners, because he had no "desire for a political future." His only desire was to establish "the supremacy of the truths on which the union was founded." As for himself, he asserted, "I shall die, as I have lived, firm in the State rights faith."

Throughout the remaining years of his life, Davis adamantly reiterated his views in speeches, letters, and interviews. He told an appreciative audience of Southerners in 1882, "Our cause was so just, so sacred, that had I known all that has come to pass, had I known that was to be inflicted upon me, to endure, I would do it all over again. [Great applause.]" A year earlier Davis had written to a fellow Southerner:

> Nothing fills me with deeper sadness than to see a Southern man apologizing for the defence we made of our inheritance & denying the great truths on which all our institutions were founded. To be crushed by superior force, to be robbed & insulted, were great misfortunes, but these could be borne while there still remained manhood to assert the truth, and a proud consciousness in the rectitude of our course. When . . . I find myself reviled by Southern papers as one renewing "dead issues," the pain is not caused by the attack upon myself, but by the desecration of the memories of our Fathers & those of their descendants who staked in defence of their rights—their lives, their property & their sacred honor. To deny the justice of their cause, to apologize for its defence, and denounce it as a dead issue, is to take the last of their stakes, that for which they were willing to surrender the other.

A reporter who interviewed Davis a few years before he died discovered that the Confederate president's "heart [was] as warm as ever for the land he has loved so well" and that Davis "did not desert during the war and has not deserted since."

His steadfastness, his refusal to desert his cause, made Davis particularly obnoxious to his enemies. He was so unlike those Southerners who after the war disassociated themselves from their past as quickly as possible in order to obtain Yankee forgiveness and patronage. Davis was just the opposite of a fellow Mississippian, Confederate general James L. Alcorn, who announced shortly after the war: "you were right Yankee! . . . we are and ever have been in the Union; secession was a nullity. We will now take the oath to support the Constitution and the laws of the United States." As proof of his sincerity, Alcorn became a Republican governor of Mississippi in 1869 and a Republican member of the U.S. Senate in 1871. He also recouped his wartime financial losses and increased his property holdings. Good Yankees approved of such "enlightened" new Southerners as Alcorn, who were "eager to keep step with the North in the onward march of the Solid Nation," as one man expressed it. They disapproved of Jefferson Davis, and their newspapers castigated him as "unrepentant" and "the greatest enemy of the South."

It may be that Davis remains unforgiven because he supported slavery, states' rights, and secession. All of these are unfashionable in the United States at the moment and have been for some time. Were Davis alive today, even the most skilled public relations firm would have a difficult time packaging him for the present market. He obviously could not run for public office, nor could he go into education. What university professor would want him as a colleague? He likely could not even get hired as a preacher. Probably he would have to turn to television. Since it is not only permissible but also profitable to satirize white Southerners these days, Davis doubtless would have his best chance of success starring in a lampoon as another comic Southern type. The plot and the characterization would have to be kept simple. To depict Davis as a man who tried to lead his people to independence might confuse intellectuals and ordinary folk alike. They might see him as a "cool dude" struggling to promote a cause most of them had no interest in and only vaguely remembered; they would either accept or reject him and then probably shift their attention to a new cartoon series. They could mistake him for one of today's socially admired freedom fighters struggling to liberate his people from outside exploitation. But such a bewildering plot might require an exegesis by either an Ivy League professor or an Eastern news commentator to explain why viewers should see Davis as a bad guy.

Yankees might have forgiven Jefferson Davis had he held his tongue and kept his views hidden. Their treatment of Lee, who did just that, suggests that a silent Davis eventually might have been remodeled by the mythmakers into a devout unionist who merely went astray for a time. Had it been possible to create such an imaginary Davis, unquestionably he would have received the forgiveness Americans grant to repentant sinners, reformed drunkards, and wayward presidents. The problem was that Davis would not cooperate. He refused to keep quiet about his beliefs, and nearly everything he said and wrote was unacceptable to Yankees.

In 1882, a year after the publication of his two-volume defense of himself and the Confederate cause, Davis advocated the totally unforgivable—a history of the South written by and for Southerners. "I would have our children's children to know not only that our cause was just," he told the members of the Southern Historical Society, "but to have them know that the men who sustained it were worthy of the cause for which they fought." Davis, full of hope and passion, outlined in this remarkable address just what he believed history ought to be and how it should be used. "We want our side of the war so fully and exactly stated, that the men who come after us may compare and do [us] justice." Davis did not call for objectivity. "I will frankly acknowledge that I would distrust the man who served the Confederate cause and was capable of giving a disinterested account of it. [Applause.] I would not give twopence for

a man whose heart was so cold that he could be quite impartial.
. . . You may ask the school-boy in the lowest form, who commanded in the Pass of Thermopylae. He can tell you. But my
friends there are few in this audience who, if I ask them, could
tell me who commanded at Sabine Pass. And yet," said Davis,
"that battle of Sabine Pass was more remarkable than the battle
of Thermopylae, and when it has orators and poets to celebrate
it, will be so esteemed by mankind."

His appeal for orators and poets to preserve the deeds of
heroic Southerners reveals that Davis understood the South's
heritage. Southerners, like their Celtic ancestors, were oral and
aural people who perpetuated much of their past in stories and
songs. Davis compared the Confederacy's military heroes with
their Scottish forebears:

May it not come to pass that in some hour of . . . need,
future generations, aware of the grandeur and the virtue
of these men, will in a moment of disaster cry out like the
ancient Scot:

O for an hour of Wallace wight
Or well-trained Bruce
To lead the fight,
And cry St. Andrew and our right.

History, Davis believed, must inspire those who learn it. "Let
the rising generation learn what their fathers did," he implored,
"and let them learn the still better lesson to emulate not only the
deeds, but the motives which prompted them. May God grant
that sons ever greater than their fathers may rise whenever their
country needs them to defend her cause. [Applause.]"

The kind of history that Davis advocated was unacceptable
to Yankees. First, it was incompatible with the so-called scientific
history taught in German seminars and popularized in the United States by Yankee professors during the late nineteenth centu-

ry. As adapted for Americans, this history stressed the evolution of New England institutions and how they contributed to the greatness of the United States. There was no place in such "objective" history for either the bard or the poet upon whom Davis wished to rely upon to celebrate Southern values and heroes. Second, a history of the South that revered Southerners and their values rather than Northerners and their values would undermine all that the Civil War had decided. To the victor went the power to write the history that justified the victory. It was that simple.

British history, as the scholar John Pocock has pointed out, is really English history imposed upon the non-English peoples of the British Isles by their English conquerors. The same may be said of the history of the United States. What passes for standard American history is Yankee history written by New Englanders or others to glorify Yankee ideals and heroes.

In the twentieth century, Northerners gained increasing control over the historical journals, the university presses, the commercial publishing houses, and the production and distribution of professional historians; consequently, the Yankee version of the American past became the history most often taught in the colleges and in the public schools.

It was precisely this situation that Mississippian Dunbar Rowland complained about in 1914. "It seems to be admitted on all sides that the people of the South are neglecting the teaching of Southern History in all our *institutions*," he informed Gov. Earl Brewer. "That we are neglecting this important *field* of instruction is made evident by the astonishing amount of ignorance of Southern and State history among the rising generation of college students. Something should be done . . . to enlighten them."

Part of the problem was that the professors who taught the South's teachers had adopted the "New South" doctrine of national unity as readily as Southern businessmen. North Carolina educator Robert Bingham announced in 1884, "the greatest blessing that ever befell us was a failure to establish a [Southern] nationalism." Bingham boasted that "the past of the South is irrevocable, and we do not wish to recall it. The past of the South is irreparable, and we do not wish to repair it."

Yet among Southerners, this teaching of Yankee ideals in the public schools was so often offset by traditions that Francis B. Simkins could label it "the education which does not educate." "This," he wrote, "is caused partly by the temperament of a people inclined to be leisurely and even Philistine. It is caused also by the survival of overwhelming traditions. Northern bias in textbooks is offset by less formal and perhaps more effective indoctrination in local ideals which survive the regimentation of the schools." Robert Penn Warren testified that his sympathetic view of Confederate history was not obtained from the school-room but rather "from the air around me."

If the air in the South was full of Confederate history, the book shelves were not in 1921 when Dunbar Rowland decided to write a biography of Jefferson Davis that would elevate the Confederate president above the forlorn place to which he was relegated by Yankee historians. Before he put pen to paper, Rowland naively asked the advice of several professional historians. Only Southerner William E. Dodd gave him much encouragement. The Yankee professors to whom Rowland wrote generally ignored his letter or objected to what he proposed. "You say that you are already convinced of Mr. Davis's 'true greatness,'" replied Charles M. Andrews of Yale University. "I do believe that one who has made up his mind on so important a point and has got his estimates determined beforehand is bound to be handicapped in the work he is to do." Edward Channing of Harvard University was somewhat kinder to Rowland. "There is no life of Davis worthy of the man," wrote Channing. "I wish you would write such a life giving the local color that we Northerners find so difficult to express or to realize." But then Channing took back more than he had given by marking his letter "Confidential" and by concluding it with this sentence: "I have asked you to regard this as *confidential*, because the study of the material that you print and the study of other material that I may find may change my ideas."

By 1935, Rowland had published his ten-volume collection of Davis's speeches and letters and had learned not to trust Yankees. "The only discontent here—and it is South-side—is . . . the return of the Carpet-Bagger and the Scalawag," he informed Sen. Pat Harrison. "We have some young men at the Vicksburg Military Park who call themselves Historical Technicians. These men are Norwegians and Yankees and know little or nothing of our . . . Southern, or Mississippi history, yet they go through our state selecting historic sites and telling the people that we are very backward. . . . In the very beginning of their stay here, they claimed that they had come to Mississippi to re-write the history of the State. This statement was made to me. What I said to them was somewhat vigorous. They are ignorant meddlers into the affairs of the state that they know nothing about." All of the national military parks in the country were "under prejudiced Northern men," claimed Rowland. "The people in charge of these parks glorify and deify Lincoln and Grant and cast aspersion on Davis and Lee. Our people resent this. I think we have a reason to do so. I think, also, that the Military Parks in the South should be controlled exclusively by Southern people. I know only too well how our young people . . . have been fed on lies from text books written by vindictive and untruthful Northern men. I have reason to know that the Vicksburg 'technicians' buy prejudiced Northern histories almost exclusively."

In a curious way, Jefferson Davis may have been as unforgiving as his enemies. For more than one hundred years, he defied the best efforts of historians—Southern and Northern—to fully understand him. None of the many biographies of Davis written in the first hundred years after the Civil War is regarded as a work of high scholarship. The lengthiest of these, three volumes written by an English teacher, has been severely criticized by reviewers. Perhaps the most interesting book on Davis written during this period was a fine character study that appeared in 1929; it was written not by a historian but by the agrarian poet Allen Tate.

Jefferson Davis might have enjoyed Tate's study, for the Confederacy's president believed that poets rather than "objective" historians were more likely to understand Southerners and their past.

Recently, as historians reckon time, three thick books on Jefferson Davis have appeared: William C. "Jack" Davis (no kin to his subject), *Jefferson Davis: The Man and the Hour* (1992); Felecity Allan, *Jefferson Davis: Unconquered Hero* (1999); and William J. Cooper, *Jefferson Davis, American* (2000). All are good books that tell us much about Davis—what he believed and how he acted.

If Francis Simkins had lived to finish his biography of Davis, it doubtless would have included some humorous moments as well as sympathetic understanding of Davis and the Confederacy. But I doubt if it, or any of these published volumes (or other, unpublished works), would be the final word on Jefferson Davis. There is too much to say about this man who lived too long for a lost cause.

Photo Credits

We gratefully acknowledge the United States Military History Institute at Carlisle Barracks, Pennsylvania, for the photos of Nathan Bedford Forrest, James Johnston Pettigrew, Leonidas Polk, and the older Jefferson Davis. We acknowledge the Library of Congress for the images of Ulysses S. Grant, Braxton Bragg, P.G.T. Beauregard, and William L. Yancey. We acknowledge the North Carolina Collection of the University of North Carolina, Chapel Hill, for the Cracker Home drawing. "A Southerner and his dogs" came from *Harper's New Monthly Magazine* (1857). The photographs of Ambrose Powell Hill and of the flag on the cover of this book are courtesy of the Museum of the Confederacy, Richmond, Virginia. The photograph of Francis Simkins is courtesy of Longwood College, Farmville, Virginia. The cover illustration is a photograph of the flag of the 3rd Arkansas Infantry, in the collection of the Museum of the Confederacy in Richmond, Virginia.

Publisher's Acknowledgments

The McWhiney Foundation Press would like to acknowledge the efforts of Daniel Price, a McWhiney Scholar, in the making of this book. He worked diligently to collect photographs and illustrations, and, with the help of Jay Hardaway, to compile the extensive index. Finally, we continue to be grateful to Henry Rosenbohm, of Rosenbohm Graphic Design, for his thoughtful design of this book and its cover.

Index

A

Adams, Daniel W., 38, 130
Adams, Henry A., 140, 142
Adams, John, 38, 132
Africa, 125
Ajax, 152
Alabama, 19, 33, 99, 138, 159, 170, 192-94, 196, 197, 198, 201, 205;
    Ordinance of Secession, 191; *peoples* 193, 194, 195, 196, 207;
    University of 3, 199
Alcorn, James L., 285
Alexander the Great, 80
Alexander, E.P., 30
Allan, Felecity, 291
Allan, William, 174
Allatoona, Georgia, 35
Allen, Henry W., 37
American South, 262
American(s), 1, 15, 46, 271, 286-88; *in Civil War* 114; *in Mexican War* 82,
    83, 87, 93-96, 98, 101, 102, 104-105, 107, 111, 135
Anaconda Plan, 124
Anderson, Charles, 50
Anderson, John, 50
Anderson, Patton, 182, 216
Anderson, Robert, 47, 50
Anderson, William, 50
Andrews, Charles M., 289
Anglo-Saxon, 2, 3, 82
Antietam Creek, 234; *See also* Sharpsburg, Maryland
Antrim County, Ireland, 19
Apalachicola, Florida, 16
Appomattox, Virginia, 276
Archer, James J., 236
Arkansas, 102, 104, 160, 218
Army of Northern Virginia, *See* Civil War Armies
Army of Tennessee, *See* Civil War Armies
Army of the Potomac, *See* Civil War Armies
Army of the Texas Republic, 166
Atlanta Register, 253
Atlanta, Battle of, 36, 122, 133
Atlanta, Georgia, 248, 252
Atlantic Ocean, 2, 9
Austin, Texas, 58
Avery, I.E., 132

Pike, Albert, 160
Pilate, Pontius, 152
Pillow, Gideon J., 100
Pine Bluff, Arkansas, 7
Pine Mountain, Georgia, 221
Pittsburg Landing, Battle of, 178-83, 186; *See also* Shiloh, Battle of
Pocock, John, 288
Polk, James K., 86, 100, 107
Polk, Leonidas, 163, 180-81, 184, 209-21, 247, 251, 261
Polk, Lucius E., 130
Pollard, Edward Alfred, 174
Pompeii, 60
Pope, John, 57, 62, 230-31, 233
Port Republic, Battle of, 118
Porter, Fitz John, 224, 227, 229
Potomac River, 234, 236, 270
Potter, David M., 136
Powell, Ambrose, 223
Prentiss, Benjamin, 181-82, 187
Princeton University, 268
Protestants, 1, 17-18, 273
Prussian, 260
Pryor, Roger A., 160, 193-94
Pugh, James L., 250
Puritans, *New England* 3; *Roundheads* 22

Q
Quint, Howard, 273

R
Ramsdell, Charles W., 136-38, 145
Ramseur, Stephen Dodson, 35, 44
Randall, James G., 136
Randall, James Ryder, 174
Randolph Macon College, 263
Randolph, George W., 154
Rapidan River, 230
Reed, John Sheldon, 1
Resaca de la Palma, Battle of, 71-73, 93
Reynolds, John F., 95, 98
Richmond Examiner, 78, 174, 230
Richmond, Virginia, 23, 37, 89, 124, 133, 155, 167, 172-73, 188, 197, 210, 215, 219, 226-27, 230, 249, 270
Ridgely, Randolph, 98